RESURRECTION

RESURRECTION

A CHANNELED TEXT

The Manifestation Trilogy: Book One

PAUL SELIG

ST. MARTIN'S
ESSENTIALS
NEW YORK

First published in the United States by St. Martin's Essentials, an imprint of St. Martin's Publishing Group

RESURRECTION. Copyright © 2022 by Paul Selig. All rights reserved. Printed in the United States of America. For information, address St. Martin's Publishing Group, 120 Broadway, New York, NY 10271.

www.stmartins.com

The Library of Congress Cataloging-in-Publication Data is available upon request.

ISBN 978-1-250-83377-8 (trade paperback)
ISBN 978-1-250-83378-5 (ebook)

Our books may be purchased in bulk for promotional, educational, or business use. Please contact your local bookseller or the Macmillan Corporate and Premium Sales Department at 1-800-221-7945, extension 5442, or by email at MacmillanSpecialMarkets@macmillan.com.

First Edition: 2022

10 9 8 7 6 5 4 3 2 1

Contents

The following are the unedited transcripts of channeling sessions conducted by Paul Selig on Maui between July 22, 2021, and September 11, 2021, before students in online and in-person seminars and a small online group convened to receive this dictation. Selected questions from students have been included.

INTRODUCTION

DAY ONE

We stand before you today in preparation for your work, for your capability and great capacity to be re-known, to be rendered anew. Each of you here has chosen, at one level or another, that the lives you have lived may be altered, re-known, sung in a higher tone, a higher key. Each of you who has said yes stands before us today in willingness—and readiness, we would suggest—for what this offering is. Some of you say, "Yes, I may. I may know myself anew." Some of you say, "Perhaps." But, in fact, all of you are here in readiness at a point in history where what may be known, what may be rendered new, has capacity to be made new.

Now, when we speak of being made new, we are speaking of re-articulation. Everything in form is in articulation. There is one note sung in this universe that you know that is in articulation as all manifestation. All things are of one

Source at varying degrees of tone or vibration. The manifestation of humanity, the idea of who and what you are and the name you have given yourselves, is being made new, is in fact being altered, and lifted, we would suggest, to a higher octave, a higher intonation. The vibration you hold is always in coherence with the reality you will find yourselves in, and the co-resonant reality you have chosen, with its highs, lows, and in-betweens, is being altered by your presence. Underline those words, friends: *altered by your presence.* Humanity itself has chosen this. You cannot agree to what you are or who you have been, but the collective has agreed to make a new choice—we would suggest a high choice—to release an idea of self that has been known through fear, known through contention, known through aggression, to be re-known in what we will call the Upper Room, which is a higher octave of resonance, a collective field where indeed all things are made new.

To be re-articulated, or made new, is an act of being. It is less a thing done than an agreement made as the field you hold is lifted and altered by agreement and energetic accord. The resonant field you hold today, wherever you may sit, is in coherence with the resonant field of all things that you see and experience. When one is made new, one is re-known or reclaimed at a level of vibration where what you claim into being, the world you see before you, is also changed. "How is it changed?" you may ask. We have said this many times, but the denial of the Divine, the great problem humanity has faced, can only be rectified from a higher level of alignment. What you deny God in, you align to in fear.

Now, to deny God in something is simply to decide that

the idea of God, or the presence of God, or the tone, which is indeed God, cannot exist somewhere. And by your decree, or your coherence with that claim, you shut yourself from the Divine in the way that we say you do. What you put in darkness calls you to the darkness. What you deny the Divine in claims you in that darkness, or at least the shadow of it. The template of reality that you have chosen to learn through, claimed in fear, enjoined by each of you through collective agreement, has chosen to shift, with your presence as the activator.

Now, as you begin to know who you are, what you are, and how you serve, the field you hold is indeed altered. It is lifted. The transmission of your field, or the coherence the field holds, claims into being that which is of like accord, a-c-c-o-r-d, or a c-h-o-r-d as on a piano. The coherence of the True Self, which we will explain later, is that which is of God, because the True Self as you cannot deny the Divine. When you stop denying the Divine, you claim a new level of alignment, energetic coherence, wherein all things indeed are made new.

Now, the idea of being made new is confusing for most of you. You think it means you pretend you weren't who you were yesterday, or that your problems are gone, or you are lifting all things to your idea of heaven. In fact, to be made new, or re-articulated, is the presence of the Divine, operating as and through you, that calls into being that which is of like accord. The body you have is the body you hold, but the body you hold is in a new coherence. The energetic field you hold is still present, but aligned in a higher template.

Now, the idea of a *template* must be understood. If you understand that there is an organizational system operating here, and that the True Self as you, that knows who and what it is, is an organizing aspect of the being you are, you can also understand that the being that you are, in this higher way, is in coherence to a reality that has its own laws and rules. We have taught the Kingdom in prior classes. We will reference it here quite often. But the Kingdom is the realization of the omnipresence of the Divine manifest as all things—exclusive of nothing, inclusive of all, the Divine as all things. When all things are re-seen or re-known as of God, the manifest world that you have experienced yourself through is indeed altered. Its intonation is changed, and what was known in fear can indeed be made new, or seen anew as it truly is—as of Source. Some of you ask us, "What does it look like?" What it looks like is yourself in a new way of being. And the world you perceive, the world before you, is the world you see without the emblazoning of fear claiming you in like coherence. In the Upper Room, which is the doorway to the Kingdom, all things are of God, and the fear you have known cannot express, because the vibration of the Upper Room cannot hold the Kingdom in fear. In other words, fear is a creation of the lower strata. When you move beyond it, or are lifted beyond it, you begin to claim a world in coherence with it. And the coherence of the Divine cannot hold fear, because fear is the denial of the Divine, and that is what it has always been.

Some of you say, "Yes, maybe. I believe this may be so. But my experience hasn't shown me yet." This is an instruction in experience, the idea of being, beyond the old, beyond the known, beyond the agreement to fear. And as you encounter yourself anew, you begin to engage in a reality that surpasses what you believed could be, because any idea of what could be is still so informed by the logic that the small self has accrued, or the idea of a reality that the small self can manage. To understand where you go in these teachings is to begin to experience the self beyond the idea of self that you have utilized to navigate a reality. It is to become the self who knows who she is, what he is, and how she serves. One's true purpose, one's true expression, at this level is the being of the Divine.

Now, already you are this, but you don't know it. You deny it, or you would refute it, because it demands something that you cannot hold. The idea that you are holy must mean that all things are holy. And, indeed, all things are, when re-known as of God.

Each of you here who hears these words is about to embark on a journey of resurrection. And the mandate of resurrection is the reclamation of all things that have denied the Divine—within the self, yes, but also within the world. This is how a world is made new. And your agreement to this journey, to this strange passage that we intend to undertake, will indeed be a text, and the journey of the text of *Resurrection* is the text of embodiment in manifestation. The texts that we will bring forth in the coming years will hold the key to deliverance, not only for the singular, but for the collective, because as the doors begin to open, as the Upper Room is full with the life and vitality of God as incarnated as each of you, the world will find itself in agreement to itself in a new way of being.

This is a teaching of love. This is a gift for each of you. You may not get what you think you will or you expected you might, because any expectation, indeed, we would say, is born of the small self. And the small self's idea of what can be is limited by all things it has known prior. When the known, when the old, is released and the new is born, the Kingdom unfolds before you. And this is the claim of the Kingdom:

> *"Each one who hears these words, each one who reads these words, will be known anew in agreement to a belief in the Creator that will surpass any ideology that has been tainted by fear or cruelly superimposed upon others through force of will. All who hear these words, all who read these words, will be in re-articulation at the perfect tone, level of agreement, that he or she can hold. And as this journey progresses, the song that is sung, the sound that will emit, the claim that will be made, will be the claim of the Divine come as one, come as all, in resurrection."*

This is the end of this lecture. We will take a pause for Paul. We will tell him when we return what we will do next. Period. Period. Period.

(PAUSE)

We have lots to talk about, but take a moment, Paul. The text that we are writing will be written through you with very little effort. The idea of the text is what frightens you. "What will this book be? What is it named? What is its action or presence in the world?" The text that we write on resurrection, which is manifestation of the Divine in form, in field, in a way that manifests or claims a new world into being, will be the beginning of a series that addresses the ideas of manifestation and the challenges one faces as one claims this path.

Now, this is a path that has been walked prior—the mystic path, the path of the sage. But re-articulation, as we will teach it, is not an intellectual endeavor. It is completely experiential. Now, religiosity has informed these teachings for some, and we must say now: This is not a religious teaching, nor can it ever be. The teaching of the Christ, or the Monad, or the True Self, finally, is a universal teaching. And while the language we use may be informed by historical meaning, our usage of the language is intended to claim you on a distinct path, and a higher path than you may have known you were even on. The path of re-articulation, being made new, as we have often said, comes at the cost of the old. And the identity you have used to negotiate your reality is the first thing that you encounter when you are being made new. The idea of self as separate from the Divine is so entrenched in the belief systems of yours that you claim it unknowingly, and the release of the old appears to you to be a death. "Who am I if I am not who I think I am?" The agreement we make to you tonight is that the death that you experience is a rebirth. It is the resurrection. It is the resurrection foretold, as the Christ, or the Monad, is re-known in form.

Now, to know the self as of God is to understand both your sovereignty and your agreement to the self as of the whole. The Monad, or the Christ, the seed of God which seeks to express as and through you, knows itself as of the whole. And the agreement we make with you is that the transit you are undertaking will benefit not only you, but all that you encounter. We cannot make you holy. You already are. But you have forgotten your divinity, and while we remind you in words, we are amply aware that the only way to reach you is to know you, realize you, as who and what you truly are beyond the small self's idea of what is possible.

The texts we have offered thus far have indeed been a system of alignment, through energetic attunement, to re-know the self beyond the old template. But to come into the new template, manifest in the Upper Room in adherence to the agreements that align here, must in some ways be its own teaching. The world before you, you see, is in fragmentation, and the fragments themselves all hold ideas of ideas that are known through history. The release of these ideas and the history that claim them is a challenging passage, because what it means is that even the fabric of reality, as you have comprehended it, can and will be re-known, because what stands before you all in such a time of change is the gift of change, the new, and the release of the old, the passing of the old, that which cannot be held in the higher octave of alignment that you have now come to.

The splintering of reality, the factioning you see, is actually the product of fear. Fear would always tell you to fear your brother, fear God, fear yourselves. The action of fear is to claim more fear. And a world in fear is a world at war with itself. But you cannot lift to the light without this passage. You cannot deny your creations, those things that have been hewn in fear, re-created, made so, from a template of fear. Now, what is fear but the denial of the Divine, and the claim we offer you, "Behold, I make all things new," will claim fear and lift it to the high octave of the Upper Room, where it may no longer be enacted upon. The attunements we will be giving you, some old, some new, are all ways of renegotiating the self that you have known as it embarks on this journey, and reclaiming the world that you are in an encounter to and with through the alignment you now hold. Understand, we said *now hold*. The gift of these teachings has and always will be a reclamation of the energetic field, through attunement, in the high octave where you may begin to know the self anew. They transition you, one after the next, to an alignment that you have not held prior.

Where you stand today, before us, yes, is in an awareness of your potential, even the supposition of it. But where we will take you, as we are allowed to teach as we wish, is to the mandate of the Divine: "It will be so. God Is. God Is. God Is." The re-creation of the body to be sung in a higher tone, the reclamation of the energetic field to receive you in your true sovereignty, and the awareness of what you do, how you be, how you enact this being in agreement to your fellows, which we will call service, will be present here, but from the perspective of the Upper Room.

For the new student, we will say this to you: We teach in a one-room schoolhouse. Every student is met where he or she sits. And the agreement we make to you tonight is not only will you be met, you will be known. And to be known is to be realized. As we sing you into presence, which is what we will now do, we will call you forth before us. And as we witness you each, the fields that you hold, inclusive of the masks you have taken to know yourselves in these lifetimes, we will release you from the idea of self that has stood in the way of the Divine as you receiving itself in an agreement to its mastery. The Divine as you knows who he is, knows what she is, knows how she serves. And its liberation, its full expression, its resurrection, is the song we sing to you now. You may say this after us, if you wish:

> *"I know who I am in truth. I know what I am in truth. I know how I serve in truth. I am free. I am free. I am free. I am in the Upper Room. I Have Come. I Have Come. I Have Come. It will be so. Behold, I make all things new. God Is. God Is. God Is."*

We say your names now, one and all, and the sound we make is inclusive of each of your names. You are all being sung to, called forward, and seen. You may join the sound we make, if it is your wish, so we sing together in agreement to your being.

On the count of three, Paul.

One. Now two. Now three.

[The Guides tone through Paul.]

> *We know who you are in truth. We know what you are in truth. We know how you serve in truth. You are free. You are free. You are free.*

We will say this now. Indeed, this is in the text. We thank you each for your presence. Stop now, please. Period. Period. Period.

DAY TWO

You ask questions about what will be. You seek reassurance for a future that is uncharted, cannot be known, and cannot be predicted at this juncture because the manifestation of change is so pronounced that what falls from the sky may land where it may. Now, we use this as metaphor, but it is indeed your experience—what falls from the sky, what lands unexpectedly, what changes a landscape or a lifestyle or a way of being. In times of great change, when change is present and all are called to witness the opportunity for growth, and spiritualization is heightened, and heightened by the cost of what is releasing, when all you have counted on, expected to be, is no longer present, you will claim what you can. You will agree to the unknown, to the potentiality of Spirit that you have hidden from prior. At this crossroads, humanity has chosen change, and the outcome we predict, and have predicted prior, is that humanity will triumph. But change is present, and some will not withstand change through their own refusal to acquiesce to the new. It is as if you are pretending that the boat hasn't capsized, that the world is different and you seek to have your tea when the teacup cannot be filled because it is upside down. Each of you says yes to the potential here—reclamation, re-creation, resurrection. Each of you says yes to what may be seen beyond the known, what may be claimed beyond the simplistic ideas of what reality should be that you have been so stuck in that you can no longer see the potential that is unfolding before you. In this time, we suggest, humanity will face itself, face its creations, and the reckoning that is upon you, a reckoning of truth and agreement to truth, will claim for you the next steps that humanity may take as a whole.

Now, your idea here is that everybody must be in agreement. "Yes, there is a problem with this and that, and we all agree that it must be attended to as we say." That will not happen on this plane. What will happen, and is happening, is an agreement claimed in the ethers, in the higher accord, in the collective soul of the species, not only to withstand change, but to utilize it for high purpose. Now, when we say *high*, we do not mean noble. We do not mean what you would like it to mean. High purpose is true purpose, and your true purpose, all humanity's true purpose, finally, we say, is resurrection, or a reconciliation with its true divinity.

Now, your true divinity is always present, cannot not be there, but it can be denied, has been denied, and denied not only at the individual level, but by the collective as well. Imagine an ice that has covered humanity that begins to shear off in an escalating heat. Imagine that what is released from its icy encasing is the flame of the Divine that seeks to reconcile itself and all things with its true purpose and nature. This is the act of being that you are attending to here. It is the act of being as the True Self as manifest that humanity is entering. Now, we say *entering* intentionally. You are impatient. You want it done on Tuesday next. You want it done before your vacation starts, certainly before your children are grown, so that you can see them in a happy landscape. But what is happening now is re-creation at a mass level, and the scale of which you have not seen in a lifetime for thousands and thousands of years. The articulation of a species, when it is growing, outgrowing old forms, manifest anew, is an act of expression. And the expression of this happens in two ways, less so the individual, although the individual is present and participatory, but primarily at the level of species when the vibrational field that the species has held is up-leveled to a new tone. When the new tone is held, a lengthy note we would suggest, the field of the body, or how the body expresses in the energetic field, is also attended to. And what the body has known through limitation is actually reclaimed in what we will call the Upper Room because that is the high strata that the Divine Self expresses in. Humanity expressing in a new tonality does not mean you have fine behavior, better manners, perhaps less difficulty. It does mean that mankind, humankind, has outgrown a way of being, and the challenges it faces now are that the creations of the old self are so paramount that they can no longer be ignored. The choice is here, and you have said yes, the species has said yes, has agreed to be altered, claimed new, and resurrected.

Now, how this happens is a long process. We use the word *long* in an illustrative way, not to tell you what the time frame is, because you can move beyond time in an escalated field. But the act of manifestation, the causal field in its new tonality reclaiming a manifest world, is a process that is now begun and has different aspects to it. The primary aspect that you are witnessing now is the collapse of structure, and this will continue for some time because the new seeks to be born where the old has held sway. Now, because you seek to protect the old—it is what you have known, it is what you believe must be so—your attention is actually moved towards preservation when it must be moved to reconciliation. The focus, the prospect, of reconciliation is different than you might think. To reconcile anything, any system or structure, any human being, any escapade or incident, to the Divine is the act of re-knowing and re-seeing. We have taught these things prior. We will continue to teach them because they are imperative to understand. At this moment in time you are busy trying to hold the walls up, to keep the ceiling in place, but the ceiling may fall and open you to the sky, to the Infinite, that which has always been present but exists beyond those four walls. Your systems of governance, your systems of politics and religion and medicine, will all be re-seen in the coming years, and to high effect. And, again, *high* means vibrationally high, not your idea of morality or right or wrong.

When something comes in at a new tone, in a new frequency, it will always disrupt the old. Many of you wonder why on your spiritual paths you face calamity or great change or a disturbance in the idea of self that you have perpetuated throughout a lifetime. This is the affect of the high tone, your own true nature, your inherent Divine Self, reclaiming what it encounters that has been hewn or claimed in a lower tone or energetic field. There has never once been a passage for humanity of this degree, and the ones you have faced prior have come through challenge as well. What you see before you today is in fact a beginning of great change, but required change, needed change, because you have been operating in fear for so very long that you mandate fear in everything you would create now. In some ways, what has happened is that the choice to claim in fear has been chosen to release, and it is not a pretty process. Understand, friends, that fifty percent of what you do in any given day is by rote, through inherent training. You know what to do because it's what you were taught and what you have seen, and consequently what you expect. The moment has come for the release of unconscious behavior, enacted by fear, that contributes to the calamity that humanity has faced and is now facing fully. You may call it illness. You may call it greed. You may call it the destruction of a planet. But these are all out-picturings, one and all, of the vibration of fear.

Now, when you understand that fear is an ignorant energy—it is not wise, it eats all things indiscriminately to feed itself, to grow as cancer, or pollute as an ocean might be— you will understand that the ignorance of fear becomes your greatest ally. You have empowered a foolish thing. You have agreed to a foolish thing. You have aligned to it, put it in your pockets, dined out with it, fed it to your children, voted for it or against it, prayed to or for it, and made choices because of it. You have done this unknowingly because it is the world you were claimed in. To understand what we teach is not to ignore fear. It is present, yes. But the choice to enact it, which is to contribute to its being, must be understood as the cause of your pain, individually and collectively. To lift to what we call the Upper Room, which is the entryway to the Kingdom—it is of the Kingdom, but because the tone of the vibrational field of the Upper Room is also in a scale of high and low, you may see it as the first note played that may be experienced at this place, from this place, in the Upper Room—you do not abide in fear because fear does not exist here. And what you lift, by nature of presence and being, to the Upper Room is made new or resurrected by nature of your presence and being.

Now, when humanity does this at a collective level, the entire energetic field of the reality you have known yourself in is altered. It is escalated. We are showing Paul the image of a screen, and many channels that can play upon the screen. You can watch any station you wish. The primary station that you are all watching, because you are in coherence with it, is a low vibrational tone, with moments of beauty, times of glory, but the presence of pestilence and pain and poverty and hunger are so present that any moment of smelling the roses is pretending that you are not in coherence with what expresses in fear or in low tone. That would be turning your back upon your starving brother or sister to enjoy the lovely sunset. By all means, enjoy it. But what we are telling you now is that the level of change that you are choosing to be participatory to reclaims all things. You are no longer denying pain. You are no longer predicating your well-being on somebody else's lack, fighting for the last piece of bread upon the table in a belief in scarcity. You are coming to a place where you recognize, finally, and we say finally, that all human beings are one. And underline the word *all*—not just those people you like, those you agree with, and those who would do as you wish. The majesty before you, when you witness God as all of its creations, its infinite wonder embodied as each individual, will show you the manifestation that God claims because you must only know yourself as of it to witness it in all things.

We stand with you now, about to take you on this journey. You may think of us as tour guides, but we are something more than that. We are not only your teachers. We are your benefactors. And what we offer you is your true inheritance. Any true inheritance is yours already. It need not be earned or negotiated for, and when we say we are your benefactors, we wish to give you what is rightfully yours, the True Self as expressed, as manifest, in love.

We thank you each for your presence. This is indeed in the text. It is the end of the introduction. The book is *Resurrection.*

Blessings to you each.

PART I

What Was and What Will Be

1

PREPARATION

DAY THREE

We stand before you in an awareness of who you are and what you have endured, how you have chosen to learn by agreeing to separation. It has been an agreement, yes, to know the self as separate from Source, and one chosen by you collectively, acquiesced to through time, and now seen anew, because the prohibition to union has been ended.

"Now, what prohibition?" Paul asks. "How could such a thing be?" When the collective endeavors to know God go beyond the systems of control that have been utilized thus far as ways of knowing God, you break through the ceiling collectively. And the ceiling was created by you, again collectively, through the denial of the Divine. The denial of the Divine, the only true problem humanity has ever faced, has been its own creation. But it has been so real, and continues to be so real for many of you, that you reinforce it by your agreement to it. The choice is here now, through the collective, with the collective, to claim autonomy from the prior systems of deceit and self-deceit.

"What systems are these?" he asks. Your acquiescence to the idea of fear as legacy and as productive to one's needs. The idea that fear is your vocation—you are here to learn fear or through fear—is no longer available. The species has agreed to move beyond a limited sense of agreement to a lower-strata creation. Now, fear is of God, yes, because all things must be of God. Nothing can be left out. But fear denies God, believes itself to be separate, and creates its own landscape, its own ideology, its own way of getting its needs met, which is replication. The idea of replication, and fear as an anchor, tethered to the lower realm, seeking to replicate, is a helpful ideology for you to understand, because the moment you understand it you can stop being participatory to it. The new agreement is made. "We may learn our lessons beyond agreement to fear. We do not need fear as our teacher to grow. We may learn in higher ways."

The triumph of the Divine over fear is not what you would imagine. The true sense of self, the one who knows who she is, what he is, and how he serves, has already risen above fear. And re-articulation, resurrection, or embodiment, manifestation, as the Monad, aligns you beyond fear. It simply does not express at the level of vibration you are coming to. But your acknowledgment of fear, that it is present, you have learned through it, been taught hard lessons by it, is also useful. You are never pretending in these teachings. You are moving beyond things with an awareness of what you have endured and what you have learned through. We are not pretending to know you as you are. In fact, we know you as you are because what you are is as we are, the only difference being that our acceleration of vibration, our triumphant resurrection, has been claimed in order to support you in your own. We stand beside you, yes. We walk with you, yes. And we say this to you, each step you take: You Have Come. You Have Come. You Have Come. And the arrival to this landscape, the Upper Room, if you wish, an enormous transition for an individual, and an enormous transition for a collective, is celebrated, but celebrated with caution.

"What does that mean?" he asks. *With caution* means we escort you beyond the desire for the small self to attend to these teachings and attempt to create from it. When the small self deifies itself, trouble ensues. Indeed, ye all are as God. But what this means is not understood by you. You are as of God because you cannot be separate from God. You can believe yourselves to be, but to know yourself as of God must imply that everyone and everything is operating in the same fashion. The deification of the egoic structure—"Give me what I want when I want it"—is the action of fear seeking to usurp a high teaching. The fallen religions, those that have passed from these planes, held truth, yes, but also claimed hierarchy. And any church that holds a hierarchy, that one's salvation become dependent on one teacher or on one master, is scaled in a lower frequency. While there are great teachers, and teachers that operate as doorways to the Divine, these teachers know themselves as doorways and do not hold edicts for their disciples. All are included, because if all were not included, the doorways that they were would be shut.

We are a doorway, yes, because we come as the Christ. Now, to understand what this means is we come as the Monad or frequency of the Christ in participation to the great awakening that is before you. We will not call ourselves *Jesus* or by any other name at this level of vibration, because at this level of vibration all names are included. The distinction of Melchizedek as title or teacher, which is the name we have offered, is inclusive of the Christ, inclusive of all great teachings, because all great teachings are in truth. And what is true is always true, eternally true. You would seek to limit this teaching by claiming it as a religion, or a discipleship to a master that is telling you what to do. We do not tell you what to do. We offer a way, and we will support you in this way as you say yes to it. Your true will is present here. And true will, Divine Will, is in fact your escort through this passage.

The passage you are undertaking, individually and collectively, is to a new level of consciousness that you have not known. Paul interrupts. We wish he wouldn't. The idea of a collective agreement to a high consciousness seems impossible to him, but the evidence he would cite for the impossibility of this is actually the evidence that it is occurring. Do you understand this, friends? The splintering of an old reality, the factioning of a people from one country to the next, is present now, yes. But it has always been present. It is just now being seen—and seen so it may heal. Pretend the rose has no thorn and you will be pricked. Acknowledge the thorn when the rose is pruned. Acknowledge the differences, the uniqueness in different people. All are here to learn in very different ways, and you must never be the arbiter of who learns what and what they should learn by your decision.

The uniqueness of each individual is still present in the Upper Room. In becoming who you truly are, that which makes you, you, in wondrous ways, is even more fully expressed, because it is not diminished through the structures of fear that would seek to inhibit you. Imagine a great dance. Some move with beauty, some move with fear, some move with laughter, and some in tears. It is a wondrous dance. All are expressing as they are, and you must never make one higher than the next. The hypocrite would do this. She would seek to stand in a higher platform, but the moment she does, she will see that what holds the platform is only relevant to her need for separation. And it is the need for separation that we seek to address here.

Why did humanity choose to know itself through separation? The idea of the fall, which has been taught poorly, may be understood as such. You all made a choice to learn the difference between light and dark, or what you would call good and evil, and in doing so became participatory to the creations of fear. And the belief in separation was born in a belief in lack, that there would never be enough and you must hoard what you have, keep it from the one beside you, lest you starve through the winter. The belief in separation from God is the result of this. The idea of God as supply, or Source, is a very basic tenet of truth. And once you understand this, you have the key to manifestation, and the texts we will be offering you will address manifestation in very clear ways. The realization that God is Source, or that there is one tone sung, expressed as all things, which may be aligned to and allow you to gift and be the recipient of gifts that are ever present, will transform a reality. But your choices prior—and you have inherited the results of these—to know the self as separate has claimed a world, or your idea of a world, in tribal structures, the haves and have-nots. You have even enslaved your brother and your sister in a belief in your self-righteousness.

The knowing of who you are implies great change, and the moment you know who you are, you know who others are as well, and any barrier that you would erect between you and your brother is the creation that you will now be attending to. Underline the word *will*. The barriers are witnessed now. The creations you've known through fear are evidential, will not be ignored. And unless you attend to them, you will continue to act with them in accord with their purview. And because they are creations of fear, they will do their job to replicate. "Well, we're told to be fearful," you may say. Perhaps you are. But to know prudence is not to be fearful. To understand the consequence of one's actions is not fearful. It is self-aware. And becoming self-aware, in a new way, is a by-product of this instruction. This is a teaching of liberation, yes. But you will not be liberated while you are chained, and until you see how you are chained, you will not release the chains, nor can you release your brother or sister from them. The chains come in different forms. You are actually participatory to them and to their creation, participatory by agreement and acquiescence. You understand when you fear you are moving in a different direction than when you have faith. But you would like to believe fear is your teacher, even though where it leads you is to greater darkness. To release the self from fear is to stop claiming it as an ally and teacher. And you must begin with yourself. Who you are afraid of is indeed your teacher, what you are afraid of, indeed your teacher, because the opportunity is to release the fear in order to liberate yourself from the morass, from the chains it would bind you to.

Now, as we teach through Paul, we have an agreement. We will only carry the information at a level that he can cohere it with or to. We will rephrase this. He is listening and interrupting. We will agree that the information we bring through Paul will not confound him to such a degree that he will turn the radio off. And we will say this now: Paul, prepare to be confounded. We intend to carry you at the top of the wave that we are bringing. That is not for visibility. It is for velocity, because it is the top of the wave that will strike with greatest impact. And this teaching is about to become changed.

"Changed how?" he asks. The information you have received in prior texts is completely relevant. It is the predecessor to what we teach today. But we are going to begin to teach manifestation of form and field, which is not addressed in the most practical ways or experiential ways in the prior texts because you could not hold the frequency of the teaching. The time has come for the authors of this text, which is we, the voice of this text, which is Paul, and the students of these texts, which is you, to say yes to a co-creation.

The manifestation of this text is the resurrection of the Monad, first in principle and then in active form. *Principle* means that the Christ itself, the Monad, if you wish, the Eternal Self, in full spring, full flower, full expression, in its own mandate to resurrect, reclaims everything that it encounters at its level of resonance. It is a reclamation, first of field, and then of form at the level that the form can hold it.

Re-articulation, or manifestation as Monad, has been taught. These are the old mysteries that have been hindered from public presence and have been buried and kept away. But this teaching is more available at the level of agreement because the density of this plane, which has been a hindrance, is beginning to separate. If you can imagine sands and grains of sands separating, the space between the grains allows for movement, and this is the movement that is required for the resurrection of form. In other words, what is so densely packed cannot be moved. But in the higher octave, the realization of who and what one is, reclamation, escalates the field, and the field in escalation escalates the vibratory accord of all and what it encounters. And it is this movement, this cascade of energy moving through what was once densely packed, that allows resurrection to commence.

Commence is the correct word. Resurrection will commence in this text. How one completes the mission, individuated in his or her unique path, will be chosen by the soul. We will stress this. The soul, finally, who has indeed come to learn, to reclaim itself in fullness, is the decider, finally, of the level of vibration that can be sustained. We can introduce you to the high tone, but if the radio you are cannot hold the tone or align to it, you will be challenged. We will give you the information, and indeed the tools, to move the radio you are to play the high broadcast. These are the attunements we offer. But you are the one, in your Divine Will, in your agreement to serve, that will say yes to the fullness of this passage.

The passage we are taking you on is to a new way of experiencing self. Self is still present, but you are experiencing self now through the edicts of history and the entrenchment in fear that you have grown in. A flower that grows in a mud patch knows the mud patch as home. What we are doing now is releasing the mud so that you may be replanted, re-articulated, in the Upper Room, where the roots you may grow will be in light, and not in agreement to fear.

As we continue these instructions, we will invite you all to practice them, because this may be seen as practice at a certain level of behavior. When you begin your day, the awareness of the Divine, even for a few moments, the presence of the Divine upon all things, will catalyze you to a higher way of experiencing the day. What you bless is what you perceive the presence of the Divine upon. And a blessing upon the day begins with the most ordinary thing, the presence of the Divine that must—underline *must*—be present in all manifestation. This first acknowledgment of the day will actually transform the day. Paul is seeing the image of the day lifting, as if grains of sand, that which make up all he sees, are separating, and the light plays between the grains. This is exactly what occurs in the act of blessing. And when the grain of sand itself is known of as God, the alchemy, the manifestation of change, is only immediate, and always immediate.

We will say this now: How you see the world informs the solidity of the world, and creating the space through the presence of the Divine allows matter itself to begin to be received in a higher state. You may say *resurrected* state, but we would say *re-articulated*. Always remember, friends, that the one note sung that is all things, that you may know of as God, is not separate from you, either.

We will say this now: This is the beginning of chapter 1. The text is *Resurrection*. We are honored for your presence. Stop now, please. Period. Period. Period.

DAY FOUR

We are here before you, one and all, and we sing before you the great note of all things, the triumphant song of being. The truth of who and what you are, present now and always, seeks to come to fruition—to flower, to bloom, and to claim all things in its scent. The beauty of your being, unparalleled in life, will be seen by you, seen by all, because the light that you are, the beauty of this light, can no longer be hidden. You stand before us praising what has been, what has brought you to this moment, the trials you have known, the fears you have endured. You understand your history is catalytic to this moment in time, where indeed all things will be made new, and the claim we sing to you, "You Have Come, You Have Come, You Have Come," the triumphant Resurrected Self that calls all things into manifestation through like vibrational accord.

Now, the who that is come is indeed no longer the small self, but the Monad in articulation, or the Christed Self in manifestation, and the blooming of the Christ is the overtaking of the small self by the essence of the Divine. Now, by *overtaking* we don't mean overriding. The small self has its place and is always useful. But the level of identification it has held has been so paramount as to negate the Divine. So the overtaking, if we use that word, is the residual affect of the Divine Self in re-articulation. When you are in re-articulation, every aspect of you that has ever been known can and will be re-known. This does not mean you are not who you think you are, as much as it means you are well beyond that. The idea of self that you have utilized to navigate this reality has its place, yes. But it is no longer the ruler, the king or queen upon the throne, directing a world through its suppositions of what should be. Because the True Self knows, wherein the small self thinks, the True Self can claim a world into being, in articulation, yes, through its objectivity.

We will explain this for Paul. Because the True Self sees all things in truth, objectively, yes, the days of the small self's opinions being the director of the claims that create manifestation are released to a much higher way of claiming manifestation. What we will endeavor to do in these teachings is explain manifestation as it truly occurs, which happens without the edicts of the small self directing the show. When we teach through Paul, we honor his limitations because they are the areas he will grow in. And for this class today, we are going to ask him to be quiet, because we will teach things he does not like or may not want to hear. The Divine Self in re-articulation is the aspect of you that is coming into being at the cost of an idea of self that can no longer be held at this level of vibration. Now, this is a process of re-articulation, and, as we have said, that which has been held in darkness must and will be brought to the light for reclamation. To comprehend the act you are undergoing, you must look at examples in nature, the caterpillar to the butterfly, the rain to the ice. All things may be known in new form, but the essence of them remains the same. And the essence of who and what you are, beyond your idea of self, remains the same. But in a re-articulated state, the mandate of the Divine operating as and through you is its own expression.

Now, *its own expression* does not mean that you don't like to go to the movies, talk with your friends, enjoy a sunny day on the beach. It does not mean you weren't orphaned or had a challenging childhood or a hard diagnosis. But the Divine Self as you, the Eternal Self as you, does not predicate its expression on what you think it should be. And it is the small self, with its history, that would seek to emblazon the Divine with its requirements for what the Divine should be. You seek a god with a crown, you seek a light that is in love, but all things must be known now in relevance to their true nature, without the picture-book illustrations that you would have accompany them. God itself, or what is known as God, is tone and vibration. It is conscious, yes. It is all things, yes. And because it is all things, it can be known as all things.

Now, the idea of God on a throne is actually somewhat useful, because it means the arbiter of reality. And a throne can only hold one presence, be it the small self, the director of the old reality who says, "I should do this or that, become this or that, conquer this or that, so that I reign supreme," or the True Self upon the throne who is an expression of the Divine, and a benevolent one at that. The throne that we teach is simply the placement of the inherent Divine as your expression. You cannot be ruled by two masters. You do have to choose, and whether it's the Monad, or what you would call God, or the edict of the personality, each one will give you your results.

Now, when we speak of results, we are speaking of manifestation, and manifestation is the being into expression—yes, that is correct—of an idea. We will put it that simply. Everything created, everything seen in form, was the first idea. And your idea of the meaning of these things, what things have come to be called and known as, the articulation of these ideas, is the reality you have known yourself in. The first idea, the first sound made, we will call it the Word, the one note sung, the energy of the Creator in action, that is then claimed in manifestation by a being in agreement to the Divine. Now, because you are all creators at whatever level of vibration you have come to, you may create in low tone, create fear and mayhem, or you may create in a high tone, a relationship to the Divine where you understand that the Source of all things is the thing that claims manifestation, and your objectivity as a small self will simply claim you what the small self thinks it requires.

We are teaching through you now, Paul, because you agreed to it once upon a time, and agreed to say yes to the level of change that holding this vibration would concur. Now, we will say this: The tone we are singing through Paul for each of you is an alchemical tone. The level of vibration we have available to us as a True Self can reclaim you in a high octave with your consent. We do not take you where you do not wish to be taken. But once you have claimed, "I Have Come," the Divine Self in announcement of its presence, you have claimed the action of the Divine upon you, and all we are doing is supporting this claim by agreeing to it. You must understand agreement, which is vibrational accord and coherence. The level of tone we sing from is of such a high level that it may override the lower and actually reclaim and lift it simply by being. When you embody as the Divine Self, this becomes the act you engage in, less consciously than you think. Imagine you are singing a song always, and the song touches the hearts of all those who happen to hear it. The heart is transformed by the encounter with the song. They do not know who sang to them. They only know they have been changed.

Now, you are the ones who have come, who are now embodying, for the reclamation of all. Underline those words, friends: *the reclamation of all.* You become the doorway or the portal for the high tone because you can hold it in your field at the level of agreement you choose or your soul will claim for you. The affect of the song that you will be singing will reclaim all things that have been placed in fear and allow them to be re-known. The being that you are, in its own expression, is what does this work. You may be walking through the park, thinking of a friend, looking out the window and wondering about the rest of the world, but your presence and thought claim the rest of the world in the song you have begun to sing, and the rest of the world is touched by the sound.

Paul interrupts the teaching: "Is this the same as the scent you spoke of earlier, the blooming flower and its scent?" In some ways, yes, it is. A flower doesn't demand to be smelled, that its scent be known. It simply opens, and the presence of its scent, carried by the breeze, also transforms the environment that it encounters. The Monad as expressed in tone and field will do the same thing. But the idea of sound in re-articulation is comprehensive to you. Now, you understand the very simple premise that any song may be sung in a higher octave. A song is a series of notes with an intention behind them. "We will call the song a lullaby." "We will call the song a tango." The notes on the piano, placed in a sequence, have an affect. While the song is sung in this reality, it may also be sung in a higher one.

Now, you are the affect of this song. The body you hold is in resonance, and the energetic bodies that you hold are also in expression, in a variety of tone. The lifting of the field you hold we describe as a transposition of vibration, tone, or music. You are being lifted, the song that you have always been, to be re-known or re-articulated in a higher strata, which we have called the Upper Room. Because the Upper Room does not hold fear, you are no longer creating from fear, and because you are not creating from fear, the need for fear is released by you. And you are made new by this exchange of vibration, but the process of alchemy or reclamation indeed comes at the cost of the old.

Now, because we may sing for you and invite you to join us in tone, because the sound we utter may override the lower natures you have held yourselves in, because the song we sing is not tainted by fear, you may lift into it. Imagine a great wind that may move through you, that may separate the particles of the being you know yourself as and inform what lives between them. Imagine this great wind is not blowing you away but re-articulating you, singing you anew, transforming what it encounters in reclamation of what has always been true. And that is your true nature, the inherent Divine, the unparalleled beauty that in fact is you.

When we sing to you now, we are singing to you throughout time. When we sing to you now, we are singing to every body you have ever known yourself in. We are singing to every memory that has clouded your perception, tainted your ability to love, and we are singing to the heart, the true heart, that seeks to open to God and to flower with God as the Christ in you comes into expression. Because we are singing through Paul, and without the body he holds, while utilizing the body, the sound we make will not be contained. It will read through the pages of this text. It will hold the reader, the listener, in its expression. And it will reclaim you as you say yes.

On the count of three, Paul.

One. Now two. Now three.

[The Guides tone through Paul.]

Be still and know. And allow the being you are to be moved, expressed, released, re-known, reclaimed, and sung anew.

We say this to you each now:

You Have Come. You Have Come. You Have Come. You are in the Upper Room. We see you in your beauty, in your right to be, in all you have known and may know, and as we say this to you, we announce this to every aspect of you, every memory, every body, every idea of self you have accrued in time, and without time. God Is. God Is. God Is. It will be so. The Divine has come as each of you. Behold, I make all things new.

Ask them to stay quiet for a moment. We will take a pause for Paul.

(PAUSE)

We ask you questions now about your lives. Who do you think you are? What do you think you are? And how do you describe service? The template you have been offered by this teaching actually transposes all of those questions to a higher way of receiving them. You think you are the name that you were born with. You think that what you are is the body or the occupation you have taken. You think how you serve is what you do for the benefit of others. While there is truth to all of these ideas, there are other ways of comprehending the meaning of them. The Divine Self as who, the I Am Self, the one who knows who it is, is the one in reclamation of the being that you are. It is not other than you. It is the truth of you. So you are giving yourself to the truth of self at the cost of the lies that you have been taught to believe should be the truth. The what that you are, the manifest what, must also be of God, because all things are of God, and how you serve is how this God Self expresses, less so what you do than how you be.

Now, the broadcast we are in with you now is indeed an expression of service, but your idea of who you are, of holding this capacity to be in radiance or expression as the Divine, impacting what you encounter, is still framed by the idea of the small self's capacity for it. Now, the small self has done the best he or she can. She always will do the best she can. But the aspect of you that is coming into being, the expressed True Self, the triumphant self, withstands all things because it cannot be conquered by anything other. The Divine as you knows no fear, not even fear of death, because the Divine as you knows itself in eternity.

Now, you've chosen to incarnate to have this life you are living now, and your expression of it may be the perfect expression for this lifetime. So, please, not one of you think we are telling you that you are doing something wrong. We are simply claiming you beyond a boundary, and a false boundary, that has been operating in your systems. Paul is seeing a coloring book. The lines have been drawn. The child is taught not to draw outside the lines. We are drawing outside the lines because you are boundless in vibration. You just ascribe to an idea of limitation.

Now, when we teach through you, Paul, and when we teach to our students, we utilize your energy field as an amplifier of the tone that we are broadcasting. But the purpose of this is to activate the student through co-resonance. Because we sing this high note, that means the note can be sung, and because you hear the note or feel the note in your field, you move into an agreement to the note, which lifts you to the octave of it and the expression of it in vibration. At this level, there are aspects of self that cannot cohere, and will fall or disassemble themselves. Now, some, indeed, will put up a fight. "If I am not the best, I must be the worst." "If I don't find love tomorrow, I will never find love." Whatever the edicts of the small self have been that have become so entrenched that you self-identify through them will be the challenges you have to encounter, because no one gets to do this while carting their dirty laundry up to the Upper Room and sitting upon it, not willing to address it. You will address the dirty laundry. You will address the old pain. You will address the circumstances of childhood, yes, not to blame your parents or blame yourself, but to say objectively, "This is what I experienced, and it is not who I am. It gives me information about how I perceived myself and a world, but it has never been who I am. It has been something that I have appropriated, a narrative, if you wish, that I seek to confirm in my daily life."

When you stop confirming the old, the old is no longer present. And the circumstances the old has claimed, be it loneliness, be it ill health, be it economic failure at the level of the personal self or the country, can be addressed. You must understand that this process of articulation is happening within and without. The country, and all countries, are undergoing this, just as the individual is—that which has been held in darkness now brought to the light to be seen and resurrected.

When a planet is made new, all things are seen anew. And the claim we have offered, "Behold, I make all things new," is indeed the witnessing of the Divine Self upon what God has created. When the Divine sees the Divine, or when the Divine witnesses the Divine, where the Divine has previously been denied, all things are made new. You will become the conduit for this sight as you integrate these teachings. They will become effortless. You will stop seeking to damn your brother, damn this one or that, these people over there, or those over here, because of the sense of satisfaction it might bring you. You will understand the cost, and you will understand that the cost is the removal from the Upper Room or the higher energetic strata to the low realm where the battles will ensue.

There is no battle in the Upper Room. This does not mean you turn a blind eye to injustice. It means you bring the light to where the darkness has been, and if you are called to action, you will act. But please remember this, friends: Self-righteousness is always the small self. The True Self does not judge, because she comprehends the unique ability of each individual to learn through his or her creations. She is not the arbiter of justice. She does not seek to punish or defile. She has come in love, and in love is great power. The song that she sings or expresses as can indeed topple walls, reclaim all things, make all things new.

We will continue this chapter when we speak next. We thank you for your presence. Stop now, please. Period. Period. Period.

DAY FIVE

What you seek in love, what you hope to find in love, indeed will be met by you. A claim of love—"I am in love, I am honoring love, I am choosing in love"—will actually alter your vibratory field to create from this place of being. As you lift your vibration, as you are attuned to the higher way of expressing, the opportunity to be as love becomes present in your field in a way that is somewhat effortless. You are no longer efforting anything, really. You are aligning. And the difference between aligning and efforting must now be understood.

The choice to embody as the True Self, the Divine as who and what you are, must be comprehended by you as a choice in love. There is no fear in this choice, because there is no fear in God. The trials you have faced historically for devoting the self to Source, in any incarnation, were the cause of much of the fear you hold now. But the prior ways of expressing, the old doctrines, are no longer holding you, and you are in fact free to lift beyond the idea of church, or religion, or doctrine that would tell you you are not allowed. To lift beyond the old, to truly be free, is to incarnate in the Upper Room, and a new incarnation, which you come to through the alignment of will in love.

Now, to understand will is to comprehend choice and the manifestation of choice. What is chosen in love will not defile you, cannot even harm you. The trajectory of love is love itself, and the path of love, the path of the True Self, holds for itself great promise. To deny the Divine in the self, or in anyone, is to move out of love and to claim the self in shadow. Once this occurs, you find yourself bound to your prior creations. The very things you have damned or denied the Divine in are the anchors to the lower realm. To release these anchors is to comprehend the freedom that comes in forgiveness. Now, many of you think forgiveness is an act of weakness. "She must know what she did to me; she cannot be forgiven." "He must pay for what he did; penance will be paid." The old doctrines, an eye for an eye, are in an equation to an idea of karma that is born in retribution. To comprehend that like attracts like—what ye measure so shall ye mete—the alignment to the Divine calls to it its own benefit. The rising beyond the law of karma, as you have often misunderstood it, is the gift of the Upper Room. This does not mean that you are not accountable to your acts. Far from it. But it does mean that your acts are now chosen in love, or quite simply the awareness of the omnipresent Divine—omnipresent, always and ever present. The True Self as you in a newly articulated state becomes the presence of this as it can and will be held in form.

Now, the denial of the Divine in the body itself is particularly destructive to humanity. A cat knows she's holy. She doesn't know what God is as you would know God, but she knows she is of the whole, and her body in many ways is her ideal expression. She is not trying to fix herself. If she has a wound, she will tend to it. If she is hungry, she will eat. She will defecate as needed, but live the life in the body in an awareness that it is who she is at this level of expression. The denial of the Divine in form for most of you claims you in separation from your vast potential to know the self in and beyond form, and by *beyond form* we mean in a newly articulated state where the laws that you have been bound by are not present in the same ways. The weight of the vibrational being that you claim yourself as moors you to the lower vibrational field. Now, while the body will always retain density because you are in form, even the form that you have taken can be ascended or lifted in scale. But this must be a gradual process for the body to acclimate. Imagine that you were lifted to the top of a mountain from the lowest valley too quickly. You would be unable to breathe. You haven't aligned to the idealization of the environment that you now find yourself standing in.

The movement of the body through these attunements

has been pronounced in prior texts. And in this text, what we intend is to acclimate the entirety of you, inclusive of form, to an agreement to the Upper Room. When we invoked the Divine through you yesterday as a great wind blowing through you, a great force of change re-creating you, we were actually supporting you in this, and we will continue to. The process of re-articulation is less about finding a better practice, a healthier habit for eating, a different way of making the body known, than it is understanding that the Divine as form is also omnipresent.

Now, you understand that the body that you have taken has a finite span of life, that one day you will be in another form, burnt in a cinder on a pyre, buried in the ground, left in the ocean for the fish to feed on. But the body itself is always alive as an energetic structure. And the energy of the body, or what was known as body, even this will move into another form. Now, to comprehend the divinity of form is a very simple act that all of you ignore. "I am holy, as is all. All is holy, as am I." But even in the speaking of these words, most of you deny form. You think of the soul, the aspect of you that incarnates and is finally realized in union with its Source. But the release of the body does not guarantee you union, and manifesting in a body certainly does not deny you union, although you expect it does.

The idea of re-articulation in form is less important than you think. It is the manifestation itself of what has always been holy, at a level of realignment where its newly articulated state can hold a level of tone, that can transpose matter. And underline that word *matter*. All matter is, is the Divine operating in a lower density. When you become more spirit than flesh, or the realization of the flesh holds spirit more fully, you in fact become somewhat translucent. The energy that you are, which is operating in two strata simultaneously, in form and without, becomes a vehicle for change. Now, to comprehend this teaching is to understand law, and there is nothing in form that can be outside of God, although the application of the form may be in denial of the Divine. Paul is seeing the image of a device of torture. It is also of God, without the meaning or the usage that has been ascribed it. To realize the metal or stone that comprises the object as the Divine in articulation reclaims your alignment to it so that it may be re-seen and re-known beyond prior edict or need. So all things are holy, although how they have been meant to use, or the usage applied to them, may be in the denial of the Divine. Every human being is of God, although many deny it wholeheartedly and live an experience that is in shadow as a result. But once you understand that the material realm is an articulation of the Divine operating in low tone, and what you are doing now is ascending in frequency as the body can manage it, and even as your sense of self can apply it, you will comprehend the fullness of this teaching.

The fullness of this teaching is indeed embodiment, the manifestation of the Divine as can be held in form, or the resurrection of the Christed Self, the manifestation of the Monad, that is the transformer and redeemer of the world. When something is redeemed, it is reclaimed, and the Source of all things, out-pictured as you, seeks to redeem what it encounters. Now, to redeem something is to know it as of God. It is

not to say, "Oh, look at that poor thing by the side o̷
She doesn't know God. I'd best teach her what she is." The o̶ͫ͜
you see by the side of the road is as holy as anyone else, and your
knowing of this is the act of the redeemer that can be claimed
in any circumstance and to magnificent effect.

When we taught in prior texts of working with the Word,
the Word as attunement—"I am Word through my body,
Word I am Word, I am Word through my vibration, Word
I am Word, I am Word through my knowing of myself as
Word"—we were claiming you each as the instrument of the
Divine that you have always been. And in subsequent texts we
examined the instrument, and the implications of beginning
to play it, and the destructive aspects of self that would seek
to deny it. But here we begin the great orchestra, the fullness
of tone, the fullness of creation, as can be exemplified by the
Divine that has come as each of you. To become this—again,
an act of will in love—is to say yes to the true purpose of
your nature, of your being, and your true expression. To understand this is not to deny the acts you have taken on this
plane. You have fed the poor. You have healed the sick. You
have done what you can to help others. And that is all wonderful, and of course may continue, but in a high regard. But
you are no longer seeking to find your holiness or to prove its
presence. It becomes the state of being where you know, and
in your knowing you act, and in this act the expression of God
is known through you. Underline the word *through*. The self
as conduit, the self as expression, the self as aligned to true
purpose in love.

Now, to benefit others in any way is to comprehend who

they truly are. Bless the one on the side of the road, but if the one on the side of the road is hungry, feed the one on the side of the road. That is an act of love. To care for your brother, for your sister when she cannot care for herself, is an act of love, and you may do this well in complete ignorance of his or her divine nature, or in ignorance of your own. God does not need to be prayed to by name to be understood, and any act of love is God itself acting through you. You do not love. You become as love. And in love you know, and you cherish your brother, and you reclaim, by nature of presence, that which has been denied love.

This is a teaching of love and re-creation. And the choice we offer you now, if you wish to take it, is to say yes to the embodiment of form and field, as you can align to it, in a choice of love. These are the words you may speak, if indeed you wish to:

"On this night I choose to align every aspect of myself to the choice to love, to be as love, to express as love, and allow the true nature of my being to inform all things to become as love, the Divine in action, the Word in form and field. I am Word through this intention. Word I am Word."

We will take a pause for Paul. We will teach you more in a bit. Period. Period. Period. Stop now, please.

(PAUSE)

What stands before you is eternity. What stands before you is always ever one thing, the presence of the Divine in any form it has taken. And any experience you have in a lifetime must be understood as opportunity to know the Divine.

Now, when we use the term *know the Divine,* we mean realize, claim, the inherent Source of all things. We do this without the religious terminology that some of you dislike, but in fact we find useful because we reclaim language as it was initially intended, and not as it has been misused by religion. To comprehend that all things are of one Source is a universal claim. It is true in every reality you could ever interact with, and it in some ways becomes the ship, this awareness that allows you to transform your own reality and integrate those realities that may be higher than you have known thus far.

Our teaching through Paul has several more texts before it is complete. When it is complete, we will work through him rather differently. And while we still may dictate books, the texts that we have written, in one distilled form, will serve as a gateway for those who read and understand and align for generations to come.

Now, we say *generations* in an awareness of eternity. Your time, and experience of time, has a great sense of confusion attached to it. And when we say *generations,* we quite simply mean that this teaching is present in eternity and may be accessed there. While the texts have form, the vibration that is the true teaching exists without the texts and may be met by anyone whose intent is to serve and to claim the highest chalice to drink from.

We serve through Paul in different ways, some of which he is unaware of. But our work on this plane has been consistent, prior to the birth of the man before you, and will continue after he is gone. The polarity of experience in a manifest world has been a good teacher, but the time has come to learn in new ways. And our presences in shepherding you to this new way of being is not only an honor, but a gift, because as we see you move, and claim an inheritance that has always been yours but has been denied, we understand that the world that you have known will be altered and re-sung in the true note of God.

> *On this day we claim that all who hear these words will sing a new song, will claim a new state of being, and lift all that he or she encounters to the true light of love.*

We thank you each for your presence. Yes, this is in the text.

DAY SIX

What you ask for, what you claim, what you say will be, from the Upper Room, can be made known to you in form. The Upper Room, you see, a place of great possibility and high awareness, announces you each in your full potential. Underline the word *full*. The ideas of who you have been, or what you have claimed as yourselves, are about to be transposed and renegotiated, re-known and prospered, at a higher level of accord. Each of you says yes to this at the cost of an idea, the idea of who you should have been or thought you were or expected to be. The triumph of the new is upon you now, and we intend to take you to a place of limitlessness.

Now, understand *limitlessness,* the idea of eternity beyond any known barrier, precluding nothing and including all. The True Self, you see, the Divine as who and what you are, knows itself in limitlessness, knows itself in fullness, and can comprehend beyond any veil that you have erected or been in accordance to. The idea of moving beyond the veil, moving beyond the screen, to the True Self in full flower is the action of this text. And the requirements of it indeed will be made known to you as you say yes, because what is before you, the unknown, yes, but only unknown by the experience of the small self, and unified at a level of agreement as the Monad, in agreement to its Source, claims all things anew.

Now, in this teaching, we have several edicts. You will be changed, you will be made new, you will be reclaimed in the high order of the Upper Room, and you will say yes to the benefit of it through the aspect of self that already knows who she is, what he is, and how she serves. As we teach, as we focus on each of you as of the whole and reunite the aspects of self that have been dismissed or dismembered through fear, through change, through alignment to the old, you may know the self in a new agreement. The Divine that has come as you, that is already in unification, will be the support for the aspect of self that is transitioning, climbing the scale, to be reconciled—and yes, indeed, resurrected—with its Source.

As we teach through Paul, we understand his requirements, his questions, which often supersede our intention for a text that is being written. But we honor the questions because they are in equation with a level of consciousness that is in transition, and to deny these things, to ignore the questions, would be to ignore the aspect of self that is seeking to grow and to comprehend.

We say this to each of you now: The idea of who you are, what you have been, who you have chosen to think of the self as, is what is being called forth and reclaimed. And the process that you will each undergo, in manifestation, is unlike anything you have experienced thus far. The transition we are undergoing with Paul, who moves to flower, the transition you each undergo through adherence to these teachings, is to the aspect of self that is in triumph and already knows itself as reconciled. The belief that you are separate from all things, the Source of all things from the one beside you, is what is being released now because humanity has chosen to move beyond the old.

In the chapters before us, we will explore several things—the idea of separation, yes, but the great potential we speak to must be comprehended experientially. We can no longer use words that by their nature diminish the process that you are undergoing. The amplitude of sound or tone that we occasionally invoke is intended to supersede the intellect to move to a place of experience, when the one note sung, the sound of the all, can underlie all things, and your experience of self as of the one tone, the one note sung, claims you anew, not only in the Upper Room, but in timelessness.

Paul is questioning already. "Is this a dictation for the text? What is the title of this chapter, if it is? Where do we go from here? And, please, how long will it take?" We will answer only one question. Yes, this is in the text, and we will give you the title when we wish because the chapter is not yet complete. The process we take you through now, reconciliation through the Monad, or the Christ, to realization, is alchemical. And the knowing of this process, which is the realization of it, is the agreement you make by reading this text. But the *yes* that you give of the free will you have is already spoken, because the Monad as you is always in *yes*, always in high accord, and cannot say no to unification.

God knows itself as of all things, and the Spark, or the Monad, the Christ, if you prefer, cannot know itself as separate, although it may be precluded from expression by the small self that would deny the inner light. These days are ending. You come into flower—first one, then all. And the *yes* that you offer, the agreement to the light expressing as all aspects of you, is the name of the book, which is *Resurrection*.

The title that we give you now we will call "Preparation," because the preparation that you must undergo here is far deeper than what you would expect. This is not a cosmetic transition. This is the transition to the new equation, in a higher alignment than you have been aligned to thus far or could imagine through the structure of personality. The choice that we offer you, as a personality structure, is always to turn the page. If you feel you must rest, must decide at the level of personality what you can hold, you are entitled to that. But as we said, the Divine as you, in its resurrected state, is the knowing that you require to align all things made new.

We will take a pause for Paul. Indeed, this is in the text. Stop now, please. Period. Period. Period.

2

NEW EXPERIENCE

DAY SIX (CONTINUED)

What stands before you, what you will encounter, is the idea of self that would deny the Divine. Each of you holds this, each of you has chosen it, knowingly or unknowingly, in your participatory natures to an incarnation in this field. The release of separation is an act of revolution, and a revolution is rarely peaceful, rarely pretty. For some of you this will mean that an idea of self that you have chosen to know yourself through is ripped from you, or at least that will be what you think. But the release of the old takes many forms, and how a soul chooses liberation is under the auspices of the soul.

Now, the True Self, in tandem with the soul, supports this realization of reunification. But what has held you back, one and all, is only one idea—that God is not. Now, the word *God* itself, confused by most of you, if seen as first principle or cause, can be re-established. In the beginning was the Word,

and the Word, the one note sung, that all else is called into
being from. The denial of this, as if you sprung fully flowered
from your mother and lived in a city that was the only place
you could be, and took a job that was your choice to succeed
through a premise of what success must be, is the way most of
you live. To remember who you are is to begin to comprehend
what you are not, and what you are not is separate, although
indeed you are individuated, spectacularly so, but of the whole.
Reconciliation, a revolutionary act, the release of separation, a
releasing of an idea of self and truly nothing more, is an act
of truth. Underline those words, *an act of truth,* or truth expressing itself at the cost of the lie that has concealed it. True
dominion comes when an individual, in a reconciled state,
cannot deny the Divine in anyone or anything. And once this
is established as the being, as the life lived, all things this life
encounters are altered by the expression of one in reconciliation. The truth of your being is what transforms this, not your
idea of what it should look like or be. You would all make it
pretty, perhaps even polite. Show us a polite revolution. Such
a thing is not possible. But it need not be bloody, and it will
be transforming, and it will come at a cost. What you have
endowed with power is your ruler. What is ruling you now,
through the schism you've created with the Divine, is in some
ways superstition—"my idea of God" or "my idea of what can
save me." To move to truth is to release the idea of God to the
resonance of the field that is God. When God is allowed to
reclaim all its creations, and this is indeed an act of will, when
all things may be made new, when reconciliation becomes the
basis of each life lived, the Kingdom is established in this field.

Now, the Kingdom, as we have taught it, the realization of the Divine in all things, is not a pretty place. It looks no different, in some ways, than the place you may live now. But you understand it as God in expression, and as it is understood as such, it lifts itself to higher resonance. It sparkles and is made new through the effervescence and illumination that is the Divine. Each of you says yes to an idea of reconciliation that is convenient to you. "I want God when I want God and how I want it, and I want to be holy in the ways I think I can be, but let's not talk about the ways I am not." Every aspect of you is holy. Even the carnal self is of God, because nothing is outside of God. And the reclamation of the idea of sin, which is simply calling back into being the practices or behaviors or ideas you have chosen to learn through and re-unifying them into their Source, which cannot be done by denying them, will offer you a level of liberation that you have not known thus far.

We say yes to you now in advance of this. We say yes to you now in preparation for what will come, because what will come will likely challenge the life you have lived, because you are so participatory to the denial of the Divine, so complicit to its creations, that you are in self-deception. Now, to be in self-deception is to be in a lie, and a lie will not be tamed by appeasing it. A lie will be transformed only by truth. And when a lie has been present and deeply embedded in a culture, the act of reconciliation of the culture may create fissions in the culture and a collapse of segments of it. And the reason for this is the intention to deny the Divine in oneself or one's brother comes at a precarious cost.

Now, as we said prior, humanity has chosen to lift, has

decided it will survive, and is undergoing a passage of re-creation that is not only monumental, but challenging at every level. Because the old is falling away as you move beyond it, because the new is seeking to be born, every step you take feels as if it is transitional to something other than perhaps you have known thus far. The individual choice to claim higher alignment is actually causal. Because the causal field that humanity has claimed has agreed to this, individuals are now accepting a potential that has been hindered, and in fact denied them, through the collective choice to separation. The collective choice to separation is going to collapse. Now, when something collapses, it often makes a great noise, and we suspect this will be the case here. But because you have denied God in your brother, henceforth denied the Divine in yourselves, because you have equated love with getting what you want from someone, or success as accruing money, what you will encounter in this transformative time is indeed reckoning, and the choices made in fear which contribute to separation must indeed be remade.

Now, when something makes a great noise, a thunderous noise perhaps, it requires everyone's attention. And if you look at the times you sit in, everybody's attention has been claimed. You now have opportunity to learn through collective event, and this is indeed a gift, only if you understand that the lesson or the gift that is being given to you is one of reconciliation. When your brother is suffering, you care for your brother. When your brother is ill, you tend to his needs. When your sister is starving, you make sure she has food. You know the one beside you as worthy of the life lived, and you comprehend the one beside you as of God, because the moment you deny God in the one suffering, in the one hungry, in the one beside you, you have denied it in yourself as well, and perpetuation of separation is re-established.

Now, the times you sit in—great opportunity, yes, thunderous noise, perhaps, to call everyone's attention forward—are times of resurrection. The time of resurrection is the time of reconciliation of the aspect of humanity that has always known truth at the cost of the lies that humanity has perpetuated through separation. And because this is occurring now, and the lines in some ways feel drawn—indeed everyone has opinions, and ideas of justice differ greatly—the only thing that will reclaim all things is truth, and truth and justice are in equation. Now, you equate justice with punishment, and that is not what justice is. Justice is a righting of what has not been righted. It is the claim of truth in the face of the lie. And the changes that occur as a result of this righting, as the result of this agreement to truth, are what humanity requires.

Now, the idea of subjective truth must be decided with and for, once and for all. Truth is not subjective. Opinions are subjective. What is true is always true and will always be true. And the idea of factions, each one's touting a separate truth, must be understood as a masquerade known in folly. This will stop because it cannot continue and will not be continued. And what will finally stand, we say, is truth in the face of the lie, in the face of injustice, and certainly in the face of man's inhumanity to man.

When we teach through Paul, we are aware of his limitations, how long we may speak while being rendered clearly, when his system needs a pause, and we will continue only for a few more moments, and continue later when his system has rested.

Reconciliation is the embodiment of truth. Resurrection, which is the presence of the Divine in fullness in form, is articulation of truth, what is always true. You can make nothing holy. You can deny the Divine in anything you wish, and that becomes your experience. It is the experience of humankind at the current level of vibration. But this transition is occurring, and the falling away of the old is before you now. Make the great sound, the true sound, which we say is "God Is," the announcement of the omnipresence that will reclaim all things, and the world you have seen indeed will be made new.

We will resume our teaching later. We take a pause for Paul. Period. Period. Period. Stop now, please.

Q: They were talking about the release of the idea of God as part of the transformation, and that kind of went in one ear and out the other.

A: Your understanding of God is based on several precepts—what you wish God to be, what in fact you were told God might be, and scriptures that tell you what God is to appeal to a specific population. They are all ideas of God, and nothing more. The experience of God, knowing God, is the closest you can have to the truth, and we will offer you this as we are allowed. We don't mean to diminish your ideas, but you cannot claim truth when you are resting in a lie. The lie may be comfortable, and indeed comforting, the best you can have. Now, you've had a god in a cloud, a punishing fiery god. You've had men on crosses. You've had beings that fly through the sky and perform miracles. All are aspects of God, but the best that humanity can know. The totality of the vibration of God will remain unknown. It is too vast to be known, but you may experience it. You will never know the ocean in its entirety. It is too vast to swim. But you may know the ocean each time you bathe in it or ride upon its waves. Do you understand the teaching?

Q: The Guides had talked a lot today about us needing to recognize or release or remake the choices that we've made in fear. I understand that sometimes as a conscious effort, and sometimes it happens in batches or feels like big chunks of stuff that fall off at the same time. When do we need to be conscious of what we're releasing?

A: It's happening anyway. You really can't control it. You're not deciding what should be released and when. You can offer anything to God, or again your idea of God, and trust that it will be met in perfect ways. But this is not self-improvement. The small self doesn't address the small self in high ways. It does the best it can with the tools it's been given. An alchemical act, one of re-knowing and reconciliation, happens very quickly, and very slowly, depending on what is requiring movement. Paul is seeing the image of the shore being eroded. You notice the change quickly when the erosion has occurred, but it has been imperceptible in its process, and one day it is seen for what it is. In many ways that is the process of change that you undergo. But undergoing this change, which is a product of ascension, not the reason for it, is something that you understand by being in it, and after the fact of it. You don't know the wave has hit you until you are in the wave, nor do you know where the wave has carried you until you are brought to the new shore. Period. Period. Period.

DAY SEVEN

What you see before you is a collective act of creation. Everything seen and that may be seen in visible form has been agreed upon by you. The reality you see is an agreement itself, an agreement to know the world through the senses, yes, in an embodied state. The elasticity of your reality is far more than you know, and there is nothing solid in form that appears solid, and even the sky is more than sky. The sky is God, the earth is God, the air you breathe the substance of God in one form exhaled in another, the Divine as all things. You seek to categorize your world—what is good, what is evil, what should be there, what should not. But we will say to you today: Until reconciliation occurs—all things are of God—you will know the self in separation. Now, it is not a great leap as you might presuppose. The idea of Source and substance in a unified state can be understood by you intellectually, but we are no longer appealing to the intellect when we teach. We wish to offer you experience of manifestation that will qualify you, in your own knowing, to know the self as of God. And *knowing* means realization.

Now, to be in a realized state is not to walk upon water. You seek to do miracles, so you might say, "I have done a miracle." You do not do miracles. You become as the miracle, in some ways, the translator of form to higher octave through your interaction with it. Now, once you understand that form itself, an expression of God, can and must be re-known, the realization of manifestation has already occurred. And we will say this: The moment permission is given to re-see anything, the Monad itself will begin its manifestation as and through that thing. In other words, the Christ or Divine Self, in its perception, is already moving to lift what it encounters, once permission is given. But permission must be given in the lower realm because your agreements in form, the manifestation as form, has claimed you in alignment to that which is in density. The fluid nature of the Divine in its most dense form is what you are obstructed by. Thought itself is not dense, the Divine itself is not dense, but your alignment through the denial of the Divine has claimed you in a dense reality. You can imagine smoke that was once wood rising through a chimney in another form, and in some ways the process of resurrection requires a death and a restatement of the form you have taken so it may move to the higher alignment. There is no crucifixion in this teaching. The death we speak of is the death of an idea that has been made concrete. You expect the ice to melt. You do not expect the rock to turn again to lava, but the rock is lava in a dense form. And everything you see and have ever seen can indeed be re-seen and re-known or realized in the Upper Room.

Now, the Upper Room is not a factory where wood is turned to ash. The Upper Room is not a place where you go about your business transmuting the material world to liquid form, to its etheric state. The Upper Room is where this is realized, because it can only be realized at a plane of vibration or octave of tone where it already exists. You must underline that. *It already exists.* Everything exists in multiple octaves. The tone of anything in its most reduced form, that which appears concretized in your vibrational reality, still exists in the etheric world, or it *is* ether or spirit, manifest in form. The lifting of all things, the re-membering of all things, to its true spiritual state is the act of the alchemist. And the alchemist knows who she is, she knows what she is, and her service is present through her witness, because she sees God, because she knows herself as not separate from it.

Now, each of you say, "Oh, let me do this. I want to turn the water to wine. I want to be the alchemist, the one who does magic." There is no magic in this teaching. There is realization. You are obstructed by your ideas and your entrainment to a level of accord that denies the realities that are present before you but have been veiled by separation from your experience. To say, "I want to be the one" is to deny the Divine, because it is the Divine that is the actor here, the one who transforms.

Now, the Divine come as you is a very confused premise for most of you. You still think it's you, and in some ways you are not wrong, and in other ways entirely wrong. The aspect of you, the Monad or the Christ in manifestation or bloom, overrides the senses, or reinterprets form comprehensive of your senses, so that your experience of the world has moved to an accord with the Upper Room, wherein all places, all things, all experience is made new. The small self, who wants the victory crown—"Look at me, I have ascended"—may be sitting happily in the basement with her crown, announcing it to no one in particular. The True Self, you see, *is* the announcement. The Divine Self in form *is* the proclamation. "I Have Come" is the sound of God in the expression of the form taken. So the small self, who would seek to put this teaching in his pocket, open up a school, hand out diplomas to the ascended, and make herself, himself, the expert, is not present at the level of articulation that we teach.

"It is not present? Then where is it?" he says. Well, the idea of self, the idea of who you think you are, is what is moved. Now, this is a mountain moving, but it is also the movement of the snail on the sand. It is infinitesimally small and fully enormous at the same time. You understand yourselves in a finite sense. Everything you experience is in fact an experience through the idea of self that you have acclimated to. But it only takes a moment to switch the station or the octave that you express through. It is a mountainous occasion, but it also happens through an incremental shift in consciousness, where you move from the singular to the plural in your awareness of self.

Now, this seems impossible to all of you, but the experience of this teaching, once it is undertaken fully, is to a knowing that expresses beyond the idea of separation. The manifest world, still present in form—you pour the tea from the teapot, you put the baby in the cradle, knowing what these things are and what their uses must be. But your realization as the who, who pours the tea and puts the baby to bed, is somewhat different. You have moved to a higher level of tone or vibrational accord, and the egoic structure, that which has been the basis of so much of your experience, is curtailed. It is not put down. It is, in some ways, assumed by the higher for its appropriate usage. "What would that be?" he asks. Well, in the morning when you get out of bed, you put on your slippers, not your wife's. You understand the difference. You understand the use and the requirements of the singular self. You are not moving beyond that. But you are moving to an inclusivity of the vibrational field where what you encounter is lifted by your presence.

It is the divine presence that opens every doorway. Some of you are stumbling for keys on a great key chain. "Tell me which lock to open. I will find my way to the Kingdom once I have the right key." The key is True Self in expression, and True Self is known in a profound humility to the manifestation of the Divine that is encountered in all things. In other words, friends, the Divine as you in its expressed state is offering itself for the transmutation or re-articulation of form to what already expresses in the higher realm. Imagine a magic trick where you say the magic ball will float on air, only to come crashing down at your feet. When the Monad is what is lifting, it is lifting the ball, or the expression of whatever it encounters, to its own level of alignment. Do you understand the premise? The Monad lifts to what its Self is, and all manifestation encountered by the Monad in its expressed state is altered by its presence. You understand an idea of Christ as redeemer, but you may also look at this as Christ as reclaimer, and we are not speaking of the personage of the Christ that you have come to know as Jesus, but the articulation of the Divine Spark in its expression in all things. It reclaims itself. The flame of the Divine, when lit in fullness, illumines you in fullness. You become the light of the world because the world itself is reclaimed by your very presence.

Now, we must caution you, and caution you well. Those of you who would seek to make this a teaching of separation through the idea of specialness will be highly challenged in your experience. "Look at me and what I am, what I can do, what I have become." You will fall off your stage and onto your bottom rather quickly because the Upper Room holds no place for self-glorification. Now, understand what we mean here truly. It does not mean you don't excel in your craft. It does not mean you don't say thank you for a compliment well earned. It is the intent of the being that you become in the higher octave that is in service. Underline *service*. True service is the expression of the Divine in whatever form it takes.

Now, to do the duty of the Divine, if you wish to use that phrase, is simply to accept it, because at this level of vibration you have moved into your knowing, and when you are in your knowing you know what to do. You know the answer before the question is asked. The gift of knowing is the primary gift of the Upper Room, and the awareness of the Divine Will that is available to you because you have aligned to it takes questioning, in some ways, out of the equation. He interrupts the teaching: "But we have to question. We have to agree. It's right to question and it's right to be cautious." You are speaking as the small self, Paul, and it is very true, at that level of tone, that you must question. This very teaching is in response to your questions, and in response to the questions of all those we encounter through our tutelage. But at the level of the True Self, you have come into an agreement with a level of alignment where the will itself, in a unified state, or braided state of expression, proffers you with each opportunity that you require to further realization. And yes, this may be service, but it may also be the requirements of the soul, as the soul is illumined to its higher expression.

The small self, you see, wants this done yesterday, and wants a paycheck for having done it. "Give me what I say I should have now. Where's the mountain I get to move? Give me the water to turn to wine." That is the small self demanding outcome. He interrupts: "Well, I must say, you said this was an experiential teaching. What is the experience, then, if we don't have realization through our impression or interaction with the material realm?" What changes is vast, and in some ways too vast to fully explain here. But the imprinting of the Divine in the energetic field that is experienced through the attunements we offer, and then made known in form, are the keys you require to go through this process. The experience of self is what is transformed, and consequently the experience of manifestation. The focus we have given you on the translation of form through vibration will be reiterated here briefly. But the body you have taken, less solid than you think, interacts with a world that is also less solid than you think. And when the thinking is transformed, the experience of body and world is transformed. Imagine you have always walked on the street not knowing you could hover a foot above it. This is an illustration, not an expectation, but the metaphor is apt. Once you know your capacity is greater than you think—you begin to express beyond the limited self that has been indoctrinated through agreement and a culture knowing itself in fear and using fear as its primary tool to teach—you can move beyond what you have known to new experience. We will call this chapter "New Experience." Indeed, it began yesterday, and we are continuing now.

The realization of the form that you have taken in a higher state is something you experience in vibration, and then in manifestation. The claim we taught you prior, "I know what I am in truth," the Divine as manifest, is indeed key here. And once you begin to work with the vibration of form itself—"Not only do I know what I am, I know what you are as well, and what that is, and that thing over there, and those things over there"—in other words, what has been stamped or labeled as solid is re-seen as of God, which is the first step to a translated reality. What you have put outside of God has called you to the darkness. The physical reality you know yourself in is in the darkness because you have denied God in it. When God is present, it is not invoked as much as reclaimed. There is God in the acorn that becomes the tree. There is God in the firewood, there is God in the burning ash and the smoke that rises. *This realization is not effortful.* And we must underline this, lest some of you go out deciding what God should be, and now how it should look, so that you can confirm the teaching in your own way. This is a teaching of allowance, and forbearance in allowance. To allow the Divine to be seen is an act of humility. To tell the Divine what it should appear as is the egoic act of sorcery. Now, when we use that word, we are simply speaking of a lower form of manifestation. "Give me what I want when I say I should have it" is never the True Self. Understand that, friends. The True Self knows the Source of all things and is always in recipience to it. The True Self is in receipt of the omnipresent Divine because it is already in agreement to it.

The world you live in is branded by the idea of lack. Any system you have that is intent on improving your lives is looking to address this idea. But you cannot address lack from the level of consciousness that is already in coherence to it. You must lift above it to the Upper Room, or a plane of vibration where you know what is required. And the lifting of the old to the new in the claim we offer you, "Behold, I make all things new," the act of reconciliation sung into being by the one who knows who he is, will in fact replace the idea of lack with the nature of Source, which is omnipresent. There can be no lack in God, so there can be no lack ever.

"That seems impossible," he says. Hardly. It already expresses. But understand, friends. Your hands are in tight fists. "Give me what I should have." They are not open, saying, "Thank you for the plenty that exists in this realm, and in the realms beyond it." You become the recipient when you say thank you. You become the observer to lack when you confirm its presence, and in that act of confirmation you contribute to lack. Now, some of you hardy souls say, "Well, let me find the lack so that I can fix it." And while this is noble and often needed, you are acting preemptively when what is really required is a new way of consequence through intention. When you feed one man, you have served him well. But when you realize that the act of being, from the Upper Room, can eradicate hunger, you have worked the miracle by being in support of true expression. There is no lack in God.

Paul interrupts: "Is this like the loaves and the fishes?" It's a good illustration. One who knows the Source of all things has access to it. It is less a miracle than you think. It is the reception of what is already so. The lack you experience on this plane, be it hunger, be it inequity, be it lack of love or compassion for your fellows, is the product of the small self in defiance of its true nature. The one who hoards her money is denying God as her Source. The one who says, "Maybe tomorrow I can lend a hand," in her selfishness is denying the Divine as well. You must all understand that you are on the brink, as a species, of such radical change that the excuses you have used to deny the well-being of your fellow will be the ash upon your faces if you continue. You may understand that the offering humanity has now to all that exists, on any plane, is its reconciliation with Source, and you cannot reconcile with Source when you are denying it. And if your actions are denying it—"I'll save the money for next year and put more in the bank and not worry about those people out my front door with their buckets out begging for food"—this choice is to deny the God in them and in yourself and the Source of all. Reconciliation is the re-knowing of self as of the whole. And your singular natures, beautiful and present, still operational in fullness, are in an awareness of the majesty of the Divine, and in the high octave cannot and will not deny it.

Now, here we go:

On this day we claim that all who hear these words, all who say yes, will move to reconcile with those they have put in the darkness, that each one who says yes will announce herself as free from the burdens imposed by lack in an awareness of the plenty that expresses in the Upper Room.

And as we say yes to you, as we announce you as free, as we see you in a reconciled state, we sing this to you in tone and in language.

On the count of three, Paul.

One. Two. Three.

[The Guides tone through Paul.]

God Is. God Is. God Is.

We thank you for your presence. We will return with more later. Period. Period. Period. Stop now, please.

(PAUSE)

When we teach through Paul, we come with an awareness of his physical self and what he can hold in vibration at any given time. The text that we are writing now is of a level of amplitude he will have to continue to adjust to. Because we are reaching our readers in vibration, while the language and the intellectual instruction is a requirement for this transmission to be understood by the intellect, the true teaching is the tone. And the resurrection of the Monad is the intent of this transmission. Each time you turn the page, you are being reminded by the energy of the book, not the intellect or what you assume the words mean, to engage in the act of resurrection that we are party to the instruction of.

Now, *party* means we are not the entirety of this teaching. While this teaching is in some ways a distillation of truth, the truth that is behind this text is an eternal truth. It exists in every landscape, without time, within time, in any realm that incarnation expresses. In other words, the idea of resurrection is an imprinting in the energetic field of all things. Paul interrupts: "But aren't there aspects of creation that are already present and embodied or resurrected?" Indeed, there are. But your presupposition is that this becomes static, an arrived state where you sunbathe on a rock in your resurrected state. Everything is in motion. Everything is in fulfillment. And while one day you will rejoin the cosmic *we*, as we would say, become participatory without the idea of self in the wonder of being, everything you see is also in evolution.

Now, as we speak, and as we instruct, we are somewhat aware of the limitations of language as can be spoken through Paul, or, for that matter, any medium for such a text. The requirement for him is to align the mind to the station we sing to him from and allow the broadcast to be present in an uninterrupted state for the benefit of the reader or, yes, the student. His interruptions are condoned because, finally, they are useful to the student and the reader, and for the presence of this embodiment to manifest in the fullest way possible. The body of Paul is actually ashift now, which means it is moving upward in its density to be able to hold the teaching at this level of tone. And the affect of this is that he becomes the doorway, less so for us, but for the presence of the Kingdom that is implicit in all of you already.

As you work with these teachings, as you embody through them, you become this doorway, which simply means the body as vehicle, an energetic vehicle, becomes the conductor for the higher frequency that prior to this was only accessible as spirit or through the energetic field. When the body becomes conduit, the body becomes participatory through its resurrection, which simply means in a higher reconciled state with the reconciliation that can be present through any interaction. You are singing the note as the note is sung through you. As the note is sung through you, you become the expression of the note. You sing this note without intention. It becomes who you be. This is re-articulation. But the note, once sung, informs all that the note encounters. It lifts all things to itself through co-resonance. And as we have often said, a new world is sung into being.

When you read this text, we would encourage you to begin to sing as this note, which requires no work from the vocal cords, but the simple intention to align and then express through this alignment, the claim "I am in the Upper Room," and the following claim, "I see you in the Upper Room," which is perception as actor, or the one lifting what it perceives to the Upper Room to be present as you read and walk the streets of your lives.

What you see before you today is merely the beginning of change. This change will continue on this realm until the bias towards separation is reconciled or unified with a new ideal. While this sounds impossible, in fact it is not, because your true natures are divine and have been repressed and forgotten. You see the graffiti on the landscape you exist in, the denial of the Divine in every form you see. To become reconciled is to truly comprehend the claim "God Is, God Is, God Is." And when this is invoked from the Upper Room, the power of the claim, which is the re-knowing and remembrance of the inherent Divine in matter, or anything perceived, will reclaim what you see in the high octave it is summoned from. Summoned and sung, perceived as and by, the Divine as you, who knows who she is, is the one who speaks these words: "God Is, God Is, God Is." And the echo of this tone—the intent is used to reconcile or reclaim—will bring forth the inherent Divine where it has been denied or where it has been refuted.

We will teach you more later. Indeed, this is in the text. Stop now, please.

(PAUSE)

Your aspirations, in many ways—who you think you should be, what you might become—are opportunities for learning and growth. We don't deny your aspirations. Even your aspiration to Spirit, to know the self as of God, is opportunity, because before anything can be made known it must be seen as possibility. Your desire for the Divine is in fact the Divine itself calling itself into being, and the denial of the Divine, the only obstruction to truth, must be seen as a choice that the collective has made in order to learn.

Now, is this useful learning? You understand the light because of the darkness. You don't deny the darkness to comprehend the light. The calamity of separation, because indeed it has been calamitous, has been to the collective in its renunciation of its Source, which has propelled you all into a kind of darkness where you have become so used to the dim light that you cannot imagine there is more. Indeed, there is more. But to rush into a bright room after a long period of darkness is deeply challenging. You must become accustomed to the light, and we have taught you in gradations, as the energetic field and now as the body can hold or manage such resolute change.

Now, while we are teaching you to hold the higher vibrational field, attuning you to it and giving you an understanding of how to navigate the emotional self to maintain balance in times of great change, you must understand that the collective is also undergoing this process. And people run from the light when they are unfamiliar with it. They believe that peace may bring them ruin because they have known themselves in war. They believe that separation is solidity with the tribe, when the tribe is much greater than they assume. Your accustomed self, the separate self, the one who chooses through separation, must be redeemed or reconciled. And this aspect of self that denies the light is the only aspect that stands in the way of triumph.

Now, indeed you have learned through separation. You've commanded the lessons of it. "I know what it means to be a victim or a captor." "I know what it means to be at peace or at war." "I understand poverty through my own agreement to greed," or "I understand greed through my own poverty." You understand your natures, and in some ways have fallen prey to the illusion that how things have been is how they will be. And those times are ending. The reconciliation that is before you is tantamount to a change in the gravitational pull of the planet you have known. Some things will seem upside down before they are righted, but in fact you've been upside down so long that you assume it to be right side up. And the challenge of this moment, this very moment, is you seek remedies to condone old behavior, to pacify existing structures, to make the pain of transition feel a bit more gentle. In fact, what may happen are sudden shifts that actually rock the planet. We are speaking both physically and metaphorically. But the one who slumbers most deeply must be brought from her bed, and if she is shaken from it and falls to her recognition that there must be more than there has been, that the world cannot be controlled by her desire to acquiesce to what was, the change will occur as required.

When humanity decides that enough is enough—"we will stop the treason to our brothers and sisters," "we will no longer decide based upon a bias of who is worthy or unworthy," "we will begin to agree that all human beings and all life forms have the right to be"—you will begin to resound in a new potential. And *resound* is the correct word. What it means is that you will lift in intonation through that simple decision: All have the right to be. And this will move enough to right the upside-down ship that has been your world. Now, when a ship is righted, it may seem like chaos. You've been under water for so long, you assume down to be up. But, in fact, this moment of great potential is the Second Coming.

Now, we will tell you what the Second Coming is. It is the

articulation of the Christ, or the Monad, or the Divine, in the material form or fabric of the world. And the realization of this, that it is a collective act of reuniting, will reclaim all cultures, all religions. This is not a Christian teaching, and these times have been prophesied in all cultures in somewhat different language and different metaphor. But the act of reconciliation, the Divine itself reclaiming what has denied it, is the challenge and the gift at the same time. The act of replication that fear would engage in—yes, fear seeks to reproduce itself at every opportunity—will be met now with a new tone.

The tone we sing through Paul that informs these texts, and in some ways are the basis of them, is the Divine expressed in tone that is available to all. When the new tone is sung, it actually claims itself in high accord, beyond the trials that fear has produced, and creates opportunity, new opportunity, for realization. Each human being is always given the opportunity for reconciliation with Source in a lifetime. This is always present, and may or may not be chosen. Because the act of will is highly respected, you may say no to the light. You may choose the darkness. That does not make you evil. It perhaps makes you afraid. But the collective, in the act of saying yes at a causal level, means that this promise of redemption, reconciliation, and resurrection is present for all in an ongoing way. It is no longer that moment of reflection and a choice to know the Divine. It is the light of the Divine peering through the clouds and striking you each in ways you will understand. God calls all things to itself, finally, because God is love. And because love may penetrate even the most dark room, those who slumber in darkness will be awakened.

Now, some of you believe that if this happens there must be turmoil. Revolution and turmoil are different. To be in a revolution is to be in a change or transition. Paul is seeing something moving in rotation. It is revolving. It is presenting to the new from a new vantage point. Imagine there was a turntable that could leave you in a different door than you first entered. This is revolution. But the manifestation of such revolution is actually to reclaim what was denied God *in* God. And the claim "God Is, God Is, God Is," the act of reclamation in tone and choice, the perceiving of what is ever true, is the revolution itself. The claim "God Is, God Is, God Is" is revolution itself. It is revolutionary, and the change it instigates, or the reclamation it enforces, cannot be limited. Any one of you can reclaim what has been denied the Divine through this intention and through this invocation. It is an invocation, yes, but finally it is what you are participatory to as you become the doorway and claim what you see and lift it by nature of presence and being.

Re-articulation of form and matter happens first at the individual level. The higher you align, the more translucent you become, which means the more light shines through you. And the light that shines through you reclaims what it encounters. You will see this in your lifetimes because this work has begun. When you say, "Yes, I Have Come," you agree to the journey before you. Re-articulation is a journey. But the manifestation of this is not understood until it is done. And we say *done*, not to say that there is an ending, but that there is a moment when the system itself is in rotation, or embarking in its new expression through the doorway that is now before it.

You are engaging now in an act of creation, and the release of the old that has been coming at the level of the individual and the collective will continue while this happens. Each of you says yes to this act of being, this expression of knowing, this choice of lifting. In ensuing chapters, we will tell you what you may encounter. But for now we only say the great work is in progress, we are pleased, and we speak you into being by our claim of truth for you:

God Is. God Is. God Is.

You may stop for now. Thank you for your presence. Yes, this is in the text. Period. Period. Period.

Q: In some of the books or in the lectures, the Guides say that, at some level, we already did our homework before becoming students of the Guides. How much is it about allowing and remembering all of the experiences perhaps most of us here already had in other parallel lifetimes, and how much is learning something new?

A: Both are always true. In fact, the soul that you are chooses this and has been in preparation for this. So that much, we will say, is accurate. We will not speak to parallel lives here, or even past-life preparation, because you are asking this in some ways by saying, "How many more pages are there until I have done with the book and can say I have mastered it?" Each of you says yes to the level of journey that you will undergo in a lifetime. The learning that we offer you through the teachings we gift you with are in some ways permission to re-member, and in some ways permission to go beyond what you believed could be. The aspect of you that al-ready knows the truth, which is the True Self or the Monad, is seeking its expression through you. When you go to the God within, you will find the answers there. There is no finish line to race to, and the learning will progress because, indeed, you are here to learn. Period. Thank you for the question.

Q: *Ask the Guides to please define, when they use the word* love, *what does it mean?*

A: The idea of love has been so confused by most of you that you would make it a doily and appliqué it on a card or a pillow. True love is God. It is knowing. It is com-passion. It is the act of creation itself. It is not an emotion, although you confuse it as such. Love is the action of God as love, but love is also present in wisdom and in truth. There are many faces of the Divine, and many ways it can be accessed. To know God as love is to know love incar-nate. To become as love incarnate is to be as the Christ who manifests as love. Period. Period. Period.

Q: *They talked about translucency and going from singular to plurality. I would love for them to speak to that.*

A: The idea of translucency must be understood. You are not becoming invisible. In some ways, you are becoming porous, which means that even the cells of the body are transmitting light, and the space between the cells is calling God to itself. In some ways, translucency means there is less density or denial of the Divine to prohibit expression. The Divine as who and what you are is always true, even at the most dense level of expression when you cannot imagine the light. But to lift to the light and become as one with the light, while in form, implies that the body itself is in a position to be a receptacle or a lantern. Now, the soul is what is becoming illumined, but the Divine Self, operating through the soul, is this light, and the body is all part of the process of realization. You have been taught that you would align to the Divine Self in some other universe, in some imagined heaven. And while there is no density, as you know it here, beyond death, even that plane holds dense vibration. To become the light while embodied is quite simply the agreement to know heaven and earth while in form. Period. Period. Period.

Q: Yesterday they referred to the Divine Self working through the soul, and I'm curious if they could elaborate on this.

A: The soul is the aspect of self that incarnates for the purpose of learning, and ultimately to the goal of reuniting with Source in realization. If you think of the Divine Self as the Eternal Self, and *of* God always, it is this light that illumines the soul, and in some ways you can say eradicates karma, or realizes all things that have been known in separation in the high order of love. So the Monad, while present in the soul, is not the soul. If you imagine a light in a lantern, the lantern is not the

light, but it holds the light. And as the light is broadcast, the lantern itself becomes the expression of the
light. Period. Period. Period.

(PAUSE)

The answers you seek are present in the Upper Room
without your asking. Your definitions of reality, preclusive in
many ways of the Divine, have been your teacher, and the life
you will live now is changed by this recognition: In the Upper Room all things are made new. Now, realization, which is
knowing, the Divine as knowing, if you prefer, is always available at this level or strata. It is something you align to. You
don't make yourself know. You align to the aspect of self that
is in her knowing, and the life you live in agreement to this
will shift you beyond what you have thought or presupposed
to be. Some of you say, "I want to know this and that. Give me
the answers I seek." But it is the small self who demands. The
mysteries of the universe, if you wish to call them that, can
only be claimed by one who has aligned to the level of vibration or tone where these things are held, and held, indeed,
they may be. The juncture you stand at, one and all, is the
choice to face a higher direction. You can be moved there by a
strong wind, a great wave, if you wish, that will propel you, or
you may ride the wave or the wind, which happens when you
acquiesce to it, do not struggle against it, and say, "Yes, I may."
    Now, each of you says yes at the level that you can. Please
understand, friends. This is not the tortoise and the hare, rac-
ing to the finish line. This is the life you live in its unfoldment.

And the life you live, your teacher, yes, will now unfold in a new claim. "I have chosen to know myself as what I truly am." The agreement in this claim is that what you already are is what has been chosen, and you are not trying to manufacture or re-create from an idea of self that you would utilize as yet another mask to perform through. Those who wear the enlightened mask—"Look to me, I will have the answers"—are hiding from the light. Those who know the answers share them freely by their expression. Now, by *freely* we mean they simply be. And the tone of their field is its own invocation, and what it encounters is itself.

The sage may have an answer, the fool may know the right question to ask and never find what she seeks. Each of you says yes to what now lies before you, and the recompense for this agreement is a life that could not have been lived without your choice to align. When you speak to your knowing, that aspect of you who knows, you must be delivered from your expectations of what you should receive. "Tell me what I want" has an outcome attached to it, has an agenda for what is delivered to you. In humility, you become the question and the answer at once. And what this means is what you require to know is offered to you as you require to know it. When you understand this, in some ways the days of seeking are replaced with reception. To be in receipt of the Divine, and the anchor of the Divine in knowing, is to be in faith, or at least awareness of the ideal of the Divine that can be expressed in knowing through an aspect of you that can be in receipt to it. You want this to be what you want so you may lay claim to the answer. And the answer of the day is a very simple one: "It will be so," the manifestation of the Divine called into being by nature of this agreement. "It will be so" serves as a translation from one idea of expression to another.

Paul is seeing the image of a record as would play on a turntable. You turn the record over. Other songs are available. It is the same record, but other songs are available on the second side. In some ways, what you are doing here is transforming an idea of what should be to what is only true. And what you sing, or what you are playing, is the recognition of the Divine that can and will know through you. Can you imagine for a moment what it must feel like to be in your knowing as your natural state, not something you strive to or for, but something that is present? Paul is seeing the image of a young man swimming in a brook. Once he is in the brook, he is knowing the brook. The brook surrounds him, becomes his environment. And he understands the rules of the brook, when to breathe, perhaps when to dive, how to navigate the current. To be in one's knowing is comparable to this. The young man in the brook is not saying, "What am I in?" His experience of the brook is now his teacher, and he knows what a brook is more than anyone who has ever painted a picture or written about a brook. His experience is what he is in his knowing. He is his experience.

Now, to know God at this level, this immersion, to know God as the brook, is to redefine an expectation that God is somewhere other. If you just sat for a moment and thought of God as the brook and let the brook carry you, you would be discovering the ease with which the current will take you. But we take you a step farther. We wish you to become as the brook, which is porous to the brook, so that you may have a sense of form or identity, while in the brook, being carried by the brook, and almost breathing and seeing as the brook. This is a small leap, but again a great one. The transition is not in your imagination. We suppose that any of you, with force of will, could summon an idea of what it feels like to be in a brook, and then call the brook God. But again, this is a teaching of reception and realization, and permission is what is granted by the self who aligns at this level. "I am choosing to know God in all ways." Underline *all ways*—not the God on high, not the God of the earth, not the man on the cross, or the one beneath the bodhi tree. You align to God as all things, wherein all things are your teacher because all things are understood as God in expression.

Now, again, Paul asks the obvious: "But what of the criminal or the heinous act or the horrible war? How do I see God there?" Through any claim you wish, because where you say God cannot be, you deny God and align to that level of abandonment. "Behold, I make all things new," a claim of realization wherein the Divine receives the Divine or reclaims what it encounters, or the majesty of the claim "God Is, God Is, God Is," which refutes this denial by the action of the presence of God in a purposeful and definite way, would be ways to approach what you perceive that could not be of God. But the temptation then has been to fix things, to say these things don't have a right to be, which would be false. Everything that is, in any form, has chosen to express at this level of vibration or consciousness. To receive the murderer as of God is in fact to redeem the murderer or reclaim the murderer in his true divine inheritance. To lock the murderer up for the safety of the town may be an act you choose, but it will not support realization. All it does is affirm separation. And until you reunite, one and all, with the aspect of self that would seek to kill another, you would out-picture it as a culture, ad infinitum. In other words, what you seek to repress or ignore will replicate, because the action of fear, to claim more fear, is what you encounter when you seek to deny.

Now, to understand God as war would be too confusing to teach you here. So we will do it rather differently. God is not war. War is a creation of the small self in the denial of the Divine. The act of war is the act of denying God, most likely created through the ideas of greed or self-importance. "We will rule those people, lest we be ruled." The realization of the Divine where war seems to be is to realize that all engaged are operating at a level of consciousness that confirms an idea that is born in mistaken awareness. To become aware of truth in the face of a lie is deeply challenging, and how you can attend to what you see before you, again from the Upper Room, is to lift all involved and re-see all of the instruments of war without the intention they have been mandated for. Do you understand this? What comprises a rifle, what makes a rifle, be it metal or wood, the lead in the bullet, is simply energy, and the reduction of energy, once again to Source, the re-knowing of the rifle without the intent to be a rifle, can in fact reclaim the rifle, and not only the rifle, but what it is made for.

The men dueling over a woman, standing in the field with their swords drawn, or pistols affirmed and ready to shoot, are operating in a misconception and an awareness of lack that has driven them to an act of violence. To know the men as of God, to know the Source of love where jealousy seems to be apparent, to realize the men as worthy of true love and not what they expect to get from one human being, can in fact re-create a scenario that seems doomed to violence. Each of you is participatory to the landscape before you, and when you confirm darkness you in fact add to it. The fallacy these days is that you must fight darkness, pull out an imaginary sword and hack away at it. All you do then is reaffirm the presence of the darkness. You cannot fight darkness. You can illumine it. But if you are acting in anger, know it or not, you are still contributing to the very structure of the thing that you wish to see transformed.

This is a teaching of love, but it is not for the faint of heart, because you believe yourselves to be so self-important, and your sense of self-righteousness, so deeply entrenched in the fabric of your being, that you presuppose what you think is right must indeed be God's will. "There should be no this or that, and I will make it so." Again, operate in your knowing. You have such limited information about why someone chooses what they choose, or how they come to the end that they have arrived at. Witnessing the divinity of the men dueling does not guarantee no one will be harmed, but it in fact reclaims them in a higher order where the acts are no longer needed. If you understood that every war that has ever been fought has been in fear, or at least the idea that there is not enough for one country and that they must have more or conquer this or that, you would understand that the history of this plane has been so born in the denial of the Divine that the small self would seek to justify any act that he or she believes necessary to confirm her reality.

You are about to lift beyond this. And in lifting beyond this, you will see the world from a different view, from a different viewpoint or vantage point. And when you look down to see how in fact you have contributed to the lower creations, you can then be accountable to them. You are not accountable to the mind or to one's acts when you are in denial. But you are all complicit in the world, or what you would call the evils of the world, because you have aligned to them and because your perceptions of them contribute to their very structure.

In the Upper Room, the alignment you hold, which does not hold fear, holds the answers that must be given for the reclamation of this plane of experience. It does not happen politely. "Please, sir, let's have no more war." It happens through the triumph of the Divine that reclaims all it encounters beyond the access to fear that has compromised it in the first place. Imagine bathwater. Go take a bath in fear, come out fearful. You have lived in this way. To release the fear allows a new environment for you to move through, and then you become as the brook, which is unintended in fear, which holds no fear, and cannot claim fear.

We will take a pause for Paul. When we return next, we intend to teach you what we will. Period. Stop now, please.

DAY EIGHT

Here we say the all that you are, the collective that you are, is ascending to a new level of agreement, where what you have known can be re-known, what you have seen, re-seen, and what you have comprehended in a lie can indeed be re-known in truth. The teaching of the day will continue to be the love that you are, in transmission for the benefit of your world. And the teaching you receive is the teaching that is required for your own knowing to begin to translate one level of experience to another. Notice, we said *experience*. It is your experience, in a new way, that is the proof of this teaching. And your recalibration is all towards this purpose.

Now, the selfish self says, "Give it to me the way I say it should be." But the Divine Self as you, who knows who she is, what she is, how she serves, is actually the one calibrating. Now, understand what this means. There is an aspect of you that in fact knows who she is, what he is, how he serves, that holds a template for a higher way of expressing. Because the template is held at this level, this is the level that it must be born through. Any endeavor you take with the divine blueprint to hammer it into the shape you think it should be would be a foolish endeavor, because all you have is a best idea of how things should be perceived from your small self's logic. The template of the Divine is within you. Consequently, the Kingdom of Heaven, if you wish to call it that, is indeed within you. And its expression through you calls the manifestation of the Kingdom into presence.

Now, logic will fail you here. You want to put the bricks in order. You want to lay the foundation the way you believe a foundation should be laid. But the foundation of this teaching has never been logic, and it has never been a foundation on this realm. From our first attunement through Paul—"I am Word through my body, Word I am Word, I am Word through my vibration, Word I am Word, I am Word through my knowing of myself as Word"—we were calling into being the Resurrected Self, or the Word made flesh. The idealization of the Word, a crucified man or the Son of God who was killed and then risen, becomes confused for you because the act of re-articulation that the resurrection presupposes is not the resurrection that you have been taught. The true resurrection has always been the Monad in a re-articulated state, and it is its radiance that transforms the world. Supplication to the Divine is necessary, yes, but only so you may assume it. You cannot conquer God. Do you hear those words? Nor can you put it in a bottle to have it do your will. But you can align to it, because it is indeed your substance. And in re-articulation, the Manifest Self has become the expression of the Divine that calls into being all which is of like accord.

Now, divinity is not understood, either. You perceive it to be a chalice, or a temple, or a perfect garden where one may meditate. To understand divinity is to comprehend Source that is in manifestation as all things. Now, we have spoken of *all*—the totality of God, God as the sea and sky and your fingertips, the dead body in the road and the newborn in someone's arms. All things. But to comprehend the Divine as all things means not only can you not exclude anything or anyone, but it requires you to move to a level of comprehension where the artifacts of history that have been blasphemed or put outside of God must now be included. Understand this, friends. Everything you see, or even remember, you are in coherence with. And a civilization that has systematically oppressed its fellows, killed for profit, warred against one another, lives in a museum of death or oppression. It surrounds you always because it is in the ethers of your experience, and the artifacts of it indeed surround you today.

So how is the Manifest Divine to translate oppression, to translate blasphemy? How do you comprehend the Divine in an idea of time that has held so much pain? Now, the pain you experience on this plane is part of your learning. You may learn without pain, but most of you will undergo pain as part of a lifetime. There is nothing wrong with it. It does not mean you are doing something wrong or being punished by something outside the self, but the legacy of pain that is entrenched on this plane is partially the cause of your own experiences. When you live in a land where no one gets ill, there is no thought of illness, and consequently it is not present in the reality that you abide in. The legacy of pain is so entrenched in this field it is as if you are moving through water that has been tainted by memory. And the self that you are, participatory to what you experience, imbibes it, or is shrouded by it, or is in agreement to it at a level of co-resonance, which creates expectation.

The idea of lifting beyond pain seems impossible to Paul—emotional pain, physical pain, whatever you may call it. But we wish to attend to something today that we have not attended to thus far, which is a cleansing or a re-knowing of historical pain, first through the individual and then through the collective or the shared field that humanity knows itself through. Now, to re-know yourself beyond historical pain is not to pretend that it never was. It is to know it anew, to claim it in a higher order, where the very resonance of the memory no longer holds the tincture of pain that would inform your experience. To be without this is, indeed, to be made new. And each of you says yes to this at the level of coherence that you may align to.

We are not teaching Paul today. He is interrupting with a thousand questions. We will continue this lecture and answer questions after.

The legacy of pain, historical data that informs your expectations, what you expect to experience, can indeed be cleared, as well as the memory of oppression, and, indeed, the memory of war. You are not erasing the blackboard, saying it never was. These have been your lessons and it is important not to forget them. But it is important to understand that holding a memory in Source translates not only the memory, but the act that the memory was born through. We will say this again: To know the Divine where the memory was held not only translates the memory, but re-creates the relationship to the impetus or event that caused the memory. In other words, friends, you are translating the environment that has claimed you in expectations.

"What does that mean?" he asks. Well, imagine you have a memory of pain, Paul, a persecution, perhaps, that seeks to keep you hiding from further persecution. You live in limitation, in defiance of the Divine, because you believe God cannot be where that event was, and you have created a signpost saying, "No God Here," that you ascribe power to. When you lift to the Upper Room, while you may not be operating in fear, your indoctrination through history will still support choice in opposition to the True Self. In other words, the one who was burned in love, scorned in faith, left behind, holds a legacy that informs behavior and also creates expectation that informs interaction and a view of the world that is still tainted by the old memory.

When we teach today and we call forth the vibration of the Word, or the energy of the Creator in action, we will do it at a level of amplitude that we have not done before. We can claim this now because the foundation of this teaching in the Upper Room is in coherence, which means you can align here and work with the octave of the Upper Room, which is what translates the data of history in the claim "Behold, I make all things new." Now, reclamation, an imperative understanding—that which has been put outside of God must now be re-known in God—must be the alignment to the present moment where God can be known. Any memory occurs in the present moment. And all time may be known through this present moment because the Eternal Self actually exists beyond the template of time. *Beyond the template of time* means it is not bound to historical data. It exists beyond it, and consequently can reclaim anything in higher order—the Divine as all things, inclusive of memory, inclusive of pain, resurrected and, indeed, re-known.

Now, the claim we have taught you thus far, "God Is, God Is, God Is," is the claim of full reclamation. In other words, friends, when this mandate of truth is impressed in a reality, it reclaims the reality. And we will say this is inclusive of memory. And the True Self as you is the one who will navigate this truth for you. Imagine, for an instant, that you stand in a field, and everything you have ever known or experienced exists in this field—your idea of a life lived, or a thousand lives lived, your idea of your own history and your perception of the world's history. Imagine the Divine has been excluded from all that you are imagining now, the small self's creations, the painful memories, the trauma you've endured or the culture has been party to, all existing in this field. Now, in this field, the Monad is present as well, as and through you. And you will say these words now very softly, so that you may know them to be true:

"I Have Come. I Have Come. I Have Come."

Now, the Divine as you, who is here and is in re-articulation assuming the being you are, may now speak these words:

"I am in the Upper Room."

You will say this now, and imagine this world before you, this field of memory, personal and collective, all ready to be re-seen. And you will speak this now to this field you stand in:

"Behold, I make all things new. It will be so. God Is. God Is. God Is."

And allow this field to be transformed.
Again, you may say the words:

"Behold, I make all things new. God Is. God Is. God Is."

And allow the field to be re-seen, to be transformed, all things made new.

Now, the energetic field that you are claiming this in is also the collective and the individual expression of a life lived. You are claiming this both for yourself and all things that may be present in a collective field, the creations of history, and we will say this: known and unknown, spoken and unspoken. The mystery of your own histories eludes you in most ways. You wish to know what happened and when, what was the cause of the pain you endured. And a culture may do the same, and a warring country the same. And this claim, spoken in truth in this field, will always re-articulate the ideas, the memories, and the manifestation the memories occurred through, in alignment to the Upper Room: again, the spoken word, "Behold, I make all things new; God Is, God Is, God Is," spoken into being and transformed.

We will take a pause for Paul. We will return shortly. Period. Period. Period. Stop now, please.

(PAUSE)

What you have chosen is to re-articulate at the cost of the known. And the choice to re-articulate at the cost of the known implies that all things must be made new, including the foundation of identity that you have known yourself through.

Now, the historical data that informs your every waking moment is always present. It does not go away. You know what a log cabin looks like, you know what an airplane is and does, but without the attachment or the meaning that has been impressed upon you, and the values things have been given throughout time. The act of re-articulation, the Monad as expressed, lifts you to a level of vibration where you can no longer agree—underline the word *agree*—which means confirm a reality that you are moving beyond.

The re-articulation of history, or the re-knowing of history, is not whitewashing, is not pretending it didn't happen. It is re-seeing it. And what has caused you the most pain in any culture, in any civilization, has had its genesis in the denial of the Divine. When you stand in the field and you claim, "God Is, God Is, God Is," to all that has been created, you are also informing the genesis, or what catalyzed events into being. The one who becomes a martyr because he holds a belief in suffering, the one who becomes a tyrant because he seeks to overpower others through his presence, is acting out, are acting out, from the implicit denial of the Divine that is reclaimed, reconfirmed, and chosen anew from the Upper Room.

The talk that you will be receiving on the intellect in days to come will claim you each in a comprehension that what you think is wisdom is merely rote. And until you know wisdom, which is the knowing as of God, you are just doing your best to sort through data to make an informed choice. But because the data has been so entrained, through logic and then through fear, your endeavor to sort through is like trying to separate poisoned peas in a pan. It may look better, it may not be as bad, but until you realize the truth, everything that you claim must be informed by its inheritance. Now, there is high inheritance, the Divine Self, the Kingdom, your true inheritance. And then there is the inheritance of the small self, neither good nor bad, but challenging in most ways, the inheritance of the small self, who you think you are, based upon who you thought you were supposed to be, what it means to be a man or a woman, or a this or a that. The ideas or trends of each day may be ever changing, but the fundamental truth of your presence, the Eternal Self, can be claimed, and in its reclamation reclaim all it encounters.

Now, the field that you stood in was comprised of many things, the artifacts or memories of personal history and the residual affect of choices made by others throughout time. The one who harmed you as a child was provoked to that harm through his or her own history. And the idea of culpability and blame begins to vanish, in a certain way, when you understand that the genesis of any act of harm, provoked by fear, is the implicit denial of the Divine. Now, indeed, you are responsible to your acts, but to claim another in darkness because of his or her acts is to deem them as separate. And if you wish to claim everyone who ever harmed you, known and unknown, in this field, and claim the offering we offered you—"Behold, I make all things new; God Is, God Is, God Is"—you will see the light that was present in them that was so denied that they could cause such harm. In this act, you release them and liberate yourself from the residual affect of your claim of their act.

Now, we will say this to Paul: We know you have questions. We are taking them as we understand them. But please let us resume as we wish.

The memory of any pain can be re-known, can be reclaimed. The choice is up to you. Most of you believe that you will always be held captive by what happened to you, what this one said or did, what those people decided, or how this country has chosen to operate, or that one. To perpetrate a crime against the self is to deny the Divine its own act of redemption through you. Do you understand this? "God can never be where the pain was" puts God in the box outside of the field. You have placed God there, and in your self-righteousness take a bow that you are correct. "God was not there."

Now, when you have an atrocity at a mass level, you have conditioning that would suppress the Divine to the level that a people or a country can ignore an injustice and perpetrate crimes against others. This has happened throughout history, and it's born in lack, a belief that God cannot be in some place, or in those people. To redeem memory is to know God where the memory was, and in the act itself that produced the memory, because the memory is tainted through the perception of the one who bore witness to the pain. To see this from the Upper Room is not to condone what happened. It is to witness it from a perspective where you are no longer blaming. If you wish to blame, enjoy your day. This is not the teaching for you. Most of you wish to blame, but pretend you don't. You wish to be sanctimonious in your behavior, but your heart speaks otherwise. To forgive another is to set the self free. Do you understand this? To punish another, to condemn another, to decide another is unworthy of the Kingdom, is to place yourself right in the middle of nothing. And by that we mean your choice to put another in darkness has confirmed your own place there.

When we teach through Paul, we must override an idea he holds that what is taught must be pleasant, must be agreeable to the reader. He wants no one to be offended by what we say. We are about to offend many people. You are rarely right. Did you know this? Even your idea of right and wrong, and the moral codes you ascribe to, are born in a history that has been tainted by fear. And your idea of doing the right thing, while it may be noble and have good effect, is primarily born in the fear of doing the wrong thing. How many of you would steal if you thought you would not get caught? How many of you would murder if it was okay to murder? You would all say, "No, I would never do that." But most of you would, and in fact you all have it in you. To catalyze the aspects of self that are capable of murder, capable of taking from another, is not to act in fear. To reclaim them is an act of love. And to know that the self holds this, these kernels of hatred or fear that can act in ways that are harmful, is to redeem the self at a level of agreement that few go to. As long as you are not acting on the impulse to harm, it is all well and good. It is fine to covet your neighbor's possessions as long as you don't put the silverware in your pocket. You understand this, yes. But, in fact, those needs, which are born in lack and fear, are the catalysts for the pain you see in the world, and they are born in the denial of the Divine.

We would like you all to take a moment now and sit with the self, and ask yourself this question: "Are there any aspects of my being that are capable of hatred, capable of judgment, capable of murder," or any other thing you can think of? If the answer is yes, we invite you to do this with us, very softly, please:

*"On this day I claim that any aspect of my being in de-
nial of its true nature, hidden from light, and the source
of greed or fear, will be reclaimed. Any aspect of self that
breeds violence will now be re-known as of God, chosen
anew, re-identified, and brought to the light so it may be
re-known."*

Again now, see yourself in a field, and see these aspects of
self that are within you also surrounding you, and align them
to the divine nature that must be all things. You may say these
words, if you wish:

*"I am free. I am free. I am free. I am in the Upper Room. I
Have Come. I Have Come. I Have Come."*

And to your own creations, now you say this:

"Behold, I make all things new. God Is. God Is. God Is."

And allow the vibration of the Divine to release you from
what you have denied, from what you have invoked in fear,
and what you may provoke in action through acquiescing to
the deed that they endeavor to make. We say this to each of
you now. We will support you in this through our claims on
your behalf:

*You Have Come. You Have Come. You Have Come. We see
you in the Upper Room. Behold, I make all things new. God
Is. God Is. God Is.*

And let the vibration of these words lift you, recalibrate, speak again through you—"God Is, God Is, God Is"—at the level of tone and choice that you have come to. We say this now:

It will be so. God Is. God Is. God Is.

Stop now, please. Period.

(PAUSE)

We would like to say several things about what has occurred, what will occur, and what will not occur. Your idea of the self in separation in some ways has been vanquished. But the habituated self that would seek to perpetuate holds an echo in the vibrational field. The exercise you did in the field was operating on multiple levels, because it was indeed done beyond time. Now, you understand yourself by the name you were born to, perhaps what you wore today, or who your best companion is, and this is all well and good, but none of this is real. They are ways of knowing self at a level of tone or vibration. We are not saying it's not true that you wore blue, that you are married to a man or a woman, or that you are of this or that race—again, ways of knowing the self that are actually temporary. When you understand the temporary nature of form, you release your attachment to form, and you allow form to be what it is, expression of God that is in fact malleable to thought. Matter is malleable to thought, and even the laws that you live by—"Humanity can or can't do this or that"—is made by prescription, and, finally, is about to be changed. The denial of the Divine, the cause of your pain, the cause of war, is about to be vanquished. But the idea of pain, the idea of war, will be reflective still in your experience for some time.

We will tell you what this means. You understand that light travels at a speed. You understand that what you see in the sky may have been extinguished long ago, but is still present in your experience. When an eradication occurs in the energetic field, while the healing may be instantaneous, at the level of the individual, at the level of the collective, it must be understood as a process of adaptability. Now, imagine there was a pitch being played in this very room that was harmful to the ear. You would do what you could to push away the sound or the source of the harm, but what you would be doing, finally, we say, is acclimating to the sound so it was no longer harmful. In many ways, you did this with fear. You adapted to fear, you learned to make choices in fear, have a bias in this fear or that. Now, what is happening here is that the acclimation to the Monad, which expresses without fear, is now present in your energetic field. But you still have the house that you bought with your ex-wife, and she still wants more alimony, and you know she is God, but you never want to see her again. You want to sell the house and forget it. Do you understand this? So the trials of history have a residual affect that will begin to play out, but like a record on a turntable, one day they will not be playing. But you are so acclimated to the pain that you will reinforce the idea of it even when it is not there. Paul is seeing the image of a man who has locked himself in a bomb shelter. "The world outside is evil. I must stay in this little shelter to know myself as safe." However, the war is ended, but the belief in war, and consequently the dangers of war, are still present in consciousness and acted upon.

There is an echo of every act etched into the energetic field of each individual and of the collective. You may call it a record. The claim "Behold, I make all things new" is inclusive of this record. It is redeemed or re-known in higher order. Well, in fact, what we would suggest is in the Upper Room you don't owe any alimony, but as long as your wife is still calling you, expect to be writing the check. In the Upper Room, or in eternity, what has frightened you the most does not exist. But as you lower your field to the old, you comprehend the self through the old associations. In the Upper Room you are free. But if you have to pay the rent, do pay the rent. Do you understand what we are teaching you?

Now, the residual affect of this teaching is indeed acclimation to the higher. The level of tone or vibration that this text will hold indeed surpasses the prior texts because you've aligned to the texts to make this possible. And we will explain this. Imagine there is a building with a twelfth floor that you've never known you could get to. You can't even imagine it from the fifth floor. But now you find yourself in the tenth and eleventh, and you say, "What's that door to? I have come so far I might as well find out." Now, the vibrational tone of this text is in agreement to the claim "God Is." It actually informs every page. And if there were those words written on each page, that might be your experience of the text. However, we write a book to comprehend in experience the nature of the teaching for the reader. In other words, without the experience of the vibrations, the words are meaningless.

We would invite you now, as you take a pause at the end of this chapter, to reflect on the life you have lived thus far. And understand this. Your reclamation is not only for now, but for always. And by *always* we mean your idea of history is included.

It will be so. God Is. God is. God Is.

We say yes to you as you say yes to all that lies before you. Thank you for your presence. This is the end of the chapter. Stop now, please.

3

RECONCILIATION

When you stand in your own way, when you confound your own possibilities to ascend to the higher dimensional reality that is indeed the Upper Room, you claim a history of lack and neglect. You confirm the ideas of separation that you have been grown by and with throughout time. Your aspirations now, if we would call them that, would be towards a realization of self beyond the known or the schemata that you have known yourself through. The escalation of vibration on this plane is what makes this so, and your amplitude is participatory to the amplitude of this plane lifting for one and all. As each of you says yes, as each of you aligns to the higher, in fact you are contributing to the higher. And the echo of your choice—"yes, yes, yes"—is confounding lack, confounding separation, which would seek to have its will through you.

Now, we said *its will* intentionally, because the small self, armored through historical data, can make a case for anything. "It will never be so, could never have been so, and how can God even be?" The proof of your experience is about to be claimed in an octave above what most of you have ever known, and like any octave comprised of notes, there are levels of agreement or tonality that are available to you. In the highest tones in the Upper Room, you have access to knowledge beyond what you can imagine. And even in the lowest tone, which expresses beyond fear, you hold an alignment to what we will call Christ consciousness for the benefit of everything you encounter. But as the scale is climbed, you are in a manifest world still replicating the known through the old ways of identifying and valuing what is before you.

Now, to align to new values in the case of this teaching is actually to claim an inheritance that was bestowed upon humanity, and then chosen by humanity to be ignored. When you said yes to this ascension process, you broke the rule that humanity had said yes to through separation. And in the claims we offer you now—the triumphant new, sung as your being, claiming the inherent divinity in all manifestation—you are reconciled to a way humanity once knew or experienced that even predates your idea of time.

Now, humanity has not always been in form. Form was taken by humanity as a vehicle for expression. The ethereal self, the translucent self, and the self that is purely vibration, which you might call soul, predates form. Soul predates form. But the incarnation into form, a passage into density, has been utilized by this species to renegotiate itself and its inheritance, and not always in the highest ways. While we say to you that each of you are party to these choices as much as anyone else, we will also say that the initial claim in these choices, born in trial and fear, predates what you would think of as time, because these choices were made while form itself was still so plastic that things could be made instantaneously. When you understand that the elasticity of form is always present, you will also understand that there has been a time when things were thought into being. They were thought into being because humanity was granted every wish. You may think of this as Eden, if you want, or the parable of Eden. But, in fact, what happened was the requirements for humanity, which were always met in perfect ways, stopped being enough. And humanity said, "Give me what I want," and in that case created a separation from the idea of Source because they felt it was their right to pick every apple from the tree and let his brothers starve, or let her sisters starve.

The parable of the tree and of the serpent are useful to understand. There is nothing wrong with knowledge, true knowledge, the knowledge of all things. But the claim of light and dark, or God and separation, have claimed you in a very different parable, which is the chaos that you now perceive yourselves in. When manifestation occurred, or the idea of separation was formed, the density of matter, in its own collective way, began to claim itself as it had been claimed by humanity. In other words, the one who operates in density claims a dense world into being.

Now, please don't think this makes you wrong. Imagine you learned a language in school, became fluent in it. That is the language that's now spoken in your household, and it has become the norm. The language of separation in density became the common tongue. Everything is indeed spoken into being, and thought is the catalyst for most manifestation. But there are other causes born through collective need. You believe that a prayer from the heart may be met by grace with very good reason. The echo of the heart claims itself through the manifest density to the higher octave. And prayer has long been the primary vehicle for intercession, not because the prayer is necessary, but because the act of prayer itself moves you to reconciliation. The denial of the Divine would claim you without prayer.

Now, are all prayers answered? No, not as you wish. The small self has its requirements: "Give me what I want. I want it now." Perhaps you may succeed at that level. But the teaching you will receive about manifestation is the challenge you face when you get what you think you want. Because the True Self knows, any prayer from the heart which claims the True Self as its presence cannot be in denial of the Divine. Paul interrupts the teaching: "Are the claims and affirmations you've given us, or the attunements, prayers in themselves?" Not as you think. The vibration of each claim is in energetic code, which translates the intent to an out-picturing in the energetic field. In other words, the equation to the higher alignment is present in the claim, and indeed in the attunements, which is why the energetic bodies are in escalation every time they are invoked. When one is in prayer, one is in an awareness of unification because the act of prayer itself confirms the omnipresence of the Divine even when the one praying feels bereft and alone.

It is the act of agreement to God that makes prayer profoundly successful as the intercessor between dimensional realms.

Now, are your prayers answered in the Upper Room? The answer would be not as you think. It is not the place to get what you want. It is the place to receive what you require, and what you require are the gifts of the Kingdom. If you could imagine for a moment living in a state where your true requirements are met by you without asking, and certainly without demanding, you would begin to have an understanding of what this level of manifestation is. Now, the idea that you should ask is somewhat misguided. It presumes that the Divine has no idea what you require, does not know the secrets of your heart. However, to say, "I am ready to receive," to confirm your availability to be in receipt of the Divine, as may be made manifest in a real need, is in agreement to truth. "I am ready, indeed," because the aspect that says, "I am ready," is the aspect that knows.

"What about supplication?" he asks. "Dear God, help me. We have all prayed that way." Those prayers are heard, but the level of intercession you seek may not always be in alignment with the requirements of an individual. "Dear God, save my marriage." "Let my child be well." "Let the bank account be replenished." "Let me maintain my idea of who I am in a community that now scorns me." You all understand these prayers, but in each case the prayer is being asked to create an agreement to a status quo or sense of being that may no longer be the requirement of the soul. You may learn through an illness, you may likely benefit from the divorce, and perhaps it is time for the child to release the body and learn in a different plane. You think things should be as you wish. Now, when we say Divine Will is available to you in your knowing, we are not suggesting that there is no desire in the heart, and in cases we have spoken of in prior texts, it is the Divine itself that has claimed the desire in the heart. "Oh, God, let me know you as I may be known, and as you may know me." That is the Divine as you in its agreement to God. "Dear God, let me know my true work so I may be of service" may be a true claim if it is said in earnest, but it is often the egoic structure suggesting that it would be happy if it were doing what it wanted. "And please, God, confirm what I want." You may do as you wish here. This is the life you have chosen to learn through. The Divine expressed in manifestation as and through you does not decide that you are no longer here to learn. Indeed, the learning continues.

The agreement we make to you tonight is that, at the level of truth, you will be met each step of the way. And what this means is a true need will be met in the Upper Room. However, your compliance to the circumstances of change that may need to be rendered for a prayer to be answered must be permitted by you. "Dear God, give me what I want, but don't take that away from me." "Dear God, do as I say, but don't touch my bank account." "Let me be of service, but please let me have to sit down to do it. I am old and have poor feet." Your decisions about how a prayer should be answered is generally the egoic structure making a demand in out-picturing. But to support the Divine, "Thy will be done," or even better, "We are one; let this be done in the highest way," will support the application to the circumstances that are required for prayer to be met.

Intercession from the high to the low is always present in love. When we teach you in the Upper Room, in fact we lower our vibration to work through the man before you. And while he may hold us, we are far too vast to be limited by form. Imagine a thimble poured through Paul of the vastness of Spirit. This thimbleful holds the magnitude of the whole, and you are the recipient of that. But the fullness of God cannot be embodied in fullness. And we speak in the fullness and the glory of God.

Now, each thing you see before you has been made into form, once ether, even the sky, once an idea, born in need, born in imagination, born in agreement to what is. Everything seen may now be re-seen, but from the Upper Room what is seen is actually restored to a level of tone that expresses with less density, and you begin to operate, in a small way, through the memory of the species that could think things into being.

Now, this is what you don't understand. Who the thinker is, is the key to this equation. If you say, "Well, my Divine Self is going to make it rain," "going to stop the war," you are in arrogance. It will be the Divine Self that is acting through you, because it knows true requirements and is not seeking glory for its acts. From the Upper Room, you move to *reliance.* Underline that. Now, reliance upon the Divine can indeed be called faith. And in this faith, your needs will be met. Paul interrupts the teaching: "Well, I have heard of people that sit on a bench and say, 'God will pay my rent,' and they wind up without a house to live in." And that is because they haven't learned a lesson. Now, you've been taught indeed God helps those who help themselves. If that same person had perhaps risen from the bench and found a job, the rent would have been paid, but the need for the rent may have been met in a rather different way. To decide that God is doing it for you, "Dear God, clean my bathroom, I've had a hard day," will leave you in filth. You have the capacity to take care of the self, and it is your accountability to any act that claims you in well-being or not.

"So what is the difference?" he asks. When a true need is met, it is present for you. Imagine you didn't even have to say what you wanted, but the waiter knew the right item to bring. Now, that's a strong metaphor, but it is actually not unrealistic, because the level of creation we are talking about in the Upper Room means that what you are claiming, claimed by the True Self in a state of unification, is known by the Divine before you can even ask. He doesn't like this teaching in the least. "But we're supposed to ask." However, Paul, we will correct you. You need to say yes to what already is. Your asking, in most cases, is a confirmation of lack. "Dear God, let there be enough for me, and can I have the last piece of pie before someone else claims it?"

The truth of this, as expressed in this teaching, is that you are in agreement to the Source of all things, hence the claim "God Is, God Is, God Is," the simple statement of being. Now, truth is truth, and what was true millions of years ago will be true millions of years from now. But the idea of time itself, simply an idea known in form or agreement to form, must be understood as a template of the lower realm. The Divine Self, expressed in the Upper Room, may know itself in form through time, but abides beyond form in timelessness or eternity. The alchemy that happens beyond time would be confounding to logic. When you are dreaming, you have some experience of timelessness, or moving beyond the laws that humanity has been bound by. The aspect of you that dreams is not bound by form, and the idea of moving beyond time is available to you there, and you can reconcile yourself with what it means in experience.

When you understand that you only think you are where you are, that your experience of this moment is filtered through a lens of collective agreement, and that there is an aspect of you now that can perceive this as idea, or a projection of consciousness, you will begin to understand the liberation that you are about to undergo. You cannot imagine being two places at once, but you are usually in many places. The aspect of you that is in thought, "I wonder how my sister is doing today" or "That awful memory is back from my childhood," is claiming aspects of you right beside your sister or in your childhood bedroom. You only think you are only here because the density of the body is residing here. You understand that thought is not bound by form, and thought itself, a key to your own creative process and evolution, singularly and collectively, can now be understood as simply one way that you may begin to experience eternity.

Imagine, for a moment, that you are in a plain or field surrounded by ticking clocks. They all have a different time. One clock says noon. One clock says three. And now imagine that all of these clocks are becoming unwound. The mechanism that turns the wheels is running wildly, speeding up, and then stopping to a halt. Now, imagine that time itself, altered in this way, was not present in this field. How old would you be here? What time of day would it be? Would the body even be what it was without a clock to measure age?

To understand timelessness is to move to an agreement of the plausibility that time may be a construct—first a construct, and then a construct that has been agreed upon by the collective to create experience known in linear form. Your experience of time is linear, but in fact you are not linear. You are two years old today, and five hundred years old. All things are true. But the small lens you operate through, again as a thimble, gives you enough reality that you can manage in a collective sphere. So it is the collective that is operating in density and a diminished sense of being. The Upper Room is where this begins to transform.

Paul interrupts: "Is this science fiction?" he asks. Well, one day it will be science, because everything we speak to has laws attached, and reasons for it. But they are not applicable at this stage or level of collective agreement, which is why we bring them to you in a decided sequence. The language of science, as we have said prior, is born in time, the jargon of time and the mechanics of a decade. In five hundred years, what you think of as brilliant will be so archaic as to be in a museum. The language of science is so limited, we will not work with it. But we will speak in a tongue of music and tone, which is eternal. And vibration itself, which you will all come to understand one day, which implies resonance and coherence, will be the language of science in the coming decades and thereafter.

We will take a pause for Paul. We are working him as we can. The ideal here is to deliver this text in an expedient way, lest he have time to think about it. We would prefer he wait, read the transcripts with the rest of you, and then decide what he feels.

Thank you all for your presence. Period. Period. Period. Stop now, please.

DAY NINE

We are waiting to speak about authenticity, and what it means to be truly the self that you have come to realize yourself as. The appliqués, the embroidery, in personality are to your benefit in some ways. The uniqueness of your expressions is part of what makes this world so wonderful. When you move to an authentic state of expression, those things that give you the sense of self are still present, but in a slightly modified state. Much of what you apply or use as personality is indeed appliqué, and the appliqué is not the fabric. When the fabric is stretched to its true nature, those aspects of self that are not authentic to self are released. Paul sees the image of embroidered work being stretched and pulled. The appliquéd beads are falling from it. They can no longer be held by the fabric that has held them. You become as this, you see, in expression. So much of what you think you are supposed to be is embroidery, an idea of self assumed by you in relationship to others.

Now, when we teach through Paul, we come in different ways, and the aspect of Paul that has to distill this vibration is questioning this instruction and the vocal tone being offered through him. When we come as a collective, at times we take turns in dictation, and I am quite pleasant as a persona coming through Paul, and it is time he gets used to it. I have great things to say and intend to say them. Paul interrupts. He is saying, "Why not *we*? You are a *we*." Indeed, we are a *we*. And this *we* is speaking as *I* for these few moments that I have the opportunity to address this collective.

Now, some of you want to know who and what we are. In some ways, we are one. In some ways, we are singular, the singular in an inclusive state of expression as the one. Now, the one is all things. And because we speak of authenticity, the aspect that is speaking through Paul is authentic, still singular, and of the *we* in simultaneity. Your broadcasts, as individuated beings, the ways you've known yourselves, are present always. However, when you lift, when you rise in light, that which is no longer true, could never be held in the high octave, not only falls away, but leaves no scar. Imagine embroidery that is unstitched. The remnants of the stitching are no longer even present. They have disappeared as the cloth itself is indeed made new.

Now, the transition some of you are in is to be supported in a very different way than you might assume. Your idea of being supported is being held to the bosom, caressed gently, as you are sent on your merry way. But do understand, dears, that the mother bird is more than happy to send the fledglings out of the nest because she knows full well their capacity for flight. And we see you now in readiness for flight—not only you who are assembled, who read the texts we write, but those of you in totality who have lifted in vibration through the storms that you have summoned to shake yourselves from your nests.

Now, some of you say, "Please let it be lovely, let it be gentle, let my poor heart sing a quiet song." But the roar of God, expressed by each of you, is indeed a cacophony, and this roar is intended to wake others from their sleep. You are not the mother birds, no. Far from it. You are birds in flight, and your call, "I Have Come, I Have Come, I Have Come," is in recognition of the true nature of the totality of the Divine that you are now summoning into being.

"Now, what does that mean," he asks, "*summoning*? What are we doing? We are summoning?" In fact, yes, you are. Each broadcast of vibration that one of you brings forth will not only awaken a thousand more through the act of being, this act of being is now in escalation, which means what was once a quiet hum is now a cacophony. Imagine a million birds learning to sing, all at the same time. You'd wish to put your hands on your ears and go back under the pillows. The Divine Self is not quaint. She is fierce, and thunderous, and magical in the most perfect ways. "Why did you say *magical?*" he asks. Would you prefer another word? I can think of several. We will go on now. The truth of your being, in its authentic state, is in a modified reality. We wouldn't say *modified* because it gives you an understanding of the value of your present life. We are not dismantling your present life. We are lifting your present life. We are showing Paul the image of dusting. You pick up the vase and you dust the table beneath it. The residue of history or the detritus of the past is being cleansed and indeed wiped away. So what was present in a dirtied state or diminished value is not only re-seen, it has been moved, it has been lifted, and the modified state of the life lived is in a new recognition. We are not just cleaning house, you see. We are lifting the house to let the light in through brightly cleaned windows. Now, some of you say, "Well, I don't want the life I have. I want a rather different life. I want a happier life with more of this and that." Well, maybe you will have that, but you must look at what you have now and realize it, which means to know it as of God.

Now, the Christ, in manifestation through each of you, is glowing brightly, and the brightness of the Christ in manifestation is what cleans the windows, dusts the table, makes all things new. The high regard we hold for each of you, one and all, is that we know not only your capacity, but how challenging it is to claim the self in an unburdened state. That is the correct term, yes: *unburdened state.* Imagine you carry your sackcloth, you carry your baggage, you carry your mother's baggage and her father's baggage, generations beyond you. It makes for hard traveling. The distillation of the manifestation that you have known yourself as, in an altered state, is in an equivalency to the true nature of the manifest Christ, which quite simply means that the what that you are, in truth, does not carry the history that she thinks she does. We are not saying you are not your father's daughter, your mother's favorite. We are not saying that generations back there was not terrible hardship, or in the current one, either. We are simply saying that while you have known yourselves as the product of such things, you have also known yourselves as the one who has inherited the pain—the generational pain, and the pain of a culture, and the pain of a world.

The idea of sin, you see, or what you believe sin to be, is the obstruction to God. And the idea of God being obstructed by acts of man, or by beliefs of man or what man has chosen to learn through, is actually accurate. Now, what you carry that you assume to be yours, that has never been yours, is indeed yours because you are carrying it. Do you understand the premise? Your mother's pain is not your own. Her father's pain was not her own. But here you have it all in a big pot, and you serve yourself lunch from it daily. The lunch that you are serving yourselves today is based upon a false premise, the idea that sin is generational and passed down, and this goes back to the mistaken belief in what some call original sin, the belief that God could deny you. You have never been denied. You've denied yourselves. And the entirety of this teaching may now be understood as a new dinner is served, and a grand one, yes, because you trust the chef, and the spoon is fine, the bread newly baked. You are not dining out on last year's heresy, or the Inquisition, or the crucifixion, or all things that were done in denial of the Divine.

"Behold, I make all things new" is spoken as the Christ that has come as each of you. It is not folly. It is not blaspheming. It is true and in beauty. "Behold," bear witness to, a world made new, summoned, called into being, by the Christ itself, i-t-s-e-l-f. The Christ does this. Now, we say you have a "Christed Self," C-h-r-i-s-t-e-d Self. And what this means is that the re-articulated idea of self aligns you to express as the Christ. So while it may be Nancy as the Christ, or Henry as the Christ, the Christ is still itself, an autonomous act in tandem with the one Creator. So you understand that you are assumed by the Christ, reconciled to the Christ, may invoke as the Christ, but you are still Nancy, you are still Henry, you are still your very selves in a highly articulated state of resonance.

The denial of the Divine, in particular, is the most challenging aspect of your experience now, because the world you've been brought up in is so inferred in this denial that it has run itself as a thread through the very cloth of fabric of your experience, *the very cloth* meaning it's so fine that you don't even see it, but it is so present that it overtakes the cloth. Now, what we cannot do is pull apart your reality, thread by thread, so you may have what you wish, but we may make the cloth new. And you are the ones, quite in particular, that can claim this with this new understanding. Paul still sees the image of the cloth of fabric stretched, and the embroidery falling away, that embroidery only which is in denial of truth. And this understanding of a new way of being, without the claims of separation present, must be understood as the acclimation to what we call the Kingdom, which is the presence of the Divine in all manifestation.

Now, calligraphy, fine lettering on a page, is pleasing to the eye. It's a lovely skill to develop. But what if what the calligraphy says is, "There is no God, there is no truth"? And it's made so lovely that you take it home and put it above the fireplace to admire the pretty lettering. That is the world you've chosen to claim, and you are the ones making the signs and paying for them and decorating your lives with them. The truth of your being, in a manifest state, may now be claimed in a way that it has not, because the level of vibration or tone that is present for you now is of such a high octave that it actually translates what is placed within it. Imagine this. You have a lantern that has the light streaming from it. Everything placed in this stream of light is altered and changed, once illumined and seen. This is an illustration of "Behold, I make all things new." And the claim of God, "God Is, God Is, God Is," first a flame in the lantern, then pouring from the lantern, and then overtaking the lantern so the lantern itself becomes the light, is what it means to have come. And the claim "I Have Come" is indeed the claim of the illumined lantern.

Now, a lantern does not light for itself. Some of you say, "I want to be the lantern. Look at all my lovely light." There has never been a lantern created whose objective was to enjoy its own light. The lantern shines for all, and it always will be so. The claim "God Is, God Is, God Is" is the light of the lantern claiming all light in recognition of itself, because all is light, even when shrouded, even when denied, and even when you can no longer say, "Please, God, let me believe." The light of God is all things, and we are here to speak today about what it means to be the risen light, which is the resurrection—yes, foretold, and yes, it is here, but not as you wish it. You prefer some trumpets, a horseman or two. You prefer a page number to check how far you've progressed. The idea of Second Coming is a secular concept, but a universal truth. And the language that we use when we teach has been in some ways useful to translate concepts to a culture that has a heritage in such language. But the idea of Second Coming, which is mass resurrection or the realization of the Divine as all, is present in every language, but in rather different ways. The Second Coming, as we speak to it, is not only an event, but a process, and a catalytic process. A forest fire is an event, but the one match to the tinder that begins the flame is also an act, and the spreading of the fire from tree to tree, branch to branch, is also a process.

Now, we are not burning down the house. We are illumining the house. And everything in the house that can no longer stay at this level of vibration is to be cleaned, and done well. You will look at this before you and say, "Oh, no! There goes the value of my home. Oh, no! There goes the church I once belonged to. Oh, no! There goes the ocean." In fact, the ocean will stay. It takes perfectly good care of itself without you. But what you have done to this plane will be made new, and you may lift it, but you will not lift what you deny, and what you deny God in, be it the ocean, be it the one beside you, be it a country or a world, will claim you in shadow. God is all things and will not be denied your permission, which is in will. To re-know the self above the old fabric, above the old appliqué, is now here and is being utilized for the benefit of all. The moment you know, truly know, "God Is, God Is, God Is," you will never be the same. We will stop this teaching now for Paul. He needs a pause. Period. Period. Period.

(PAUSE)

We would like to begin and we will continue for a few more moments because the teaching is imperative and you need to understand the obligation to your own needs that must arrive through this experience. When the idea of self and the appliquéd self is met in a higher octave, the translation of one's experience is vital to understand. It is not that a teacup is not a teacup. It's that who holds the teacup, who tastes the tea, who pours the tea is altered, and the experience of all things is actually translated. Imagine a film, once in black and white, that has been painted in color. The painting of the color would be what you assume should be there. The grass should be green, the flower pink, and the sky bright blue. But in this translation, your expectations of what should be are going to be denied. Now, you can decide the sky is still blue, because the collective has agreed to this, and the spectrum of color that you choose from is rather limited. You don't know the color of the sky. You know how that idea of color is filtered through the lens, and how you perceive and invoke is predicated upon what things have been. As you are aligning to the higher, the senses in a refined state are actually operating in tandem with the Divine Self in order to support your experience. So to believe that the body and the body senses are operating separately from the Monad would be to your detriment. As the soul expresses through your being, in its own learning, it accrues information to its benefit. But the self that you have known yourself as has also accrued evidence to the detriment of its experience, because you've been chosen and been choosing with a rather limited menu. Your father said, "Look at the beautiful green ocean, look at the pretty blue sky," and the child that sees the ocean as other becomes in complicit nature to the creation she was expected to see.

Paul interrupts the teaching: "The ocean is green. Don't

go on, please." Your idea of green, yes. But it is an idea. Now, the translated experience, from the Upper Room, is the manifestation of the Divine that may be experienced by one who is no longer operating in limitation. If you simply think of it as limitation—"This is the order of things, this is how the hands on the clock are to move, the tides are supposed to flow"—you will see how you've ascribed meaning and patterning to your entire lives. In the altered state of the Upper Room, when you understand time as construct, you become limitless in some ways because the operating system, if we may use that term, is no longer limited or bound by linearity, and the senses themselves can be invoked to have the experience of the higher, and translated to the being in a way that is comprehensible to you. In other words, friends, if your senses were to fully activate now, if you could fully see the world before you, you could not manage it. You would have to sit in a state of wonder, or at least horror, that things are not what they were.

Now, the brain itself is in some ways the filter of your experience. It is utilized by the senses in wonderful ways. Now, when the Monad or the Divine Self is in its expression, and the senses themselves are acclimated to the Upper Room, you will begin to have the experiences we speak to. Now, these are not experiences you should usher in or mandate should be. You become aware that there is more on the menu than you were taught to believe. And the moment it's there on the menu, it can be tasted, partaken of. Your agreement to be in body in a limited state has been part of the calling of humanity and how you've agreed to know the selves. But the altered state humanity comes to actually has an obligation to move beyond limitation, and because the senses are how you experience your world, they must be in acclimation to this transition. The authentic or True Self sees beyond the spectrum, hears beyond the tones available, and touches, or experiences and feels, beyond what the skin would fathom.

When we operate through Paul, his system is in acclimation to the service he provides, which is how we are speaking through him and how he knows what he knows when he knows it. When he is unplugged, the system itself, which has been appropriated through this work, is still operating in a refined state. But his sensitivity to this acclimation is a process he has to undergo. The same is true for all of you. Now, the benefit of this is not to do as he does, but to be as you truly be, which simply means a vibrational being whose senses have acclimated to a higher degree, and consequently there is more information, and then experience, available to you to distill. Imagine you are a painter, and suddenly a color appears on your palette that you could not imagine was ever so. To begin to utilize the paint is somewhat of a challenge. "It is not a peach. It is not a brown. It is not an orange. What am I to do with this? It resembles nothing I know." But then you look back down at the palette, and there are three more, and then the old ones are changing as well, and the richness and vitality of the spectrum is now revealed, and it makes all things so.

The beauty of your beings is unbeknownst to any of you. If you could see yourselves as we see you, you would weep in joy. We know who you are, because you cannot be other, and we sing your songs for you so that you may learn the words.

We Are Here. We Are Here. We Are Here.

Stop now, please. Indeed, in the text.

(PAUSE)

What we ask of you now, if we are allowed to ask, is permission to align you to the next level of vibration that is accessible through your prior work and the attunements done thus far. The release of the old has been primary in these teachings, in alignment to a new potential. And the manifestation of the Divine, come in form as each of you, is the agreement that has been made to the reader of the text, or the student of the work, who has truly said yes—at the level of heart, the level of soul, and at the level of expression. What that means is when you have said yes and made an agreement to move beyond the old, you are escorted across a border, not to the Upper Room, but to the next level of vibration that can be accessed there. This is a border of consciousness. It is less a shift in the vibrational field than a reckoning, a true facing of self as what one has been in order to become what one truly is.

Now, this is not a pleasant experience for the aspect of self that demands things be as they were. And we will say to each of you, if you do not wish to cross this border, you may wait until the time has come when your soul says *now,* your heart says *now,* and your expression says, "It must be so." This is an agreement to a new life, a new way of expressing, beyond a system of agreement that has precluded your light from truly shining. To cross this border means to enter into a new way of expressing the self, beyond the field that you have utilized to claim an identity, and beyond the identification through matter that you have used to claim what a reality must be. Each of you says yes to what is before you now. Each of you says yes to what stands in the way and must be moved for this crossing to occur. And the reckoning you may face is to a residual idea that you are not present across the border. And for most that is what stands in the way of realization.

Now, you are forgetting an idea of self. You are releasing what was not you, and you are saying yes to what truly is. When we teach through Paul, we have requirements for him as well, and he is as you at this juncture of change. So we will say to him: You must also say yes, with the heart, with the soul, and in your expression. Each of you says yes at the level that you can come to, and when we say this now, we are saying it not only to you who are before us, but you who hear these words in another time, in another space, and in another reality. We are accepting all of you across this border. We are saying yes to you each, and we welcome you each on the other side. The small self's will, which has undergone change through this expression, the idea of self, which has been altered through this encounter, is present now as well. And as you agree, say yes to what is before you, you will be moved in vibration to the next level.

We invite you to say this now after us:

"I know who I am in truth. I know what I am in truth. I know how I serve in truth. I am free. I am free. I am free. I am in the Upper Room. I Have Come. I Have Come. I Have Come. It will be so. Behold, I make all things new. God Is. God Is. God Is."

. And when we sing and make this sound, the sound will echo through the pages of this text, through the room we sit in, and throughout time. You may remain silent. Let this wash through you as a being of light, as your true being of light is reclaimed and altered at this crossing. On the count of three, Paul.

One. Now two. Now three.

[The Guides tone through Paul.]

Be lifted as one, and know the True Self as expressed in the form you have taken.

We say this now:

Everything is changed. Everything is new. It will be so. God Is. God Is. God Is.

Stop now, please. Period. Period. Period. Yes, this is in the text.

(PAUSE)

Paul, to the assembled students: "Anything anybody wishes to share? You just want to be in the quiet of it? Just be in the quiet of it then."

(PAUSE)

This is about respecting the process that they are in. And the process that they are in is engaging itself through your body and energetic field. The system that you hold has been altered to produce a new alignment. Underline the words *to produce.* To claim and accept what is produced is the passage you undergo. In other words, the border has been crossed, but you have not yet acclimated to the new land. The system has been altered to support this and will continue to align to a new level of agreement.

Now, the choice we make with you is to attend to your passage as you grow comfortable in a new way of being, less a new body than a new way of being. And the choice that you are offered is to maintain this new alignment, or, if you wish, revert to the old. We will say this to those of you who wish to revert: You are going to be challenged by that choice because you've had a taste of what it feels like to know the self in a new way, and while the comfort of the old and the old pain may call to you, we don't expect you will stay very long.

We sing your songs for you, not only so that you may learn the words, but so that you may sing to others. And your vibrational being is what sings to others. When we return with this teaching, we will explain how this occurs.

Yes, you may include this in the text as the end of this section. Period. Period. Period.

(PAUSE)

When you ask questions in love, when you make a claim in love, when you choose in love, you claim love. It is always the answer. To know the self in love is indeed to know the self in alignment with the truth of your being. When you have a vendetta, when you seek an action against another, you are always in a low vibrational field, and the claims of justice made in such a way perpetuate a low alignment. This is true in a culture, a civilization, and, yes, at the cost of the Divine that would now be seen.

When you perceive injustice, or you perceive someone acting in fear, you must begin to see it as opportunity to know truth in the face of the lie that is being perpetuated by the one acting in fear. The one acting in fear has lost her mind, has lost his sense of self, or alignment to love and truth, and to reconcile them is to be as love in deep forgiveness for what an imagined wrong might be. Now, we said *imagined wrong* intentionally. The imagination will conjure anything, and even your idea of justice is born in a misconception of right and wrong. Indeed, ownership itself, as you prescribe meaning to it, is an illusion. The bodies you have, while yours to care for, are not your bodies. They are of God. The air is of God, and the property you think you own is of God. When this is fully understood, the walls will come tumbling.

Now, you care for your body, and you care for the body of the one beside you as if it is your own. Make no mistake here. As long as there is one child hungry, one woman starving, one man in need of medical aid, there is work to do. The work of your hands is always present here. If you have something to do, please do it, but if you trust God to be your director from this amplified state that you have been taken to, there will be no question of an action, and the lines between one another will begin to blur. Now, you don't hold your brother's debt for her or him, you don't take on someone's issue as if it is your own. You reclaim the issue and the one before you in the high accord you have been taught.

The issuance of this teaching, finally, is world peace, but you don't understand peace because you believe it to be the cessation of war. Now, war is a symptom of fear that has been systematized by cultures, by governments, throughout time. And the mercenary acts committed in war—starving a people, even slaughtering a people—cannot be acts of God, but acts of the forgetting of God, the denial of God, and the refuting of God. And the claim "God Is," in all ways, the realization of this claim, in all ways, is the realization of peace where other things seem to be. Now, we say *other things* because the list is too long, and the denial of the Divine has taken so many forms that you are so confused as to what is or must be God and what can never be. We will tell you what can never be of God. Hatred can never be of God, because God cannot hate. And the love that is God can reclaim even hatred in the Upper Room by one who has embodied as love. To embody as love is to be love in transmission, and the acclimation to love that some of you will now undergo is an acclimation to a province that few have truly known. To become as love is to reside in the vibration of truth.

Now, imagine you lived in a kingdom where a lie cannot exist, and even to perpetuate a lie could never be, because there is nothing for the lie to hold. A lie can only hold when there are ears to receive it and senses to agree to it, or a moral code born in agreement to fear that would support it. When you understand that a lie can only be told in fear, even a lie perpetuated upon a people, you will begin to understand that the Divine Self holds a capacity that the small self never could. The small self will condone a lie, perpetuate a lie, if it is more convenient to know the lie than to accept the truth. The Divine Self cannot align to a lie. It is impossible. So as the Divine Self in a risen state, you are actually immune to a lie. It cannot hold you because there is nothing for it to be held by. The action of fear, to claim more fear, can only be perpetrated upon one who holds the vibration of fear in herself.

Now, you can't imagine becoming fearless, but in fact it is the Christ, the Monad, the True Self, that is already expressing beyond fear, that is immutable and pure. The Pure Self knows. It has been said that the Christ is without sin, was born without sin, and this is true. The Christ in each of you, or the Monad or True Self, is without sin because sin does not exist, as you might think of sin, without fear as a basis. Vanity itself, a form of fear, greed itself, a form of fear, gluttony itself, a form of fear, which all hold their ideals in the basic premise of lack— that there cannot be enough, that there will not be enough, that there can never be enough. And the plenty that awaits you in the Kingdom is present always, but you have been starving for truth because you have been dining upon lies. To transmit the truth, to reclaim another in truth from this place we have brought you to, is to know the truth of them when they deny it. Knowing is realization, and your realization of the truth, in any instant, will surmount the lie and move the vibration of the lie because it cannot be held at your level of vibration.

Now, Paul interrupts: "I can think of many lies I believe. I know they're not true, but I'm comforted by them. When I think of the body, how I would see it fixed, when I think of my relationships, what I wish they were, I understand that the basis

may be in a lie. But how am I made new when I have invest-
ments in what you say can never be true?" When we took you
to the field and invited you to see all of your creations before
you, inclusive of things you've created or inherited as creations,
and announced the claim "God Is, God Is, God Is," the rec-
tification began. The sealing is done in the etheric. It is done
in the energetic bodies. The manifestation of the claim in the
physical form you have taken is the last step in incarnation.
So the True Self, the purified self, the self who knows itself
in truth, is already done, has always been done. The Christ
within you has never been tainted by fear, because it cannot be
tainted, nor can it be tempted, nor does it hold vanity or envy
or greed. The Divine as who you are, in an articulated state,
manifest fully, is congruence to love and to truth. There is no
fear in love, and truth will not deny the Divine.

Now, some of you say, "Look at the atrocities committed
by the church. Look at the terrorists who claim to act in the
name of God." We will answer this very quickly. Any religion
that damns another is not operating in truth. Any religion that
condones the harm of another is not acting in truth. But all
a religion is, is a structure to hold beliefs that may have been
spoken in truth, but the walls built around them, with their
murals and parapets, may have been corrupted by the fear of
humanity that would seek to encase God in a temple, a church,
or a mosque. God is in all places, and any place you know of as
holy is your temple, your church, and your mosque.

The gift here is true freedom, the reclamation of all. World
peace is not what you think. It's realization of the kindred nature of humanity. It does not mean you don't grieve. It does

not mean you don't toil. You may grieve or toil as you wish. But it does mean one thing. The requirement for arms, the requirement for battle, the requirement for deceit, all of which are born in fear, are released to the high octave which you are now present in and for. Your idea of justice must change, for you believe justice to be retribution. And that is God's will. It is not yours to decide. The law of karma, or cause and effect, has been so misunderstood to mean punishment that you forget you're in school, and any encounter must be seen as an opportunity to learn. Now, the idea of justice being God's certainly does not mean that there is a God that will smite or offer retribution for a crime committed. The idea of karma can support this, but not as vendetta, but as an offering to educate. You do not kill what you know to be holy, but you murder freely in your denial of the Divine. The gift of the Kingdom in the frequency you hold is to become peace. The term Prince of Peace has been spoken prior, and all this means is emissary. If you look at a father in a kingdom, and you wish to use that terminology, the prince is the one who inherits the kingdom. You may choose queen and princess if you enjoy hierarchical structures, but the true meaning is so simple.

The human being you are is now activated to have one foot in this world, one foot in another, and traverse the realms in love. "How is this possible?" he asks. "I was taught to believe that if you have one foot in spirit and one foot in the material, you fall on your face." We will adjust the metaphor for you, Paul. You are in the world, yes, an actor in the world with other actors, those engaging in the business of being. But the reality you know yourself in has been altered in vibration. In the past, we have said you become the doorway. Now we will say this: The border you crossed earlier allows you to open the doors of the world. This is very important. To be the doorway is to know the self as conduit. To open the doorways is to hold the tone of liberation. "I am holding the tone of liberation. I am holding the door, and the keys to all doors, in love. And I am realizing each one I see, engaged in this act of being, in their truthful states." Underline *Truthful*. Capitalize it, please. Always Truthful because the Eternal Self that you witness as them is ever true.

Your conditioning thus far has claimed you in a template, an entangled one wherein you see your brother as your enemy, or your sister as your competitor. You are being taken to an equality that you have not yet known. Now, equality terrifies you. You believe there must be a victor, a winner at the game of what you call life. This is perpetuated by you, and indeed it is a lie. If you can believe for an instant that there is one of you who is more loved by the Divine than the next, not only are you being foolish, you are being vain.

Each of you here is deeply loved. There is nothing you could do, in any world, to alter that truth. And even any act done in the denial of the Divine is already forgiven. Did you hear those words? An atonement, if you wish, but true. There is nothing you could do to put you outside of the Divine. But your belief in fear, your desire for hatred, requires you to do this for yourself.

We love you as you are. We teach you as you prepare for this great journey in anticipation of embodiment. Period. Period. Period.

Yes, this is in the text. Stop now.

DAY TEN

When we teach you about yourselves and the varying aspects of you, we are calling them forward to be witnessed. We witness each aspect of you in this instruction, the small self or the idea of self that believes itself to be separate, the True Self that knows who and what it is, and the varying aspects of self that have taken on identity through prior incarnation or experience. All are present here in a unified state to be receiving this teaching.

Now, the True Self is present, not as student, but as instructor, and the activation of the Monad, and the release of a time, experience, that you have known yourself through in linearity, claims you outside of time, where all things may be made new and indeed reconciled. The act of reconciliation, calling home to pasture those aspects of self that have been disenfranchised, abandoned, cast out, must all be collected to be re-known.

Now, you cannot do this yourself. You are incapable of it at the level of personality. The Monad, however, in agreement to its nature, has capacity to redeem and reclaim any aspect of the personality structure that has become fragmented. Your idea of self is in fact only a fragment of who you truly are, but you have made it so very important that you claim your entire being through its lens. Your idea of self as outside of God is the issuance of this very small aspect of self that has not been reconciled.

Now, when you are in trauma, when you are in fear, when you have to negotiate safety in a lifetime, there are aspects of you that indeed may splinter, may be caught in a web of fear and feel as if they will never extricate themselves. When we work with you today, we seek to finalize a claim of reconciliation—that the fears you've held that have become trapped in the energetic field and hold themselves as sovereign independent entities or states of consciousness must now be claimed into the unified state so that liberation may truly occur.

Now, a splinter is a piece of something, so none of these aspects are truly separate from you. But when you are traumatized, undergo great fear, the splinter itself may actually claim an identity and reinforce itself when a new fear is encountered. The idea that the body you hold holds sense memory of past events is very true, but the energetic system holds the detritus of an activated fear. Think of it as a blemish, something that gets infected and on occasion bursts open to inform the entire being. When we work with you on this, we are not making you better. We are quite simply telling you something very different—that no aspect of you, even what you think is darkest, is outside of the love of God. And this reunification of the splinters, or the parasitic energies if you wish to think of them this way, must be seen not as an act of exorcism, but as an act of reclamation.

Now, what a parasite is, is something that lives off something else. When a splinter occurs, a thought form, if you wish, that becomes ennobled by fear, it uses fear to catalyze itself, to know itself anew. So it is fed by fear because it is of fear. It's how it was created, and its own action in the energetic field is to claim more of itself. Now, it believes it is supporting you, or protecting you from further harm. It is not evil. It is simply a disenfranchised or abandoned or rejected idea that refuses rejection and demands re-entry into the being. If the only way it can claim this is through further trauma, it will perpetuate an issue. You may call this psychological. You may call it energetic. It really matters not. All we are telling you is whatever these splinters are were once of the whole, can be re-known, and indeed healed.

Now, when we speak of healing of the mind, we are not telling you that you are ill. But we are happy to tell you that you think you are, and you may be imbalanced because the seas you've been riding upon have been in tumult. To claim peace in the mind, or balance in the mind, does not take away identity. It simply aligns you to the Monad that is the sea of great peace and calm. The claim of the Monad upon what we will call the splinter—"You are as I am"—is a very simple claim. "You are as I am" is reclamation. "I cannot perceive you as outside myself because I am all things."

Now, the nature of the personality structure will attempt to use this to do distance energetic work. "I am going to my memory. I am going to retrieve it, make it better than it was." We are operating differently now. Reclamation happens in this present moment. And the energetic field, the identity you hold, in utilizing itself in agreement to Source, is the aspect of you that is brought into unification. (We will say this now: Please be still.* We have resistance from the channel, and if this is so, we will have to stop dictation.) Our requirement for this teaching is that anyone who reads these words who is suffering in the mind may know peace. And this distillation

---

* Spoken to students in the room.

of a teaching can be understood very simply as a reuniting of aspects of self that have been orphaned, splintered, cast into darkness.

Now, while we have taught reclamation in past teachings, we have never discussed them in quite this way, because the amplitude of vibration from the Upper Room would not hold in fullness until this next step was taken. Understand, friends. Most of you entered the Upper Room and hung out happily in the foyer, thinking that's as far as you were allowed. But because we have lifted you to the next level of vibration, the alchemical act of reclamation that can commence can even calm the most stormy sea. We will say this now on your behalf:

On this day we claim that any aspect of self induced by trauma, claimed by fear, that is now operating in separation, any life lived, held in trauma or fear, that claims imbalance in the present day, any thought or invocation of damnation of self or others that has been left in the vibrational field that must now be cleansed, will be done, will be reclaimed, will be lit by the brightest light so that they may be assumed in a high state or octave of love.

On the count of three, Paul.
One. Now two. Now three.

[The Guides tone through Paul.]

Be received by us, as you are, as you hear, as you say yes, as you know. Allow any splinter, any fragment, any orphan, any parasite, any fear, that lingers in shadow to be received in love. We come forth now as a great wind. We sing now as the vibration of love. And as we call all forward into reconciliation, we offer you these words:

You are free. You are free. You are free.

Period. Period. Period. Stop now, please.

(PAUSE)

When you have been challenged in your own experience, denied love, or accosted in fear, when you have been used, or understood wrong-mindedly, you begin to self-identify through the issuance of the experience. You believe it to be who you are. While this was never the case, the self that believes these things creates an investment in maintaining its identity, even if the identity is a mask of pain. You take comfort in your pain. "Look at my sad self. Look at the tragedy I have endured. Look at what I lived through." But if you perceive this as a badge of honor, or you think that the couch born of historical pain is where you must sit, you will continue to self-identify through the very things that you deem calamitous.

Now, this is a very simple teaching of a frame, the frame of the mask of pain, the frame of a distorted reality, the frame of the one so harmed, he or she cannot be redeemed. What you say cannot be redeemed you have made stronger than God. It becomes idolatry. And even this terrible habit, or that awful predilection, or those thoughts that keep you up all night cannot be stronger than God. You understand this, yes?

Now, the tone we sang informs the pages of this text. It's a vibrational tone that holds an intention. The intention of the tone we just sang was to reconcile aspects of self that have been dismissed, abandoned, or denied. When something is re-claimed, it may make itself known. It may be re-seen in a new way. Don't believe for a moment you have taken something back, because it waves goodbye from its old sense of self as it rejoins you in the light.

Because we love you, we will never add to your suffering. Because we know you, we will always sing you to sleep if you require it. And the tone that we sang, informing these pages, is present for you through this simple invocation:

"I hear the song of truth. I am reconciled in truth. And I know myself as safe and loved."

Period. Period. Period. Yes, we will say this is the end of the chapter. We will call it "Reconciliation." Period. Period. Period.

4

FREEDOM

We are with you now as you journey forward, as you see what you see before you with new eyes. We are with you as you walk. And we encourage you, on this walk, to remember who you are and can only be in truth. The Divine as who and what, long this teaching, has been made manifest in the energetic fields of those who hear these words and align to the very truth of them. At this level of alignment, what you are claiming is nonnegotiable. And we will say what this means. "This is a little bit of God. That's a little more God." That can no longer be claimed. The triumph of the teaching, ultimately, is reclamation of identity and manifestation of form. And the denial of the Divine, vanquished at this level of triumph, the Divine as risen and resurrected can now be sung by humanity, one and all.

The echo of this teaching, the residual affect of it, will

be in the fields of all of you for the rest of your being. How you operate with this attunement at this level of alignment is in some ways up to you, and in other ways completely the purview of the Monad, in tandem with soul, to realize itself at the level or octave it can now come to. Choice is implicit here. The choice, once made, sung in the energetic field, is an echo in amplification that encourages what it encounters to be re-known. And the intention you hold—"Behold, I make all things new"—realizes what is seen, claims what is seen, in the template of the Upper Room.

Each of you says yes to what stands before you now. And as we continue this work with you, we will say these words: This is a teaching of re-creation and alignment that can now be made known in manifestation. And the cultures you have grown through, the worlds you have known yourselves in, will be touched and moved and reclaimed by you as you walk this journey onward.

Yes, this is in the text. It is the beginning of the next chapter. Period. Period. Period. Stop now, please.

DAY ELEVEN

When we speak to you about what will come, we are looking at probabilities. The choice to ascend, which has been done at the level of the causal being you are, in tonality, in frequency, in choice, is a manifestation of the Christ that may be known in form. The choice to align at this level of agreement has consequence in the life that you live and in the world that you share. The choice to embody, which is to realize this manifestation, again comes at cost. The choices that would be made in fear, perhaps convenience, the choices that would be made in anger or in deceit, will be reckoned with. And this is true for each of you and all who hear these words.

The teaching of the day is frequency, and alignment beyond an idea of what you could think or conceive of as the small self. The touchstone for you now must be experiential. You are no longer looking for the answers written on the walls, but the experience of the wall itself. And the wall itself, in experience, releases the need to be a wall, and you step forward beyond a separation that you have utilized to be in comprehension of a reality. *Comprehension of a reality.* Understand that phrase—to comprehend something, to give it meaning in understanding, a relational way of being in engagement. To comprehend a reality also implies that there are other realities that may be comprehended, and this is where we take you now.

Now, choice is essential. We are not disregarding past experience here. We are actually utilizing it. You are not forgetting who you were. You are re-knowing who you are. And the information from history that is necessary for you will always be available, but far less available will be your attachment to it—what should be, what must be, in order to conserve an identity or a template of reality that is actually now in motion. When you look at your world and the level of confusion that you are all experiencing, you are looking at a reality that's in flux. "What we thought was so is not so. What we want to be so isn't so, and what is so?" And you grapple for kernels of truth within the lies that you have been aligned to.

Now, when we speak of these lies, we are not speaking of a particular edict, but a way of being in the world where your ascension, or idea of self in a higher template, has been precluded by a belief that it could not be so. And, indeed, that is a lie. Now, when you learn truth, essential truth—what is true is always true—you begin to have an experience of confusion because what you thought was true is still present. Imagine you stand in a room with mirrors. You have used the distorted mirrors so often that you appear to yourself in distortion, and indeed agree to it. Where there may be a true mirror in the room, you might disregard it because it's not what you were expecting to see. The rational mind, the self that you understand yourself through, will make excuses. "Well, this can't be the right mirror. Everybody else says the distortion is true." In this process, you are facing the true mirror, and what was never true comes forward to be seen, to be released, so that the true reflection may maintain itself.

Now, the world you live in is operating in great distortion, has for a long while. You have been fighting since you first chose to pick up a stone. You have been arguing since you decided you must be right at the cost of another being wrong. And you don't understand silence and the beauty that is present in it, so you begin to fill all space with information, sound and chatter, to distract you from the truth that is still present. The cacophony of choice made through fear is actually reaching a crescendo, and we say *cacophony* because there is a level of pitch that may be sounded that is so deafening you are rendered into silence through the sound itself. This is one way to learn. But since we cannot imagine all of you sitting peacefully in awareness, we understand that you may create the circumstances for that quiet to ensue.

Now, this is an internal quiet, but it may also be an external one. The world that you live in now is so busy deciding what it is, how it should be, with the factions participating in what they want or would have be, you don't even know what is. Finally, we have to say that what is will be re-known and seen in truth. And the very fabric of your reality, twisted into a knot, will release those things that cannot abide in the higher octave.

Now, the choice to align at this level must be a collective one. There are teachings that would choose one above the next. "Let these ones go to the mountaintop and avoid the flood. Let those ones perish in the sea of darkness." These are metaphors for high and low choice. But that is not what we see happening here. Finally, we suggest that humanity, in a time of reckoning, sees not only itself and its creations, but the affect of these creations upon one another. Imagine that you were foisting a lie upon a group of people, unaware that it was a lie. When you understand the lie and you align to truth, the residual affect of the lie spoken is still present and must be attended to. How this is attended to at the level of the collective is done in several ways—personal accountability, of course, but also collective accountability for acts done and choices made in fear. Now, recrimination is not the answer here. We have spoken of this prior. But the true answer is love, loving into expression that which has been defiled, claiming the lie in truth at the cost of what the lie would perpetuate. The damning of one's brother or sister for what they have chosen or believed will only get you more trials.

Now, imagine there's a sinking ship. Some of you would be running for the boats that might save you. Others might be helping your brothers or sisters. What we are about to tell you may be shocking, but the boat is sinking and you are the life rafts yourselves. Now, what this means is that each individual, in her choice to align to the higher, supports those around her in a lifting. This is not a lifting to an ideology or to certain politics. It is not about getting your way. It is about the expansiveness of the light and the tone that you are holding, which can hold another, and can hold a thousand more. In this expansion, you are claiming service. "I know how I serve."

Now, some of you believe that this must be an act you undertake. Paul is seeing someone running around with a butterfly net trying to save the butterflies. No one will listen to you this way. No one wants to be saved. They want to continue in the ways that they have known, perpetuate the idea of self at whatever level they have been comfortable with. When we say the boat is sinking, we simply mean that the structure that you have all utilized to determine what reality should be is actually in collapse. And the systems that support this reality, be they economic or religious, whatever they may be, will indeed be re-known. But as the tide comes, washing away the old, the new is present, and you, each of you, in the manifest light you hold, become lighthouses to the storm, and others will see the light and be lifted by it. To become the lighthouse is simply to know who you are. See a lighthouse before you. See its beams radiate and fall across the dark waves. The lighthouse is not trying to be. It is asserting its function. And this function is to illumine and to guide to safety.

Now, understand *safety* in a new context. You all believe that safety is the known. It is not the known. Safety is where you come to in a liberated state when you are no longer determining your well-being on a set of ideals that you have inherited. "I am safe as long as I have a job, as long as my partner is faithful." "I am safe as long as the children are well and the air is clean and the water is drinkable." Your ideas of safety are predicated upon several things—your idea of what should be, and the basic sustenance of the form you have taken. The form does need to be sustained, but if your belief in lack is such that the water may dry, the air may be unfit to breathe, you will do what you must to create better circumstances for yourselves. In fact, what you see on this plane, in this physical realm that you have chosen to embody in, is a degree of lack of love, a lack of awareness of divinity, that has claimed all things in separation. You defile an ocean when you don't believe the ocean to be holy.

Now, your idea of safety must be re-understood as operative from the Upper Room where you cannot be attacked by fear. We use the word *attacked* in an illustrative sense. Imagine you stand on a dock. Below the dock, the sharks are feeding. Best not to hang your legs down below the dock. You will come up without them. You understand that the positioning is not so much avoidance, but understanding the requirements of what it means to be safe. Now, when a world is being recalibrated, which is in tone, when everything is changing at once, your understanding of where to hang your feet is confused. What was safe one day is not the next. Your idea of self is changing so quickly that you don't even know what hat to wear when you leave the house. Allow for change, and allow the change to be beneficial. From the Upper Room, your perception of self as the one changed is not claimed by fear. It is the act of fear that would seek to reclaim you in the dark waters, without the light that you are calling others to the safety of the shore you sit upon.

Now, the shore you sit upon can be understood as the Kingdom, or simply another level of vibration that you have aligned to in such a way that your reality has confirmed your new stand or way of being. The reality that you know yourself in now is not seeking to confirm the old. When we said there was a wall with writing upon it, and you read the writing on the wall, whatever it may say, you are actually confirming the wall. When you move beyond the wall, when the wall crumbles, you stand in a new field. And a field is always present in these teachings when we wish you to understand the idea of dimensional reality. The octave above the one you have known yourselves in is in resonance, claiming things to it at that level, and within that level there are gradations, again an octave in the Upper Room with highs and lows and in-betweens. Each of you who says yes to this passage will actually trespass the wall that we are teaching you of, move beyond it. Paul interrupts: "Isn't the claim 'I am free, I am free, I am free' doing this?" Indeed, it is. But it is the passport to the Upper Room, and you may be in the Upper Room and still experience the self in separation. To begin to move towards union requires an acclimation to a higher level of intonation than you have held thus far. To become one with Source in your realization, while knowing how to care for a body, how to navigate a shared reality, is a transition few make. But we are teaching it anyway, because the species you are, in its collective agreement for change, is aligning at this level, even though you don't see it yet.

The splintering you see of the reality you have known in some ways may be seen as the bricks in the wall falling to dust—each brick, each claim of separation, contributing to the structure of reality that you have known. When the wall is dissolved, when it has fallen with a great sound, or silence, you have a comprehension of being that has been withheld from you before, and by this we mean the wall itself was preclusive to your inheritance. Now, this wall does not exist in the Upper Room. But even in your initial alignment to the Upper Room, you are still held in some abeyance from full expression by the attachments you hold to a literal world or a manifest world that you don't believe can be moved.

The teachings you've received thus far have been preparing you for this transition towards unity, or reclamation of body and form and experience from the vantage point of this lighthouse or the Upper Room or the Kingdom. Each creation you encounter at this level of amplification is not only chosen to be seen anew, or agreed to be seen anew, it is claimed anew by your very vision, by your very presence, and by the invocation of being that we have taught you. "Behold, I make all things new. God Is. God Is. God Is." If the lighthouse beam had a call to it, it would be as such: "Behold, I make all things new; God Is, God Is, God Is"—reclamation at the highest level of intonation that an individual can hold while maintaining form.

The maintaining of form will be discussed later in this text. But for now we wish you to understand two things. The body itself is now undergoing change in preparation to hold the level of tone that is required for this transition, and the psyche or the mind is having to be released from one state of agreement to a new one. "What does that mean?" he asks. Well, you are so entrenched in your requirements for reality that you supersede or decline what is available to you beyond it. Paul sees someone in a car with a map in their lap, trying to chart a course. The old map is what you are using to determine a reality that for all of you is uncharted. It is present now. In fact, you are beginning to experience it.

You may say these words after us, if you wish:

"On this day I choose to be reunited with my own sense of agreement to what expresses beyond the known. I am willing to be taught by the new and allow the old to be confounded. I am willing to have an experience of being that aligns me fully to my true nature, and I will not inhibit this by my idea of what is supposed to be. As I choose this, I create the circumstance for this evolution in my life and in my field. And as I say these words, I know them to be true. I know who I am in truth. I know what I am in truth. I know how I serve in truth. I am free. I am free. I am free."

We thank you each for your presence. We will take a pause for Paul. Period. Period. Period.

DAY TWELVE

When we present through Paul, we have an agenda. Every class we offer has an intention behind it. And the intention for this morning is recognition of where you stand in your own way, what you choose as obstacle to become your teacher. Now, every obstacle on this path must be seen as opportunity, but the recognition of an obstacle can be a hindrance when one wishes not to look. How one perceives herself, himself, through the faulty mirror we have talked about prior is to understand that you cannot see with a distorted lens what can only be seen in the light of truth.

We invite you each today to stand before a mirror. It can be any mirror you wish, small or large, but the reflection in this mirror will hold the truth of your being, and the intention here is not to look away, not to deny what you see, not to excuse what you see, not to pretend that it's not there. The choice to recognize the self, blemishes and all, hindrances and all, will support you in a higher way of seeing self. But this cannot occur when you refute truth for the convenience of the known. *The convenience of the known* means, very simply, "I don't want to see what I don't want to see because if, indeed, I saw it, I may have to address it and change." Recognition in truth is the teaching. And the articulation of the Monad that comes at the cost of the old will be what translates your experience as perceiver of self.

You stand before this mirror today in a willingness to see. Now, the self that sees has predilections still. "Let me like myself. Let me approve of my body. Let me not think about those terrible things I said one day that must mean I am a this or a that." Your idea of what you should be, or would believe yourself to be, either high or low, creates an obstructive filter. Now, when a filter is taken off a camera lens, perhaps what is seen is true. But what is here to be seen is not to be judged, but recognized in neutrality. Understand this, friends. It is you who decide what is worthy or not, what is good or not good, what can be shared and seen and what cannot be. And the recognition in this mirror will not fail you if your intent to see clearly is presented in fullness. See yourself in this mirror and allow the reflection to claim you. Any ideas of self that are imprinted in this reflection, any disfigurement of self that you have accrued through wrong idealization, faulty perception, choosing to see in fear, or choosing to deny truth, will now be met by you.

We are going to call the Divine, the true spirit of God, into the perception you hold, so what is reflected back to you will be in truth. Now, we are not giving you the perfect reflection that is indeed how we see you. We are showing you how you obstruct through an identity that you have claimed in agreement to fear. This is the first step of this exercise. Let the mirror be illumined in truth, and see what you see, and allow yourself to see what is revealed for you. Don't decide what it means to see in this way. Allow the experience of sight or perception to be the gift that you are given. You don't clean a dirty room without identifying the dirt, nor do you release a false idea of self without an acknowledgment that you have adhered to this for some time. Paul is seeing the image of Band-Aids being pulled, scars being revealed, tokens of history burned into flesh, pain that has been held in the body, attitudes of scorn and grief, rage and frustration, all being seen in this mirror. Because they have been present as how you would reflect self, they may now be seen to be reckoned with.

Now, a reckoning is a facing of self and one's creations, and this reckoning is a deep gift, because where we intend to take you is to a level of vibration where you will no longer hold even the recognition of what once was, because the idealized self, True Self, if you wish, will be present and occupying its place.

On the count of three, we are going to claim all of you in the brightest light you can bear. Now, when a light is so bright, it reclaims what it encounters, and re-creates from them what they can only be known as in truth. You have an alchemical act of expression. And the claiming we do now for you is not to make you better, but for you to understand that what is seen in this faulty mirror of personality, what is now being seen in truth, that which you have used to know the self in small self ways, may now be reclaimed in a new mirror that reflects truth in a high way, not the hindrances to truth or the obstacles to true perception.

On the count of three.

Now one. Now two. Now three.

Be received by us and allow this mirror to be illumined in perfect light, to recognize only the Divine that is the true reflection of your being. The hindrances you've held, the obstacles in perception, being claimed by this bright light, will be known anew. And the claim you may make now with us, "Behold, I make all things new," spoken to this mirror, will rectify any wrong, reclaim all darkness, and choose itself to be known anew. To choose itself to be known anew is the Divine reclaiming every aspect of being that it encounters in its true glory.

We speak these words for you now:

> *On this day we claim that all who hear these words, all who are present for this recognition, will allow the scales to fall from their eyes, layers of deceit, layers of fear, and what has been chosen to deny the light is now re-chosen to reflect it. We know who you are in truth. We know what you are in truth. We know how you serve in truth. Indeed, You Have Come.*

Now, because this is a meditation and an act of expression both, we wish you now to surrender to the energy that is present for this meditation, an alchemical act of recognition and re-knowing. Paul is feeling the energy around him as if from a shower, moving away or reclaiming what it encounters. You may all do the same, or simply allow what is transpiring in the energetic field to be laid present for you each to re-know the self in truth.

The agreement we are making with you today is to a process of release of what has held you at bay, and what you would take to the Upper Room unknowingly because you don't understand that what you have chosen to know yourself through has been in hindrance to the truth of the Divine that is present as all things.

We see you each as you can only be seen. We have said prior, your beauty is unrecognizable to you. The depth of beauty in all of you is beyond your recognition. We hope now, we trust now, we claim now that you will begin to see this, because the mirror you are now presented with will be the mirror of truth.

Paul is seeing a mirror. He sees a round one before him, and he sees a reflection that has not yet been seen. We invite you each to see a new mirror before you, that which is yet to be seen through, that which you have never been reflected by from the lower strata of recognition that you have known yourselves through. Allow this mirror now, from this place in the Upper Room, to grant you the gift of true sight. And *true sight* means moving beyond appearance to the recognition of truth. Let yourself see your reflection, unhindered in your beauty. And let this recognition be imprinted upon you so that you may perceive your fellows in the same legacy and vibration of truth.

The claim we make for you now—"It will be so"—is the mandate for articulation at this level of agreement. See the body you have known, see the expression of the energy you hold, see even the idea of self, unencumbered, unhindered, in its glory before you. And as you say these words, let them be heard through the entire field, spoken into infinity by the one who knows who he or she is:

"I am free. I am free. I am free."

And let yourself be known, unhindered, unadorned. Simply be, as the Monad, come in expression in the beauty of who you are.

Now we will teach you something other. When you align at this level, you become an authority in truth. This does not mean you hold opinions. It doesn't matter what you think or believe. But what does matter is how you claim truth, and the truth that we speak to is the legacy of the Divine that claims what it encounters in love. You must understand, friends. There is no punishing God that would smite its creations. The legacy of pain you've endured on this plane has primarily been the out-picturing of selfishness and the denial of God. So you must now be generous in truth, and all that you may meet must be met in a mirror that does not claim their fear, or their appropriations of fear, but claims them in the beauty of their being.

Now, understand this beauty is not a compliment to their appearance, but a recognition, and true recognition, of how they can only be. You will become as the mirror that you looked in, that holds the perfect structure, the perfect reflection. To be the doorway to the Upper Room is to welcome all you meet in their agreement to it. And if you are judging your fellows, you have denied them entry. If you are claiming your fellows in darkness, you are no longer present in the Upper Room as you may think. And we say this for Paul: Yes, an aspect of all of you is ever present in the Upper Room, but by denying the light in another, you have moved to a lower gradation of tone and scale.

Now, being the perfect mirror to what you see does not mean you condone acts that are harmful. It does not mean you ignore things that you would otherwise think poorly of. It means that the being you are *is* the sight of God, the claim of the sight of God, and you become the reflection of the Divine that is ever present in all manifestation.

An idealized self, or what you would assume to be an idealized self, would be the one who is never ill, never frustrated. But we will say something other to you. Your humanity is intact. Your ability to feel all feelings is still present. But in this articulated state from the Upper Room, you are the welcoming of your humanity in every form it has taken in others. God cannot deny its creations, and consequently you cannot deny them either. The love that you may hold for your brother is not romantic love. It is the same love that the Divine knows for *all* it sees, for *all* experience. You are not the arbiter of truth. You are the one who claims truth where the lie has been held.

We will say this to each of you now: We have completed the first half of the text. We will say thank you. We will give you titles when we wish. We are pleased for your presence and thank you. Stop now, please.

DAY THIRTEEN

What is before you now is a reconciliation of that which has been denied or refuted or abandoned by you. These aspects of self, including the sexual self that has operated in distortion, must be brought forth for reconciliation.

Now, the sexual self must be understood as precious as all, but in the cultures you've been brought up in, it has been distorted or made shameful. And the denial of the body and its precious divinity plays out in consort to the old shame of the sexual self. To reconcile the sexual self is to allow every aspect of it to be brought before you and seen and agreed to.

Now, to agree to the sexual self is not to make it good or make it bad. It's simply to accept it. "This is who I have been, how I have desired, how I have used this energy, how I have denied this energy." And to comprehend this simply as so is the first step in reconciling it. There are aspects of self that you deny that you are completely unaware of, but are acting upon, and how you attend to these aspects of self must be done in a similar manner. Any memory that has been buried, any pattern that has been ignored or denied, that has not been made conscious for you, must also understand itself as of Source in order for reconciliation to occur. And the manifestation of this, in some cases, is making visible those patterns or aspects of self that have been dis-assimilated, or put aside, or refuted and denied.

"How does this occur?" he asks. Primarily through one's agreement to them. Now, you don't understand, when you look at a beach, that there are grains of sand that you may think of as poisoned that inform the beach. But, in fact, they are there, and an aspect of you that operates as such a grain of sand upon the beach of your energetic field can be re-assumed through the agreement to it. And, in fact, the willingness to agree to it makes the choice to align beyond it—inclusive of its presence, but beyond it—a far more easy task.

Now, imagine you have an aspect of self that has been so denied that it creates its own kingdom, its own way of operating, an orphan of the self who has grown up independently and found sustenance where it can. You may consider this an aspect of self that operates in separation and claims an identity beyond even the host. This aspect of self believes itself so neglected that it will do anything to revenge or get the attention of host, so reconciliation may be possible. You may consider this an aspect of self that seeks revenge, but this is not so. This is an aspect of self that seeks attention and energy wherever it can find it. This is reconciled by you in a slightly different way. Because you understand that the thing operates with a self or independent structure, the act of reclamation must become inclusive of its own creations.

Now, imagine there is an aspect of you that hates the world, that has been operating somewhat independently, wreaking its own little havoc upon the life lived. The one who wonders why the relationships fail, why he is always betrayed, may be in benefit of the acts of just such an aspect. The reconciliation of the product of the structure, or spore of identity, must be reclaimed as part of the whole. So, in other words, friends, not only your orphaned daughter must be reconciled, but the things the orphaned daughter has done to get attention or in its belief in separation must also be attended to.

Now, the work we have done with you thus far with mirrors is highly beneficial, and we will do this a little bit differently. The reconciliation of an aspect of self that has created an independent structure, through the announcement "God Is," must be done in a way that is inclusive. If you use the claim "God Is" as some form of exorcism or renunciation of this aspect, you will find this aspect agitated and fighting back. Any aspect of you that has been refuted actually requires only one thing, which is love and acceptance. Because these spores or energetic grains of sand that operate in poisonous ways have done the best they can as a result of your refusal of them, you must understand that they have been participatory to your entire experience upon this plane.

Now, imagine there is an aspect of you that is created at the age of seven—a terrible incident, an attack, an altercation, a time when you could not be safe or heard. To reconcile this aspect of you, which you may be unconscious of and has spawned a series of beliefs that have claimed you in action, must involve a reconciliation of the idea of self that was present at that time. The identity of the seven-year-old is actually as formed as the one who is ninety, but it is operating differently. It has accrued less formal experience on this plane, and consequently the impact of all experience is far greater because it has been selective in some ways about what can inform it because it's receiving less data than can be accrued over ninety years. The reconciliation of the child, or experiencer of trauma, the one who believes him or herself to be separate, can be known in totality.

Now, we are saying this intentionally. *In totality* means as of the whole, and to reconcile a self that has been splintered, fragmented, or denied, and now operates as an independent structure must be seen as the act of redemption that the Monad is capable of. It is not the small self picking through a beach full of sand to find the poisonous stone. You would spend the rest of your life searching. But reconciliation, or being redeemed by this aspect of you that we call the True Self, is the gift of being, in a reconciled state. The manifestation of this claim, "I am free," means less that you are free of the old behaviors than that you are no longer acting on the impulse of the original act that created separation or fragmentation from self, the sexual self, the self who believes he must be loved no matter what he does and is punished by an angry mother or disappointed father and then believes himself to be bad, the one who is left behind by accident, or suffers an encounter of the body. Any form of accident that terrorizes and makes known fear in such a way that fragmentation occurs must be comprehended as something that can be held in total reconciliation.

Now, to understand redemption is not to understand the idea of sin, but to understand that the true value of anything that has been discarded or refuted is known by the Monad or Creator. You wouldn't want that thing back in the house that you threw away two years ago. But the aspect of you that we can call redeemer knows full well the matter of fact, reason, for its displacement even if you do not, and can reclaim for you, and will, as it realizes itself through this old fabric of history that has become distorted by way of your fear or experience of separation.

"Well, how does it occur?" he asks. "You have given us a few examples now, but how does this occur? How are we redeemed, or how are we reclaimed?" In the Upper Room, you can imagine a chamber. Now, we use the word *chamber* intentionally, because it is enclosed. And what happens in the chamber may be separate from your experience of the Upper Room as a state of consciousness or vibration. We invite you now to imagine this chamber in the Upper Room. And what is held in this chamber is a level of velocity or vibratory tone where these aspects of self that have been denied and dismissed can and will be reconciled.

Paul imagines himself stepping in, seating himself on the floor of a white chamber. The energy is still, and is about to lift. When we sing through Paul now, we will be singing into this chamber. If you wish to place yourself in the Upper Room in a comparable chamber, we will sing with you as well. The tone that is being sung does not eradicate. It includes. It reconciles or redeems. While we are singing, we wish you to imagine that any aspect of you that you have put enshrouded in a dark space, were ignorant of or denied, will be revealed, and in this revelation, being seen or accepted or acknowledged, will then integrate into the totality of your expression and not operate separately from it. In this tone, the energy of love will be so present to deny any fear that may have accrued around this. And fearlessly, you may allow the return of this thing to be loved and integrated as of the whole precious being that you are.

On the count of three, Paul.

One. Now two. Now three.

[The Guides tone through Paul.]

Be received by us as whole. Be received by us in unification. Allow any fragment of self, any dissociated aspects of you, any shards of self that believe themselves to be independent or outcast. See them in reconciliation. Allow them to be loved in this residual tone we sing. We are singing through the

energetic fields of all who hear or read these words. We are announcing your presence in wholeness as we speak. And we say
these words now on your behalf. There is nothing you could
do or could have ever done, nothing you have ever believed or
chosen, that can put you outside of the love of God. It cannot
be so. Reuniting aspects of yourself in the True Self, the act of
the Monad as redeemer, or Christ as True Self, is the gift you
receive now. We invite you to allow the Monad to complete the
task of reconciliation, which is integration, or allowance of the
whole, in acclimation to the old energies that have been re-
turned to you in a new high state of vibration. You were never
wrong. It was never right. It simply was. Whatever happened
simply was. You do not deny what happened. You give it permission to be re-known.

> *On this night we claim that all who hear these words are
> re-known in totality.*

And as we speak now to Paul, we remind him that any
experience he has had that has caused fear or separation is
being reconciled as well. The being that he is, is in re-for-
mation and the integration of it is less challenging than
he thought it would be. He sees a window now. There are
patches of dirt still, a few cracks here and there that are
being repaired gently, wiped away and cleaned. The distortions of self, the motes in the eye, if you would, the grains
of sand that pollute the beach or the experience of self, are
being re-seen, and you are unencumbered by the distortions
they prior offered you.

We will stop this dictation for a moment and then we will return and teach some more. Paul, take two minutes in silence. Then we will speak some more. Period. Period. Period.

(PAUSE)

How does one know herself as changed? How does one understand that the landscape he walks upon has been altered? The senses are the first thing, and the responses you have emotionally are the ways you will begin to understand that what has operated in separation has been claimed anew. The out-picturing of your life, you see, when informed by such fragments or distortions, play out in accord with them. We have taught you frames prior, that how you frame expectation of a life lived delivers that life to you. And the distortions that you have utilized, and in some ways claimed as identity, have wrought a life born in distortion. The one who believes her body is shameful makes choices in shame. The one who believes his sexuality is evil will deny his sexuality or act in poor accord. How any human being is reconciled at these levels must be understood as transformation. Not as fixing. Transformation. To be transformed or made new is to be redeemed, reclaimed, and made new in the Upper Room through the Monad, who is the redeemer.

Now, this is a choice some of you will make. You will attend to the changes that come, and then begin to refute them, because you actually cannot imagine the self as beyond the old structures. Imagine someone who lives in a lovely apartment. She moves to a new country. She redecorates the apartment in the new country to resemble the one she was in. Now, imagine you were living in squalor, or in shame, or in a dispossession of your life that precluded the body's love for the life lived, or a shame of the body that would deny the body sensation or intimate touch. You can move in squalor to another country. You can't redecorate the room in the new country that we take you to in the old way. So some of you choose instead to look out the old view, beyond the old soiled curtains, to a view that at least you understand.

When one becomes liberated from aspects of self that have operated in fragmentation, there may be a period of feeling dislocated in your own experience. Now, because you are attuned to the Upper Room and the work that we do with you occurs there, you may always be present here, in this high light of knowing who and what you are. But the aspects of self that feel dislocated, you expect to be there. Now, imagine you lived in a world where the doorways were only four feet tall. You become so used to stooping as you enter a doorway, it becomes an automatic response. Now the doorway is twelve feet high, but you stoop because you are used to stooping. Soon enough, our friends, you will stand erect. You will walk through these doorways unhindered by distortion and past associations of pain.

The denial of love will be what we address next in this teaching. This has been a chapter on reconciliation, yes, but of aspects of self that have known themselves without love. And realization of the love of the Divine cannot be excluded by a splinter that says, "I will not be loved anymore."

We will title this chapter "Freedom." We will continue with this chapter when we return tomorrow. Thank you each for your presence. Stop now, please. Period. Period. Period.

DAY FOURTEEN

We'd like to begin by discussing your lives as they have been lived thus far. Each one of you here is in an encounter with the unknown every day upon your awakening. But because the known has been so present, because you operate in the field of the known, the choices that you make, informed by history ever-present around you, consolidate an idea of a world that is actually an idea and very little more. The truth of your being, in a resurrected state, operates in a higher amplitude than the world you have known thus far. And the equivalency you create, once you articulate as manifest, is to a different level of resonance.

Now, the resonant field you know—that surrounds you, that provides you the choices that you see each day—is not so much replaced, but re-known from the higher. And the ingredient that you must understand now, as discussed in realization, is truth. You are moving to the level of truth where what is in a lie can not only be seen, but re-known in vibration. Underline those words, *in vibration*. The claims we made for you yesterday when we took you to a chamber where you might be re-known were in truth. The realization of who one is, beyond a narrative that you have superimposed on the lives you have lived, releases you in all ways from an idea of self that is claimed in shadow. Re-articulation or manifestation in a higher octave reclaims identity beyond falsity, beyond the ideas of scarcity or lack, because you have gone into an agreement with the True Self, who knows far more than you were taught as a small child. The Manifest Self, who operates in this world, or a world made or seen anew, is the self that claims the manifest world in co-resonance with it. The denial of the Divine is no longer present in this octave at this level of tone. So the agreement you are making as we take you forward is a reconciliation, not only with the Monad, but all things in equivalency to it. Do you understand what we are saying?

The triumph of this teaching, we will have to say, is renewal and manifestation at a causal level, where the manifest plane is reintroduced to its true nature through the process we are engaging with you now. The choice to align at this level, the agreement to come forth as this manifest light, the choice to be, as this articulation, in a resonant field that claims all things in accord to it, is to become visible. We will explain what this means. The small light in your bosom, that burns brightly always, overtakes the being you are. You are illumined in this way, and the agreement to this light to call all things to it is actually visible. "Visible in what way?" he asks. Imagine the clouds part and a beam of light makes itself seen. This light was always present, but was precluded by the clouds. In this way, you begin to understand that you are not the light, but the vehicle for the light's expression. And the denial of the Divine cannot be held by the light. Visibility means that your encounter with darkness, or what has been held in shadow, will release darkness. The tone you sing at, the vibrational echo of your resonant field, can and will be anywhere that you are taken. This is not just the walk to the post office, where what you encounter is re-seen. Where your attention is, you are, at the level of vibration. And the agreement to be where you are called, to lift what you see or is there for you to claim, by nature of presence, is the act of the Monad in a re-articulated state.

Now, this is true without the body. The presence of the Divine is not limited by form. But your expression, while inclusive of form, is not limited by your form, either. And the realization that you can and will be, in multiple environments having multiple experiences in simultaneity, will be a surprise to you. "How does this happen?" he asks. "It sounds uncomfortable and it doesn't seem real." We will say it is already so. You have a memory. You are summoned to that level of vibration. You think of a trip. You imagine yourself where you go. But at this level of tone, the vibrational field you hold, which is consciousness, is going where it is required, and its echo is translating expression to the high tone as it is required. Understand, friends, that the light does not decide upon what it shines. It simply is. And at this level of tone, you have made yourselves available for this action. To be in multiple ideas of reality simultaneously is not so far off from your current experience. You have an idea of who you are that informs each walk you take, calls each thing you see into agreement with the consciousness you have held. You have dreams where you are broken free of the limitations of the physical realm. And you understand that your alignment to Source claims you in a higher octave. All of these are ways of operating in multiple realities, although these realities are filtered by you through the brain to a level you can comprehend. Your agreement now towards a less limited expression is simply saying, "I am free of the limitations of experience and expression that the life that I have lived thus far has claimed me in."

Now, this level of realization must be experiential, and those of you who go seeking it—"Let me see myself in Paris while I dine in Oregon," "Let me see myself when I was ten, be back in the classroom where I was harmed, while I wash my feet in the ocean on a sunny day"—once you understand that realization is experiential and not a token to chase, you understand that every day is this opportunity for a higher level of expression. Paul interrupts: "I imagine people seeking higher levels of expression. Everybody wants the experience. But in this case, isn't this experience born in equivalency?" Absolutely correct. The equivalency you hold in any moment is claiming your agreement to any reality that you encounter. Underline the word *any*. There are more realities than you can fathom. Some of them need not be discussed. Some of them are present now. Some of them will claim you as you are aligned to them.

You all stand now at a precipice of agreement, where what manifestation means can and will be inclusive of a higher level of tone that translates environment and reclaims you and what you encounter, what you claim in consciousness, in the Upper Room. As the doorway to the Upper Room, you are claiming all things in like accord. But your experience of this act can and will be altered by your own consciousness as the filters you have used to diminish expression are released. When we spoke to you yesterday, we instructed you that there are aspects of self operating in some independence from self that create experience and bind you to the lower realm through their own justification of fear or what they require to survive. Without these inhibitions operating in the energetic field, you become clear of those aspects of self that would claim you outside of the Kingdom. Once you can rest in the Kingdom as an awareness—it is possible to receive and perceive the inherent Divine as all things—you move to new requirements of how you operate and how the energy field you use to work with reality can superimpose itself and reclaim all things.

Paul asks for clarification. The idea that the energetic field, unhindered and unbound by the data of history as it has been, that the senses themselves become inclusive of higher experience, translates your own expression and way of being in a world. The idea of superimposition simply means that all things are lifted to the higher, or higher template that is held in the Upper Room. The template for the Kingdom is simply what is. It is simply that one note of Source as manifest as all manifest worlds. And when you agree to align to this level, embodiment occurs in the stages that it can be held by the individual. Some of you will ask, "Well, what does it look like? What does it feel like?" It feels like who and what you are as liberated, in awareness of the truth of what you see, in a reclamation of the primary relationship with the idea of the Creator that can be held at this level. We said *idea of the Creator* because until that is experiential and simply known, you will be aligning to an idea that will make itself known through you.

The triumph of the teaching, again, is resurrection, and the amplitude of the self at this level of alignment to support a world made new. You all seek to justify the old, still. "Well, this is my bank account. That is my mortgage. That is my family. This is what we do and who we speak to." While these are all ways of knowing the self, they have little to do with who you truly are. And while you may maintain these things in the Upper Room, they move into right place, *right place* meaning an agreement to what is that is useful, that is part of your experience here, but is simply another expression of the Divine that you may know God through.

We sing your songs for you so that you may learn the words, and re-articulation is its own song. And its agreement to the one note played, to expression of love, to embodiment in love, is the gift that you give through your own agreement to it.

We will stop now for Paul. Period. Period. Period. Stop now, please.

DAY FIFTEEN

We ask you questions today about what you think you are, what you assume yourselves to be, and how you would calculate an identity based upon the principles you have inherited—what makes a good man, a good woman, what makes a good life. The ideas you hold, born in history, are useful in a template that binds you to the three-dimensional reality that you have been in adherence to. But because you've lifted to what we call the Upper Room, which is realization of the Monad in principle, you have been overwritten, in a certain way, by truth.

Now, *by truth* means what is always true. And any culture or society will create the rules it requires to survive, perhaps at the cost of others' survival. In the Upper Room, the idea of oneness, or pluralization, becomes a principle that you are adhering to. Now, a principle is not an idea, as we teach it, but a fundamental truth. And the truth of plurality is that you are all of the same stuff, no matter how hard you deny it. And the realization of this, even for one individual, has ramifications on the collective. Some of you believe that you do charity, acts of good, to serve the soul's progression. And while this is true at a certain level, in any act of charity you are being reminded of the gift of being that is always extended to another through a realization of unity or oneness. To move into this level of consciousness—unity or oneness—requires a realization that the old ideas, useful as they have been in navigating this world that you have known, are not nearly as applicable in the other.

Now, the question Paul has is "How do you navigate two worlds? How do you realize the self in the Upper Room, pay your taxes in the lower? How do you love your brother as yourself when your neighbor is bothering you?" You ask questions, you see, Paul, born of the old template, as if you would overlay the old template upon the Upper Room to see which rules are still pertinent. In the Upper Room, there is one truth, and the ultimate truth is "God Is," which may be known or splintered in other ways that would support your realization of the great truth.

Now, understand, Paul, that each of you is born to realize the self through a manifest reality that you have chosen to align to. The choice to align to the higher does not necessarily vanquish the lessons that the soul has called to itself for the purpose of an incarnation. If you came here to learn love, you will indeed learn love. If you came here to learn courage or selflessness, you will learn those lessons as well, and call to you the circumstances and people that will be your best teachers.

Now, the experience of this in the Upper Room is somewhat

different than you've thought. Of course, you have friendships, relationships, those you cherish, in the Upper Room. But you also have those you have never met that you are no longer excluding from the light that you are. And your inclusiveness, which simply means allowance of all beings to be, is the step you are required to take in the claim "God Is." You imagine a boundary around yourself, Paul, that invites some, refuses others, and while we understand your requirements as a personality for this, you do this at a cost. To love another as yourself implies that you know self-love. Few of you truly do. You still believe you are the lover, whereas it is God that loves through all of you. And the alignment to God, as we teach it, is indeed the alignment to love. And God cannot exclude any of its creations from the love that it holds for all—the claim "God Is," a claim of inclusiveness and totality.

Now, you can imagine for a moment that you are as an ocean, and that the waves of your being touch every shore that it is participatory to. This ocean that you are touches everyone, not only that you encounter, but that you hold in consciousness. And the realization of "God Is," in totality, is as becoming the ocean, inclusive of all.

Now, you don't understand yet, Paul, what your role is in this mission. It will be revealed to you in time. But because we expect you would stop dictation if you comprehended this fully—you would not want to be accountable to great change in the world—we will continue now with this bit of information for you. The texts that are being written through Paul are keys to freedom, and keys to re-creation. A key will only work if it is put in the lock and turned. A key without a doorway is somewhat useless. But we say to each of you now: You are all the doorways. And the keys you are being given open you to service to be as the ocean that reclaims each shore in its own perfection.

Now, Paul imagines himself separate, comfortably separate. "I will decide when the lights go out at night, what time I rise in the morning, what I will eat and what I will choose." And you understand yourself in singularity in the ways most do, the idea of autonomy in free will, what is chosen by you to learn through that appeals to your idea of safety and comfort. We are about to do away with safety and comfort as you have understood it. And this is not to mean that you are unsafe, or even uncomfortable. But the idea of comfort that you have chosen, Paul, and many others as well have chosen, is decided by the self that mandates separation. And the inclusive self, the Monad in realization, cannot hold that vibration. Underline *cannot*.

Imagine you have become too big for the house you have lived in. You push up against the walls and ceilings, and the baseboards themselves. The walls begin to tumble, the ceiling breaks free, and you are yourself, unhindered from the sense of boundary that you have utilized, for the idea of comfort and safety that you have utilized, to navigate this realm. Now, the embodied self, the one who comes as she truly is, does not hold the same requirements for safety. Paul interrupts: "Pardon me while I say this. But there are times when people bother me. I don't want to pick up the phone at two in the morning. I don't want to let someone in the house that I don't feel comfortable with. What happens to those needs?" Those needs are present in prudence. You are still choosing, but the choices you are making, not claimed by fear, move to an inclusivity where what you are calling to you is always of God. Now, underline that, please—*always of God.* Because the self that is realized here, who knows who it is, who knows who others are as a result, is not predicating separation by its presence, it claims inclusivity because this is the light you have become. And realization of this, as the doorway to allow others entry, is not that they will steal your silver or bother you in the middle of the night, but that they will be lifted by your agreement to them.

You abide now in the Upper Room, whether or not you know it. This is for you, Paul, yes, and many of our students as well. Abiding in the Upper Room simply means you realize the self at this level of tone or octave. And the inclusivity that is present now is something that must be understood as the product or result of outgrowing the old house. The one who abides in the old house, with its windows and curtains and locks, knows a life that is separate from Source. This does not mean you don't live in an actual house and you don't close the windows when it rains. It means that the being that you are, that would rest in comfort of the known, has outgrown the known and the idea of safety or comfort that is predicated upon isolation or the denial of others' presence.

You all say you seek love, or you want love, or you wish to be in love, but your idea of this, in almost all cases, is inviting somebody into the small house and drawing those curtains in an isolated way. When you have moved beyond the small self, in inclusivity, the realization of others has no effort attached. Do you understand this, all of you? You are not seeking to

realize the Divine in others. In the Upper Room, they are realized because you are there to realize them. And from the Upper Room, what is seen is of God. The habits you've formed
about exclusivity, that some of you would call boundaries and
others of you would call barriers, must be seen now in a different way. Paul interrupts: "Well, what is a healthy boundary in
the Upper Room?" We will answer that shortly, Paul. We wish
to tell them first that this level of realization, at the cost of the
old, has its own requirements for fulfillment. As every stage
you make in your progression forward has a border or a doorway you cross in ascension, each has its own requirements.

Now, the idea of a healthy boundary has been discussed
in prior texts. If somebody steps on your foot, by all means
please say, "You just stepped on my foot. Please don't do this
again." If they continue to act in this way, remove yourself or
do what you require to protect yourself. This is true. You have
a body. You are responsible to its well-being. If the house is on
fire, get out of the house. You understand this much. What
you don't understand, Paul, is that the one that you would
deem as having an unhealthy boundary is operating in fear, or
trying to negotiate an identity through proximity to another.
When one tries to negotiate identity through another—"Tell
me who I am as I wish to be seen"—they are claiming you in
lower vibration. The antidote to this is to be in the higher,
where they cannot claim you in their fear or selfishness, but
you may claim them. "I see you in the Upper Room. I know
who you are in truth, what you are in truth, how you serve
in truth. You are free. You are free. You are free." Now, these
are not words that are spoken to pacify. You are not petting a

cat that you think might scratch you unless it is pacified. It is the realization of them from Upper Room that reclaims them beyond their own history and needs to attach through the lower vibrational field.

Your own ascension, Paul, as it progresses, has had requirements. And releasing those who seek to attach at the lower has been uncomfortable at times, but a requirement for your well-being. This is true for all of you. What it does not mean is that you are going through your address book, crossing out names of those you assume must be in low vibration. It simply means, in your alignment to the higher, what has been negotiated in fear is re-known in love, and what falls away is what is no longer required, what cannot be held at the level of tone or velocity that you have now aligned to. All of you will undergo this. We say this for Paul, who is concerned. He believes people will say, "Well, time to leave that job, time to leave that husband or wife, time to move away from all I have known."

Any action taken at this level of realization is claimed in love and not in fear. You are not picking something off of yourself that has taken root there, to disentangle and liberate yourself. These things fall away as you unattach to the requirements of them. And your own requirements have been present in every relationship that you have ever had. Underline that, friends: *every relationship*. They are there as your teachers. Not all teachings are pleasant or comfortable, but the soul has mandates for growth and will call them to itself as it requires them.

The agreements we have with you about your well-being, as you undertake this journey with us, is that you will not be fooled, you will not be taught poorly, and you will always have choice to agree with what we say or choose something other. We step with you for as long as you wish to walk, but the soul that you have, the arbiter of your own experiences, is there for your counsel. And the Monad or True Self that is your True Self in freedom is the one you will finally answer to.

We will teach now what it means to be free of an idea of self that predicates her well-being on how she is seen by others, how he is perceived by others, and the idea that a self should be esteemed in certain ways. Again, your idea of comfort, even within a community, is to have a sense of self and the role that you play. The baker knows her place in the community each time a loaf of bread is gifted to another. The child knows itself in relationship to its parents and teachers and understands that its well-being and growth are predicated upon those relationships. But when you come to a certain point in these teachings, even the idea of how you think you should be and be seen must be replaced with who you truly are. Now, *truly are* does not mean you don't bake bread. It does not mean you don't go to school. But it does mean that the True Self, who holds no label or no descriptor within community, can actually hold the community and lift the community in vibration without being seen as the one who does so. You are releasing the need to have a name tag and a job description that is in service to an idea of self that is operating in limitation.

Paul interrupts yet again: "But we still bake bread if that is what we do?" Yes, you do. But your sense of worth, and requirements for knowing self, have moved beyond that act of generosity or craft or skill. You have simply become who and what you are. And how you are perceived by another does not need to fit a descriptor that would be attached to you for the comfort of the known.

Again, you have outgrown the old house. The old house has fallen away. Some of you will begin to understand this experientially. You will actually feel the expansion in your energetic field in a way you have never done before. Others of you will suddenly realize that you once thought you were your job or your role in community, and you no longer experience that. There is some discomfort here, but very, very little. Each of you says yes to the level of agreement you have chosen.

We will say this now for Paul: We will stop this dictation and resume tomorrow. Period.

DAY SIXTEEN

We stand before you today in reckoning of past creations, where you have denied God, where you have chosen to see something other than God, where you have denied the True Self that is in fact here for you to reconcile you with the truth of any situation you have been accountable to or known yourself as party to. The realization of the Divine as the fabric of your life, the very fabric of your life, is what will re-create your life.

Now, Paul is seeing fabric stretched. You have imagined your lives as embroidery on this fabric, the things that happened to you, the things that you would object to, the things that you encountered that were your teachers. But the fabric itself, that which these things are stitched upon, can indeed be rendered new through the redemption of a life by the Monad. To be redeemed is to be reclaimed. We are not speaking of sin. We are speaking to where you have chosen, knowingly or unknowingly, to deny this fabric, God itself, when it has always been present. Now, to reconcile at this level is a requirement, because the issuances of what you would call karma, those things stitched upon the cloth that scar the cloth or impede the cloth from full expression, have never been who you are, but it's what you have created through the act of denial. And to reclaim the self and the life lived must involve a reconciliation, not only with past action, but the denial of the Divine that has impeded your true expression.

Now, the value of what we take you through today cannot be underestimated. What we are doing with you is reclaiming the life that has been lived with a mandate for a new encounter with past creations that will lift you beyond cause and effect, as you have known it, to a realization of the omnipresent Divine where it was most obscured by you—and underline *by you*—where you chose the other, denied truth in ignorance or in a claim of fear.

Now, when we teach through Paul, we do our best to override his resistance. When we speak of karma, or past acts, or the idea of an encounter with fear, he becomes anxious. "Please, no more rough seas." Well, the world you are expressing in, Paul, is *in* a rough sea, is *as* a rough sea, and all of you are being lifted to the top of a wave that may carry you to the new, lest you be pummeled upon the old as it crashes down. Our reconciliation with you must then entail a reclamation of the life lived, inclusive of past choice. The ramifications of these choices are already present in your field. Again, think of embroidery, or stitching upon a piece of cloth or a veil. To lose the embroidery on the veil is to release the ideas that have accrued value that were stained there in fear, stitched there in anger, claimed in anger, that you now wear as embroidery or stitching in what you would call the auric field.

Now, when a life is made new or reclaimed in the higher octave, the residual affect of past choice is still present in the life lived. To reconcile this with the higher octave is not to deny past choice, punish the self for past choice, or to be fearful of the ramifications of it. It's to simply comprehend that what was, was. And the action we take with you now, reconciliation with the idea of history where you have been participatory and actor in the effect of the denial of the Divine upon the template you live in, must be decided and can be so. When we say *must be decided*, we simply mean it's your agreement to this level of re-creation that allows it to come into being. Again, we say this to you, Paul: This is a necessary step for everyone, to release an idea that has been informing your experience, based on past choice or fear that still holds ramification in the life lived.

We will say these words now on your behalf:

On this day we claim that the realization of the Monad in the energetic field will reclaim and re-see any aspect of self that has engaged in the denial of the Divine or refuted the Divine out of fear, knowingly or unknowingly. And because we claim this for each of you in True Self, in true alignment, in a mandate of love, we may support you each in a level of resonance where this reconciliation can occur without a bias or fear of what it will entail.

We will imagine you see, Paul, yourself stepping under a shower. When you enter the shower, you are not clean. The purpose of the shower is to wash the body. When you are lifted to this level of resonance, while things fall away of their own accord, what you are still accountable to are the ramifications of past choice. And in this case we mean the denial of the Divine in whatever form the acts have taken. Our agreement now is that this will be done in love, in freedom, and in an agreement to be re-known beyond prior choice. When you make this claim, "I am in agreement to be known beyond prior choice," you are giving permission for the movement of the old and the reconciliation to the new, which releases the stitching or the embroidery or the manifestation in the energetic field of the denial of the Divine that still claims you in alignment to your fear or your agreement to fear.

We say this again for you each: The ability we have to truly know you, to bear witness to your truth, can and will supersede what is not true and has never been true. And in this agreement with you, not only are you re-known, you are redeemed, because the energetic field you hold can now claim its alignment to the Monad, the truth of your being that is without fear, the Pure Self, untainted, unaggrieved, the aspect of you that is the Divine come into manifestation at the cost of any idea or prior action that would refute it.

Paul interrupts the teaching: "Well, are there consequences to the past actions or past thoughts we've held, once this happens?" There is residual affect, but you are no longer creating from these blemishes or this embroidery upon the energetic field that still serves as attractor to what you would call karma. This is not wiping the slate clean. It is releasing the need, the first need, to deny the Divine, which claimed all the difficulties that followed. This recognition to release the impulse, the desire, to refute the Divine will reclaim you and release the creations that you chose in accord with this.

We say this now in alignment to your truth: The aspect of you that is free already, that has aligned to the Upper Room, is the aspect of self that is in fruition, is in bloom, through this treatise. This aspect of you, sinless if you wish, without fear if you wish, is what reclaims each of you. And your disavowal of your responsibilities to your own denial of the Divine is an inhibitor now that is being addressed in love and in efficiency. And we say *efficiency* because the tone that we operate in is reclamation, and the mandates of fear that you have chosen and are now accountable to—again, the stitching in the field—can be lost so that you may understand that the fabric, the very life lived, is God in its expression. The life lived, and all encountered, is God in expression, operating in varying tones in agreement to will.

Now, the reconciliation of Divine Will with the will of the personality structure has been discussed, but we will return here for a moment so that you understand that the choice to agree to this level of clearing, or reconciliation with your own creations, is the claim of the Christ within each of you. The desire to align to Divine Will *is* Divine Will in accord with your true nature. You have become who you truly are. You are no longer aspiring to it. You are released from the old as you become of the fabric of the Divine in perpetuity. "What does that mean?" he asks. It means that you are born anew, that the creation of your expression, unblemished, unadorned, an expression of the Divine that has come in its unique way as you, is in perpetuity or continual unfoldment. When you are releasing at this level, you are not reclaiming what you release in the lower accord. When an aspect of self is reconciled with Source, it is re-known as of the fabric of the whole because it is no longer denying it.

On this night we claim, on this day we claim, in this life we claim that all creations made in fear will be reconciled to truth, and the truth of the Divine that indeed makes all things new.

We are not your shepherds. We are your teachers, as you wish us. You become the shepherds as you walk forth, because the light that you are, untainted, unadorned, claims all it encounters in love.

We will stop this dictation for the day. Indeed, this is the end of this chapter. Period. Period. Period.

PART II

The Birth of the New

5

A WORLD MADE NEW

DAY SIXTEEN (CONTINUED)

When you stand before us and we see you as you truly are, without blemish, without blame, we see the Divine incarnate come as each of you, the embodied light of the Monad come to sing, come to express, come to reclaim a world in love. The teachings you have received thus far in embodiment in the Upper Room, in the recalibration of the energetic field that can now support the Monad in expression, have been testament to your willingness to grow with them. And because you grow, because you agree, because you allow and say yes, we are privileged to continue these teachings, as we are allowed to speak through Paul and address you wherever you sit, wherever you be, at whatever level of consciousness you have aligned to thus far.

The fear for some of you is that you will not be who you wish on the other side of this journey. There is no other side to this journey. The journey is the experience. The manifestation of the Monad, while an event, yes, is a progressive one, both in the individual, and in humanity, as humanity begins to claim its true inheritance.

Now, when you see chaos around you, you are seeing the residual affect of fear, and the chaos you see today precedes reclamation or an uncovering of truth that is an allowance for each of you to realize the self in the midst of your past creations. Your past creations are things thought or done, intended in fear, intended in love—it really matters not. But because you are creative beings, you are accountable to the creations you've made. This is true at the level of the individual, and also at the collective. In times of great change, when the collective is witnessing the residue of past actions, one seeks to look away, revert to the old, claim an identity born in yesterday's newspaper, the comfort of the old, or the idealization of what was supposed to be. What was supposed to be is not so. It is merely a relic or an idea of the time it was created. And what mankind, humankind, is facing now is not apocalypse, but a great wave of change that must be attended to at every level of society. You think in secular ways—"my country," "my community," "my needs"—but this is in fact an experience undergone by the species itself as the species recalibrates and prepares itself for a new incarnation, a new way of being expressed, without the historical data, what you expected to see and is no longer commandeering your futures.

Now, when the old signposts are released—what you expect to see, expect to be there—you believe yourselves to be lost. You seek the relics of the old to tell you where you stand. The relics of the old are not present now as you think they are. Much of what you witness on this plane is residual affect. And the level of vibration on this plane is in great shift, and consequently the structures of old are in deconstruction because they cannot be held at the higher octave of vibration that is now present. But you see the old signs, the memories of what was and how things should have been, while beginning to understand that you are in a new field that has not yet been named, not yet been decreed this town or that.

What we are speaking of is the Upper Room, a field of consciousness that is present now and is manifesting, whether or not you believe it, on this plane of experience that you abide in. It is a translation of matter, a realization of the new. And the manifestation of the new—if you wish, new signposts—will be created by you at a higher level than you were able to prior. In some ways, what is beginning to happen is that the old foundations are being uncovered and then removed. You must begin to understand where you have been party to deceit through your own choices and creations, how you have contributed to fear through your denial of the Divine. And the choice to manifest in the Upper Room consolidates the energetic field in a new tone that will not hold the old fear, so the new foundation may be built for humanity by those who are no longer claiming the mandate of fear for their own experiences.

Now, a mandate of fear is very simple to understand. The inherent denial of the Divine that this plane of experience has been operating in is fraught with the denial of the Divine. It informs all aspects of it. And fear is known, always, as the denial of the Divine. In this amplitude that we teach you now, the Kingdom and the Upper Room, the Monad expresses as each of you. And the octave you sing in, a new way of expressing, beyond fear, codifies itself as an exemplar in everything it sees and experiences. The manifestation of the new is where we come to in this text—how the world is made new, not through doctrine, but through vibrational accord. Each of you contributes to this world through your acknowledgment of your own true nature. The true nature of the Divine expresses as you, claiming itself into and as all things.

Now, the recovery of the old, those things that you are responsible for or accountable to that were claimed in fear, built on foundations of fear, must be seen as what they have been—perhaps well-intended, but finally, we would suggest, corrupt, through the indoctrination of fear into the systems they hold themselves in. This is true in commerce, in religion, in every structure you can imagine. The edicts or mandates even of education, what can and cannot be taught, will be releasing to a new potential, because the information that is going to be available soon, on this plane of experience, is going to require a reframing, not only of history, but what humanity is. The acceleration of tone here in some ways is opening the old, the old craters, the old libraries. The old ways of comprehending what humanity is has the requirement of re-knowing what it encounters. And the teachings you have received in humanity's history have primarily been distortions based in ideas of what once was. The catalog of humanity's history, which is actually trespassing many realms of experience, far more than you know, is becoming available in archetypal forms that can then be accessed.

"What does this mean?" he asks. Well, you look at iconography or emblemization to comprehend what something is. You understand what an eagle is through the depiction of an eagle as much as you understand the eagle through the bird in flight. But to comprehend the eagle, to truly know the eagle and its information at a level of archetype, is to be realized as the True Self that can know the inherent Divine as eagle. When something is re-known at this level of congruence, the information held by the other, the data that it has accrued throughout history, becomes available. And the process of re-knowing the object or thing as of God, which is the act of alchemical reclamation, the embodiment you hold in agreement to the embodiment of something else, manifests an alignment and agreement to the Divine that cannot be denied. And the information held within is then available.

You sit at a time in history where archetypes are being invoked without comprehension. "This is the divine feminine," you may say, or "That can never be of God because it doesn't resemble what I say God is." You are looking at ideologies here, and from the outside. To align to a vibrational stream from the Upper Room is to truly know it, and the names that are bandied about, some heretically, some in sovereignty, some in true denial of the Divine, some in an agreement to it, can be in fact known.

Now, the language of old has been filtered for you. The names things are called now in most ways are convenient to understanding. The reclamation of language itself is about to commence here, and what this means is the reliance upon what things have meant are beginning to dissolve. Much of the confusion humanity holds now about what is truth and what is not is an expression of this. What used to mean one thing now means another. But the truth of anything can and will be expressed, because the truth of all things, we say— underline *all*—must be of God. Now, again, understand that God is the one tone played, the one note sung, that expresses as all manifestation. And this simple realization is an act of restoration that in some ways releases language from the dominant form of communication.

When we teach through Paul, we utilize language. But the energy we broadcast to him is being translated into language so that you may comprehend it. The energy that expresses as language is finally intent. It is also of God. And when you begin to understand that you may begin to know without words, claim without words, and see without the old descriptors informing what you see, you will understand the transition that humanity is about to undergo. It is a shift of expression. Paul remembers a time when the telephone was plugged into the wall and you lifted a dial and pushed buttons, while standing before the machine, never to be moved. You have other ways now of communicating through devices, but you don't understand yet that these are actually symbols, mechanisms, and where you are heading, in embodiment, is to a level of knowing where you have access to a continuum of information and ways of communicating that are not bound by time or space.

The shift humanity is undergoing will take four generations to align to a world that is knowing itself in peacefulness. And we use that word intentionally. You are now outgrowing form, watching form disassemble. This does not mean you are warring.

It means that the physical transition that humanity must undergo towards a new template of incarnation is a progression. The texts we have written through Paul are in fact blueprints for this progression. Those of you who attend to these teachings now, hold the teachings in the resonant field and reclaim the world in a high octave because your alignment holds the key to the liberation of others. But this does not mean that the world resembles what you think it should in the timeframe that you would use to authorize a lifetime.

Now, some of you may say, "Well, what's the point? It takes too long." The species is in transformation. You are learning new language. You are becoming liberated from an old frame or template that holds the denial of the Divine as the primary factor of expression. Imagine a loom that has been sewn through with thread, and each new thread contributes to the denial of the Divine. You are all party to this weaving. But the loom is broken. You cannot sew more upon it. And a new loom is being claimed, a new reality woven, a new idealization of your true potential being realized in form.

The gift of this teaching for some of you is simple permission to realize your own worth as of God. But you underestimate the gift of this, because the moment this is realized, you gift this to everyone you meet, not by intention, but through the co-resonant field you hold. For others of you, you have come in preparation for these times. You have come with the key of liberation in your heart. You seek the ignition of the Divine Spark flaming through you in its true light to illumine a world. We say wherever you sit, you are where you must be for this grand adventure to continue. Do not underestimate your role here.

The Divine is present in each of you, and we sing this song now for you:

> *You Have Come. You Have Come. You Have Come. Behold,*
> *I make all things new.*

The key to the Kingdom is your own agreement to it.

We thank you each for your presence. Indeed, this is in the text. Stop now, please. Period.

DAY SEVENTEEN

What has been before you, what has stood in the way of your progress, has been shifted through the work that we have done thus far. When you meet an obstacle now, see it only as opportunity, and nothing substantial, nothing that can hinder you from your True Self moving towards full expression. *Full expression* must be understood as manifestation, and the Monad in an articulated form.

Now, the bodies you have are undergoing a process, re-calibration to hold the higher tone. The vision you have is being moved higher, so you may see the higher template as it is presented to you to see, and the life that you have lived, not paused, but re-assumed in a higher qualification of expression. *Qualification* simply means that what you have come to in a resurrected state, as the Monad claims all things to itself, is a re-knowing of the idea of being.

The idea of being can be understood quite simply as the experience of self in a new articulated state. The challenge you

face now, very simply put, is the process you've chosen to engage in, because as things are made new, as you are revoking
the old through the reclamation of the new, as you are seeing
what is true in the face of what has not been true, as you are
agreeing to truth at the cost of a lie, the act of being is the act
of resurrection. Now, you think of resurrection as a thing done,
when in fact it is a process of re-conceiving the vibrational
field in the tone of God at a level of amplitude where what
could be hindered cannot be, where what can be known will
be, and what is sung in truth through the vibrational echo of
your presence has its own qualification to resurrect that which
it encounters.

When we spoke last, we spoke of generations, and the time
that you will understand humanity processes a reconfiguration
of self and the manifestation of new life in the face of what
once was. Paul sees a field now that has been cleared of debris.
All things are now possible in this field. The deconstruction of
reality that you are currently undergoing has time, still. Build-
ings fall, not all at once, but one at a time. And the structures
of civilization that cannot be held in the Upper Room indeed
will be re-known—some repaired perhaps, others lost to
history.

Now, reconciliation with acts, things done in fear or in the
denial of the Divine, must be understood as part of the process humanity engages in. As long as humanity defines war
as something productive and not destructive, you will attend
to your world through war. The awakening to the destructive
nature of war is about to be seen at a scale you have not, and
this will cause pain, and also be cause for celebration, as arms

are finally put down in the awareness of the futility of violence as a means to claim peace. Destruction, you see, is not
always negative. A house infested with termites perhaps needs
to be razed, and a new one built on a strong foundation. And
a system riddled with fear, under the name of greed, under
the claim of separation, may also be banished, or re-known
in a higher way. To release something that no longer serves
you, at the level of the individual, is an alchemical act—often
very challenging because you don't seek to face your creations
unless you are forced to.

Now, imagine what you go through individually, in the process of transformation, out-pictured on a country or a planet.
That is what is happening now and will continue. The choice
to deny past acts, egregious acts, acts known in fear, simply
perpetuate the violence that has now come to a head. And
realization of futility—"There is no point in these acts except
a kind of destruction that we can no longer continue"—will be
the way that humanity finally says no to what it has chosen in
fear. To reconcile to the idea of peace must claim an agreement
that peace is a potential, something that can be claimed. But
thus far, your ideas of peace, born in a notion that if nobody is
fighting on Tuesday, Tuesday is peaceful, but the expectation
that by Friday you will be fighting again, is what has claimed
you. To realize peace in the Upper Room is the beginning of a
great shift, not only for the individual, but for the consciousness of the whole. To meditate on peace for ten minutes a day
would support the energetic field in an alignment to peace.
When one meditates on peace, one need not imagine something peaceful. One must turn the radio station that holds

peace and align to it. To turn to this station is to simply set the intention, "I am aligning to peace."

Now, from the Upper Room you have access to stations, if you wish, that the density of the lower realms have precluded you from playing. And the agreement to the Upper Room—"I am in the Upper Room; I Have Come, I Have Come, I Have Come"—is in some ways the key to realization of what is already present here. We underline that phrase: *what is already present here.* You are not seeking peace in the Upper Room. You are not seeking God in the Upper Room. You are aligning to what is always present and is now accessible through the vibrational field that has been altered to agree to this in manifestation. Underline those words, *in manifestation*—which simply means not only is this held, it has become who and what you are. To become as peace is to align to the Divine that is as peace, or the aspect of the Divine that can be claimed in this way. While you will never know the totality of the Divine, because it cannot be known, you are able in fact to align to the aspects of it that are present here, and available, and gifted to you through your agreement to them.

"What might these be?" he asks. We will suggest peace is foremost, and love, and freedom. Wisdom, we would suggest, accrued through experience, is not what you access in the Upper Room, but the affect of experience there. Wisdom is accrued. Knowledge may be aligned to. Now, when you align to knowledge in the Upper Room, it is as if you are entering a vast library and you have a bird that sits by your shoulder that can call the correct page to you from the many volumes that are always present there. Paul interrupts: "Is this what one would call the Akashic Records?" In fact, it is beyond that. What is truly available at this level is universal knowledge that exists beyond lives lived, but great history and a great creation of wisdom that has been imprinted and is shareable by those who claimed it and would offer it now. Consciousness never dies, and you can align to a system where in fact you are taught by a great being, because the imprinting of the great being's knowledge is actually available to you.

Now, you don't go into this library demanding what you want. You enter this library with your head slightly bowed, in agreement to the manifestation that you are about to encounter. To have the head slightly bowed is to acknowledge the omnipresence of the Divine in all of its creations. You are not a supplicant, but a recipient. And the one who comes in gratitude will be fed. The one who comes in arrogance will be set aside until he or she learns what it means to truly receive. To begin to access higher wisdom does not make you a teacher. It simply makes you in agreement to an experience that you have undergone that has transformed idea, and then, consequently, manifestation. Everything you can imagine was first idea. And to move into congress with great thought, high truth, is to be transformed by the encounter. Because you are moving beyond time, and accessing lineage that is in perpetuity, eternally present, at this level of vibration, you can enter the stream of knowledge from any place and move to any time.

"Can we be fooled here?" he asks. The only one who would be fooled would be the one who is in a lower vibrational field, creates his or her idea of a library, and then demands to be taught what she wants. To be in a meditation on peace, and in an alignment to peace, is not to just sit and be peaceful. It's to know or realize peace through that alignment. Information is not peace, and true knowledge, true knowing, is also not informational, but experiential. The one who comes out of the library saying, "Well, I have the secrets to the universe, and only I," is the one who has been fraudulently expressing what she thinks she has learned in the lower field. The one who comes from the library in the Upper Room is now present *as* the knowledge that has been conferred upon him or her.

"Well, what is the purpose of this?" Paul asks. "If we are curious, do we go?" In fact, what we are giving you now is great access to truth that has been withheld from humanity, because the level of vibration that humanity has claimed has not been high. And the potential for the misuse of this information, what humanity would do if she understood how things truly worked, can now be claimed in a very different way. In the Upper Room, you are not in agreement to fear. The one who is truly in the Upper Room cannot fear, can be taught, can move to agreement of what has always been true, hold it in the energetic field, and as it is held in the energetic field, it becomes a template for humanity.

Now, imagine this. Nobody knew what a hat was. Once upon a time, there was no such thing as a hat. One day someone covers her head, and someone sees it, and two weeks later there is a hat store down the block to meet the demands of the new idea made into manifestation. When the energetic field has been inscribed or claimed in a high level of truth, it becomes visible. Underline the word *visible*. It can be seen, not so much with the naked eye, but by the soul that encounters what it sees. Recognition happens at a level beyond the senses, and recognition is an aspect of knowing. To be recognized as the one who knows is not to open up a school. It is simply to move into a conversation, without language, in energetic concourse to what is true. In other words, you are meeting each other in energy, and the dialogue happens at that level. The one who perceives truth sees the opportunity to align to it. This is done at the causal level, and the manifestation of this is the creation of a new template that is actually held in the energetic field of humanity.

The progress of humanity, as we have said, over generations, is the acclimation to this new level of vibration and the true knowledge that is now implicit in the structure of the being that you are. That one little hat is now a hat store, and finally a hat factory, with them all over the world. In fact, what happens here is not so much contagious as co-resonant. The visible self that holds the key makes the key available to what it encounters. In the past, we have spoken about becoming the doorway, but to become the doorway simply means you are giving access to what you encounter to what exists in the Upper Room, and then the Kingdom. We say *and then the Kingdom* because the level of vibration of the Kingdom, entered and claimed through the Upper Room, is at a level of amplitude that must be claimed in stages. If the light is turned on too quickly in a very dark room, you will all hide your eyes from the glare. The one who demands they stay open may go blind. We bring the issuance of light in gradation, through each text, to support the reader through acclimation. Imagine water rising to the level of the dam, and then breaching the dam. The river then flows unimpeded, but the dam cannot crack wide open and destroy the town. The town must be prepared for the new river that is about to be born.

In times of great change, the desire is always to consolidate what has been most valuable to you. You pack one suitcase for a terrifying journey. You bring what is most valuable to you. What is most valuable now is truth, and your alignment to truth and the inherent truth that is the Source of all things that can and will be claimed in all things. Underline, again, *all*—reclamation of *all*. Again, the dam breached. The river covers all. The new is made present through your realization of this.

Paul interrupts the teaching: "Sometimes, when you use these metaphors, I wonder what level of destruction you are talking about." We are talking about deconstruction, Paul, not destruction. We are talking about the house that is rotted through, finally falling down so that the new may be built. We use metaphor to teach because it's the easiest way to convey the ideas we present to the most readers. As we teach, we understand the reasons that you wish to consolidate the old. We certainly do not make you wrong for them. But we are now telling you that humanity is ascending, and that this is not an act that is necessarily comfortable or graceful, and that the challenges that it presents can be remedied by riding the great wave of change, by claiming the potential for the new that is born in the release of the old, to not be fearful in the face of great change, but to be gratified that you have come to bear witness to a new life, a new world, and a new way of being expressed.

We thank you each for your presence, and we will stop now for the day. Period. Period. Period.

DAY EIGHTEEN

As each of you says yes to the claims you have made thus far, articulation progresses, the act of manifesting, the process of becoming the True Self in a new state, a higher alignment, in recognition of a world made new. "A World Made New," is the title of this chapter, and where we intend to take you, one and all, through a process of agreement that everything can be changed through alignment to truth.

Now, understand truth. It is impartial. It is not kind. It is not violent. It is not loving. It is simply what it is, a recalling of what was before an overlay occurred, or a disfiguration. Each of you here, who hears these words, are perfected beings, whether or not you know it. But the alignment in the lower vibrational field in many ways has disfigured or altered your ability to express at this level. The challenges you have all faced have been operating through systems that agree to this disfiguration.

Now, that is a challenging word for Paul. We will try to give you a better example. Each of you in your perfected states, aligned to a lower vibrational field, has amassed evidence of separation that you continue to foist each day upon a shared reality. And consequently the shared reality has been disfigured or altered from its perfected state through the continual reliance on false ideas, what you think is, at the cost of truth.

The requirement here, as we lift you, as you agree to be lifted, is that what you encounter, at whatever level of creation it has manifested at, can and will be re-seen by you.

Now, re-seeing something is actually a passive act. You are not fixing something you see. You are not taking the piece of dust from your neighbor's eye. You are seeing your neighbor anew. And in this new sight, you are receptive to the innate perfection. And what has accrued evidence, or we would suggest *disfigurement* from the true state of being, is re-known, known anew. Now, to know anything, truly know it, is to know truth, and in truth a lie will not be held. Re-articulation involves a passage of re-seeing past creations. The collective creations that you witness now are present to be seen anew—not to be expected, to be altered to your liking, but seen anew, and therefore lifted and restored.

Understand the idea of restoration. You have a perfect painting. As the eons go on, as it amasses dust and filth, the true beauty of the original painting has been obscured. As you are lifting now this painting to the higher light to be re-seen, what it has accrued will be seen. For the last forty years you thought that painting in the hallway was a deep brown. In fact, it was a vibrant pink. The deep brown will now be seen as not what was true, what has simply accrued, and the release of the old will take place in the stages that can maintain the perfection of the original painting. You don't take a rag and rub the painting canvas so difficultly that you erase the original image. You are lifting what has always been precious, that has been denied its worth, to the light of all things.

"*The light of all things*—what does that mean?" he asks.

Well, again, the one note sung, the one tone played, that is all things, is original light. And original light, without the detritus that it has accrued, will be blinding. So you are lifted to an awareness of true perfection at the level that can be held in form. This is imperative that you understand this. Imagine you have been in darkness so long that at the end of the tunnel you see a very bright light. You rush to the light with your arms open, only to find that the light is at a level that you cannot hold it. We take you there, one text at a time, so that you may manage the level of change that you will have to align to, to hold the new.

Now, why do you bother with this, you may ask. You can be comfortable in the old, go about your business as you have. Well, we will tell you this. The old is releasing, so the comfort of the old is not present as it was. We have said this many times, but when the sleeper is awakened from his bed, some are awakened with the kiss on the forehead, some are turned over because they refuse to budge and have a hard awakening on the floor. We make this as graceful as we can, and we invite a new student reading this text to kindly ask themselves to be patient in their comprehension, not only of this material, but of the vibration that is the truth of this text. The tone of this text is the tone of resurrection. It is a massive change, an altering of the field where the detritus is released and you are liberated, really liberated, from an idea of self that would continue to amass evidence of separation. Realization at this level, alignment to truth at this level, is not always easy. But it is much easier than getting rocked from your bed and awakening in a world that is so changed that you don't know how to put your shoes on.

We are singing through Paul with a level of vibration that will summon the sleeper, and the one who is half awake will rise from her bed, stretch her body, and say, "Yes, indeed I Have Come." A world made new. A world in re-articulation. A world where the canvas has accrued so much dirt, so much evidence of lack and separation, that you have lost even any idea of the inherent wonder of what it means to be born, and privileged to have a body, to experience through the senses the Divine that is all things.

As you walk this plane, one and all, as the light you truly are, the act of reclamation at a mass scale will be understood by you as the lifting of the old painting to the light that requires the old to be re-seen. As witness to this process there is only one requirement—that you not embellish what you see with fear or any descriptor that would deny the Divine. Paul interrupts: "There are things we see that we cannot condone. There are levels of cruelty that are not of God. How do we see these things and not be in response?" You are lifting what is seen by the presence of the Divine articulated as you. There is no effort at this level of alignment. There is only agreement. "It will be so." The Divine will be seen where such error has accrued evidence of the darkness. It will be made new through the presence of the Divine that is higher and more potent than the idiocy of darkness.

Darkness is a child that was raised in a dark room. All it knows is darkness. It cannot imagine other. When the light is brought to this room, even that child is made new. And all who live and act at that level of idiocy, responding only to darkness, require your love. And this mandate, "I will not be afraid," will claim you as the liberator of even the most heinous thing that the small self could imagine. All things must be of Source, or nothing can be. And even that dark room, that has only known darkness, has accrued its own authorization to claim a template, can and will be re-seen.

If you would imagine, for a moment, that every darkened space on this plane of experience has the potential to be re-seen and re-known in truth, you will have taken an enormous step in your understanding of the true power of God. There are those who say, "We will vanquish the darkness," meaning that they will destroy it. You do not destroy darkness. It is not destroyed. But it may be illumined, lifted, re-seen, and this is done in love because that which is so dark it can no longer even imagine the light has done the best it's known how. Re-articulation of the darkness is the claim of the risen Christ. You must understand this. All things will be made new.

Now, when something is liberated from a very dark place, it will fight to maintain the small rule that it has held. It will do its best to maintain an idea of separation because it believes that its livelihood, its very existence, depends upon it. Those of you who see us imagine us as high. When you are witnessed by darkness, you are seen as a light of great fortitude. And your choice to bear witness to shadow, wherever it appears, is to claim the Upper Room as a bastion, a place of true safety. We will explain this. Fear does not express in the Upper Room. You are not taking a sword into the dark room and fighting

imaginary demons. You are bringing light to the darkness, reclaiming what was held in shadow, and the darkness is re-seen.

The idea of redemption, restoration at this level, has been
confused. You comprehend in some ways the idea of personal
redemption. But you don't understand that this act of redemption is now happening at the causal level on this plane, which
is what is incurred when shadow is exposed. The release of the
old, which we have discussed already, is indeed a requirement.
But to make darkness visible means that there is enough light
with which to perceive it, and it must be made visible in order
for this re-articulation to occur. Once again, the old painting in the hallway covered with layers of soot, underneath it a
pristine creation—but if you don't realize the brown was once
pink, you will not lift the painting to be released from its altered, disfigured state.

We sing your songs for you, yes, so that you may learn the
words. But once you are this song, once your vibrational field in
manifestation is at a level of tone or pitch where it encounters
darkness without fear, you are the song in full expression that
teaches the song through co-resonance to all you encounter.

We will take a pause for Paul. We will return in two minutes. Please stop now.

(PAUSE)

"The Birth of the New" is the second half of this text, which
we are now writing. The first half of this text is called "What
Was and What Will Be." We will stop this dictation for the day,
and we will say this to each of you: The ramifications of this

teaching on your individual lives will become present rapidly. So simply say, "Yes, I see the truth in all things. I have no need to fear. I am well, all is well, in this Upper Room that I align to."

We bless you each for your presence and say good night. Yes, in the text. Stop now, please.

DAY NINETEEN

We are before you today with answers about your lives. "Why did this happen?" "How did I undergo that?" "What was the purpose of this event or that one?" Everything you undergo in a life—high, low, in-between—is party to the evolution of the soul. It does not mean you chose it. It simply means you aligned and agreed to it. When you are lifting from the old, the things that you will encounter are those creations that were known by you that had residual affect on the perceptions you now hold. In some ways, what you are doing is seeing to re-see, unknowing to know. Now, to un-know, in this example, is simply to decide that the assessment that you made at one time of what something meant can be replaced by a higher knowing. There are ways you understand yourselves through events in life—the death of the parent, the birth of the child, the markers that claim you in a new trajectory. But even these things, whatever they may be, are often misunderstood. The trajectory of a life has a patterning to it, and the soul in all ways is the keeper of this pattern, which simply means that what you have come to learn will be presented to you because you are in alignment to it. And these events of a life, which are there to support learning, will contribute to the full evolution of the soul.

"*Full evolution of the soul*—what does that mean?" he asks. Well, each soul undergoes a process from the time of its inception. In many ways, the learning it undergoes while in form is to contribute to the whole, the vast awareness or collective consciousness that humanity has claimed. Imagine you are one light in a million lights. Your small light contributes to the whole. And your own experiences, which seem to be in isolation, are never in isolation, because every life currently lived on this manifest plane is contributing to the whole. You believe yourselves to be separate. You are not separate. You are in an illusion of separation.

"But the soul is separate," he says. "It comes with its own learning, its own requirements. How is that of the whole?" There is a collective soul as well. You may think of this as collective mind. And the choice of the species to evolve beyond its current limits is not an act of God as much as it is a collective agreement to move beyond a bias, or system of separation, that has been accrued over time. The collective, made of the individual, is present in all ways.

Now, you may have autonomous learning while being in the collective, but you seem not to understand that the collective learns through individual experience. In some ways, the commonality of the plane you have chosen to express on, this world that you have known, is the availability for common experience. There are ways of knowing self far beyond a single self. The fullness of this experience is inclusive of all aspects of you, beyond even the idea of singularity. You still hold consciousness, you see, but you are actually party to and present for collective agreements, collective awareness, and a comprehension of the contributions that all make to the whole.

Now, to move beyond the idea of singularity into pluralization, or collective form, does not deny you singularity. It simply adds to it. The raindrop is of the whole. It is of the pool it lands in, as it was of the cloud it came from. While the experience of the raindrop is singular, it is never not of the whole. And how you have perceived yourself in separation has greatly limited the awareness that is now available to you. If you wish to imagine, for a moment, that the consciousness you hold is not bound by form, and you could enter into any world and learn from what world you enter, you would actually be accurate. In fact, this is already happening. There are aspects of you, beyond form, that are in experience in multiple strata, accruing other information and experience, and aligning to Source through these experiences. Because the soul is always in evolution, it cannot be static.

He interrupts: "But isn't there a time when we rejoin the puddle, become one with the whole?" Of course. But your experience is contemplative, in a high awareness of what is, inclusive of the old ideas but participatory to the new. You are not lost in the whole. You are reclaimed in the whole. And the awareness of self that you have utilized at this level of vibration is expanded to the degree that you are of the whole mind, the whole mind of God, if you wish, or consciousness itself. A restoration to Source, while maintaining a body, is a teaching of resurrection. He interrupts: "*A* teaching or *the* teaching?" They are the same. While there are many doorways in, the access to Source is known by you through one principle. We will call it the Monad or the Christ, but all it simply is, is the imprinting of the Divine as itself, as the who that you are, the what that you are, and how that expresses, which is service. It is the Monad, the redeemer, that which reunites all aspects, that is the doorway to the manifestation of Source that is the Kingdom, and the realization of this, which you might call high awareness or an awakened state of being.

Now, to become awake does not make you more awake than the one beside you. It simply means that you are no longer obstructed by the ideas of separation. The ideas may remain in some ways, but they are not obstructive. While you maintain a body and an experience of singularity, your presence on this plane will always hold an idea of separation. But the agreement to this as nonobstructive allows the energetic field to utilize these ideas in an agreement to the Source of all things. In past teachings, we have reminded you that the belief that the body is separate from Source has claimed separation in all of the material world. To understand that the body is of Source, and then begin to have an experience of this, is to move towards reclamation of all manifestation. And the eyes with which you see, those eyes that perceive the Kingdom, become the awareness, or the vehicle for the awareness, of a sense of self that is of the whole while in maintenance of form.

You have heard stories of those who have risen, those who may appear in more than one place at once. What is being discussed here is a level of articulation when form itself, in agreement to Source, is transposing itself in a material sense. While this is not this teaching, it is actually an affect of it. The idea of solidity and separation preclude a uniting of matter and spirit at the level that most of you might seek. But to become resurrected is to be able to hold the vibration of Source, beyond the old limitations, in agreement to the Source of all things. It becomes malleable, you see, by your experience, which means what you see in the higher octave, no longer holding the density of form, can be re-known, reshaped, or made new.

Paul sees a ball of clay that can be formed into many things. This is a metaphor for energy that can be claimed in any way you wish. The oscillation of the field you hold, in a high state, can transform matter itself to the degree that what is being realized is realized as of the same Source as all things—again, that one note played in this universe that is in manifestation as all things. The alignment at this level, to become the clarion call, to become the note sung, is to claim that note as what you see. And you become participatory to the reclamation of a world through your knowing of yourself beyond singularity, of the whole, and in agreement to Source.

When a world is made new, it is not so much fixed as reseen. The perceiver of the world, at any level of vibration, confirms the world seen. And in your dense form, you qualify yourselves to see denseness, density, the amassed tone of vibration in a lower state that you are conforming to in a co-resonant field. In the lifting to the Upper Room, we have done much with you to release the obstacles or ideas that would support separation. When an idea is active in the energetic field, it will always seek to confirm itself as manifestation. Do you understand this? Any idea held in the energetic field is active and claiming in vibration. When the collective is active at this level, with a common fear, a common enemy, a common anger, the level of vibration in a low state coincides with event, things that occur for the collective to know itself through the experience that it is claiming. You are contributing to the knowledge or the awareness or the understanding at any level of vibration.

Now, once you understand that what has been active in the self is also active in the collective, and your idea of self, informed by your idea of the collective, is also creating, you will begin to understand that what may operate as what you would call a negative in the lower field becomes a gift in a higher. In other words, friends, "We are all afraid of this or that," in the lower field, which claims a people, a civilization, in coherence with that fear, is re-known in the Upper Room, and what is seen for individuals and the collective is the true state of being, the one note played.

The releasing we have done with you is to support you in two different ways—to release the ideas you've held that are activated in the field that will confirm fear or separation, and the agreement to the whole to release the same. Once you understand that you are party to world change through these releases, you will understand what it means to be in the Upper Room for the support of all you encounter. The True Self, you see, not holding the basic ideas of separation that have committed you to fear in the lower, becomes the liberator of what it encounters—the Monad again, or the Christ as redeemer. This is an act of energy in co-resonance. It is truth itself in co-resonance to truth, and it is what will transform your world. It will not be a new invention. It will not be learning how to be polite to your neighbor. It will be a reconfiguration of consciousness, without the obstacles, detritus, self-centeredness, known through fear, that have established separation.

Now, you understand self-centeredness as the idea of *me*. It also operates at a societal level. When a society is operating in separation, the *me* becomes the idea of self that is as familiar as others are—"my neighbors," "my race," "those who practice my religion." When you understand that the move to a pluralization, or a comprehension of the whole, also lifts the tribe that believes itself to be separate, there are no more borders, no more factions. There is one humanity, expressing in love. While this does not seem possible to you today, the template has been set for this. And what you perceive now as violence and destruction, man against man, brother or sister against brother or sister, is the last hurrah of fear, an idea playing out in the energetic systems that is being lifted because the vibration of this plane is being transformed.

Realization of this allows you to ride the wave, to put down your arms, to see your brother as your friend. Realization of the inherent Divine in yourself claims the inherent realization of all. Realization is knowing. There is no occurrence you can undergo in the Upper Room that will claim you in fear as you begin to trust that the Upper Room is a foundation where you may remain. Those of you who go back down all the time are primarily doing this because you think that there's a bomb shelter in the lower realm that would protect you from occurrence. "I will go hide in a dark place, defend my home from a dark place. I will fight for myself in my limitations."

We will say this now for Paul: The teaching you are getting

today is present in the text, yes, but it is also enacting itself upon the readers as they read these words. We are granting an understanding of what we teach to those who are receptive. You are included in this because you are a student of this text. To understand that maintaining the vibration of the Upper Room is not holding on by your fingernails when the lower realm is shaking, it's to understand that the basis of truth is foundational. To be foundational in truth is faith, and an awareness that who and what you are, at this level of tone, beginning to experience the self as of the whole, is not done just for self, but for all you may meet and may never meet.

This teaching is in the text. We will stop for the day. Period. Period. Period.

DAY TWENTY

We have come to teach you about the reliability of the Upper Room as a place you may claim identity through. In the Upper Room, the idea of self is in fact translated to the higher idea, or the True Self, that can and will be expressed here. The maintaining of the Upper Room in vibration is understanding that there is always an aspect of you that is present here. And as you begin to rely on this aspect—the Monad, or the Christ, or the True Self—to be as you here, your environment, in re-articulation, begins to command a new experience. A new experience means that what you have expected in history, used to mandate a reality, is no longer present, and the understanding of the truth of the claim "Behold, I make all things new" is seen by you experientially, a translated reality, a reality transposed to the Upper Room.

Now, while this is very confusing for most of you—you want to understand how it feels, what it seems like—it's actually really very simple. In the Upper Room, the idea of self, translated to the Monad, claims a reality in equivalency to itself. Without the mandate of fear prescribing what should be, what is already true is seen. When what is already true is seen, it is re-known from this vantage point in a re-articulated state. So when you appear to be seeing suffering, you understand the inherent divinity that must be present in the individual suffering and you reclaim it, thereby translating the individual to a higher strata of vibration.

He interrupts the teaching: "Does the suffering end?" It is re-seen, it is re-known, and in a new equivalency it cannot be what it was. Now, indeed, an individual has free will. One may choose suffering, and indeed one may learn well through it. But it is not a mandate of the Upper Room. And in this place of re-knowing, you must understand that all things can and will be re-known, inclusive of those things that you thought could never be seen anew. If you would take one moment now to think of an aspect of the self that you think can never change, will never be healed, and you reclaim this aspect of you in the Upper Room and align it to the truth of the Divine that is omnipresent here, you will begin to understand that you become the exemplar of the changes we are speaking of.

When you are re-known at a level of identity, the action of being is so simple as to be misunderstood by all of you. The idea of *being* holds many meanings. Very few of them are accurate. To be is to allow. And to allow, at this level, is to agree to the Source of being. In agreement to the Source of being, you become the actor of the Source of being, not through the intellect, but through the innate knowing that the Divine is present and responding to the requirements of the moment. At this level of knowing, you are not arguing about the right or wrong thing to do. You are simply being in the right moment, or in the right action, if indeed an action is called for.

When one knows who she is, the requirements of being are translated. One is no longer seeking to prove herself. One is no longer acting out of fear, or seeking to justify her acts. One is knowing and allowing. And allowing the self to be, at this level, is to become the principle, or the Word in action. *The Word in action.* When we once spoke through Paul, many years ago, we said that the Word was the energy of the Creator in action. This is as true now as it ever was. And to be activated at this level of assumption—the Divine has assumed the will, reclaimed the aspects of self that were denied the light—the True Self, in its own mandate to express as the Divine, is what is acting, what is teaching, what is allowing this progress to be in a continuum.

Now, the continuum here can be seen as truth or Divine Flow. The idea of Divine Flow simply means that you are un-impeded in your receptors, that the agreement of the Divine to flow through you is ever present, and consequently you move in the Divine, live in the Divine, and therefore have your being there. Each of you says yes to this first as an idea. But the manifestation of this, which is what is being taught here, is born in agreement and allowance. You are not scaling a wall, fearing you will fall. You are allowing the wall to release itself so that there is no hindrance.

Now, the cultural beliefs you hold will stand in the way for a while more. You understand yourself through these structures, but in time these too fall away. They don't disappear as much as your allowance of them is translated to the Upper Room, where they are no longer impediments, simply ideas that have been chosen by the collective that you can choose to move beyond. Any structure through the collective is an agreed-upon structure, and what is agreed upon, first and foremost, is the simple idea that makes a thing a thing, the need for the wall which predates the wall. The wall is simply an expression of what you think needs to be there. When thought is changed, or the need for the wall is no longer present, at the level of idea the wall will dismantle itself. It will no longer be present because it cannot be present at this level of amplitude. And the need for the wall, a directive of the lower strata through collective agreement, is not present in the higher.

He interrupts the teaching: "So if some of us are aligned to the higher, where there is no wall, what about those who are aligned in the lower? Is the wall still there for them?" We are speaking of transformation now, less so in individuated sense of reality than how the totality of reality begins to move when those who are higher release the need for the old. You grant permission through this to the collective. When the need for an idea that has been held by the collective is no longer fostered by individuals, the new may be born and aligned to. In other words, as we have said, by becoming the doorway to this realm of vibration, the anchor for it that can align others to their

true nature, you are releasing an idea of self that has perpetuated a reality in separation. Your inclusions of those who believe themselves to be dispossessed or separate translates their
experience. There is less speaking involved in this agreement
than the expression of knowing. When you know who you
are, you know who others are. As they are known by you, they
release the frequency of separation because you have shown
them, in your articulation, that there is no need for it to be
present. You are ushering in a new expression by allowing, and
the being of yourself is what claims all things new.

Now, to teach "Behold, I make all things new" as a claim
of truth is a requirement at the initial stages of embodiment.
You must begin to have your own experience of how this claim
operates and what it will do in an invocation from the Upper
Room. You will not operate as this claim, "Behold, I make all
things new," from the lower strata. It does not express there.
But in the Upper Room, you are holding the new template, and
it is the new template, or the higher octave of frequency, that
is claimed in this choice. Now, to claim, "Behold, I make all
things new," is to agree to the Monad as redeemer, or the aspect
of the Divine that reclaims all things to its own true nature.
You are not the one doing this. You are the vehicle for it. But
as the will itself is still being moved to a higher alignment,
the choice is made by you for some time still to operate in the
claim, or the invocation of the claim, which is an agreement to
what already is.

As you maintain the Upper Room, as your vibrational
field becomes aligned here, the act of making things new has
no thought attached, no intention attached. It is the affect of

being. Think of it this way, please: Imagine you have a lamp. You turn the lamp on. The light is bright, and you understand the light while it is on. This is the choice to embody in the Upper Room, and the claim "Behold, I make all things new" is simply the intention to pull the string or the cord on the light. As you are established there, the light that you are is perpetually lit. It is perpetually bright. And the need to illumine through a choice or activation is no longer present because the being in the Upper Room is what substantiates the old claim. You have become the light. Or the Divine as you, in your allowance to it, has become the light that reclaims or redeems.

When we teach through Paul, we are aware of his questions. Some of them we will take now. Others, we will wait until the chapter we teach addresses the questions more directly. But his question now is a very simple one: "Who am I in this Upper Room? What does it mean to be me in this new state of vibration?" It simply means, Paul, that the old claims you have made on self that deny the light have fallen away. And that which has diminished the light, refused the light, embellished the darkness that you once thought was, is no longer present. You are redeemed at the level of the Monad.

Now, the idea of Paul, the man of a certain age, with certain gifts, certain choices made to know himself in form, is still present, but in a re-aligned way. Again, we have used the metaphor of moving to a higher place where the view is different, but how it feels in the higher place is also different. In the past, Paul, you have looked at moving through life as walking across a minefield. "Be careful where you step. There could be danger ahead." There is no minefield in the Upper Room.

There is peace and knowing. There is agreement to Source, and consequently, while you may watch your footing for some time to come—it is an entrenched habit for you—you will soon come to understand that the idea of the old self who needed to protect in this way has been released, and the level of freedom allowed you now is beyond what the small self can fathom.

The personality structure for all of you, in many ways was predicated in separation. The moment you are told you are separate, or agree to separation, you begin to accrue evidence for it. And the societies you live in are predominantly based in an idea of separation—every human being for itself, brother against brother, what have you. Once you understand that in the Upper Room you maintain individuation while beginning to experience plurality or oneness, you no longer seek to justify separation. You move into allowance of the innate Divine that is present in all human beings and in all manifestation.

We will conclude this chapter today. When we reconvene, we intend to teach you who you are beyond any idea that you could be separate. Period. Period. Period. Stop now, please.

6

THE WAVE

What you are offering now, what you are agreeing to, is to become the light incarnate at a level of vibration where your encounters with the world are transformed by nature of being. Again, underline the word *being*. How you be at this level of vibration, in an encounter with the manifest world, is what alters the vibrational field of what you see and experience.

Now, the residual affect of your presence on this plane, the act of being, is a transformed world. Because you wish evidence for this, we intend to offer it to you. If each day you would take ten minutes in the Upper Room in an agreement to the Source of all things, you will begin to find very quickly that your encounter with the manifest world is an encounter with Source. And the radiance of your vibrational field will be felt by you as you walk, as you speak, as you are embodied at this level of vibration. The tone you are singing, you see, at this level of agreement, the one note played in articulation as all things, summons all things to its like accord.

Now, as we have said so often, you can make nothing holy, but you can deny the inherent holiness in anything. It is your presence that reconvenes, resurrects, and reclaims what it encounters in this note or tone. You are remembering, re-understanding, and comprehending anew the level of tone that you are aligned to in an experiential way. As we teach through Paul, as we sing through him, as we are remembering him, we are remembering you, those who hear these words, in this encounter with the light that he is and that you truly are as well. The wish of some of you is to be the light at the cost of others, and you must understand now and always that you are the light for others. The lamp is not illumined for its own benefit. It is illumined to shine upon all it encounters. The Resurrected Self, the one that has come in form, in some ways is an antidote to the ills of the world. Because it shines its light on the denial of the Divine, the denial of the Divine is released, and what is seen instead is what is unfiltered, un-tarnished, unblemished by fear or the residual affect of fear as you have known it on this plane.

Now, we said take ten minutes each day, but the purpose of this ten minutes is not to align you to transform the world, but to give you the experience of what is already occurring at this level of tone. The frequency you now hold, you see, is at a level or pitch where what it encounters it claims, and reclaims or resurrects. And your experience of this can be very simple. Understand that the claim "Behold, I make all things new" is a claim of reclamation, and the new that is seen is the vision held from the Upper Room. Your own perception, you see, will become, in a way, an assessment of your own vibrational tone. When your tone is lowered, your experience of the manifest plane will be more dull, will not feel as bright, not as alive, as the level of vibration that the Upper Room calls to itself. Your experience here is a first step in comprehension that the teachings you are being offered have an affect on the encounter you have with the life lived. There are some of you who still think that this is a teaching of feeling better, and while you may feel better, and can feel better, at this level of tone, the purpose of the teaching is the realization of the Divine in reclamation that alters the physical realm.

Now, the physical realm is altered, not by taking an axe to what was and building with the clay what you would have be in its place. The new is known by the reclamation of the Source of all things. Some of you have been so busy trying to get what you want from God that you stopped asking what God might ask of you. And to ask that question—"How can I serve?"—will actually align your will to its own capacity for a higher expression. The residual affect of the choice to serve is the embodiment of the Divine as may claim itself in the manifest plane. This is an act of translation or transposition from lower to higher.

He undermines us by teaching what he would like today. This is his question: "Show me what I want to see so that I may know that this is so." Instead, we will offer you, Paul, the experience that we are speaking to. And if you allow us to lift you now in vibration and tone, and open your eyes and see what you see now, you may be quite surprised that the landscape you experience appears differently, unshrouded and re-known. What you believe, though, Paul, is that this is only your experience. What you don't understand is that the landscape is translated and lifted with this encounter.

As we do this for Paul, we intend to do it with all of you. If you would take a moment and simply be, and allow the affect of the tone we sing to be in an encounter with your vibrational field, you will have the experience of altered perception and a re-seeing of matter in a higher tonality. The tone we sing through Paul is at a pitch that will move you in form and field. You need not be present the moment that the sound is made. You need to align as the sound is made, wherever you may sit, and it will be present for you. We are without time, unencumbered by the mandates of time, so we are with you as you read, as we are with him as this dictation occurs.

On the count of three, Paul.

One. Now two. Now three.

[The Guides tone through Paul.]

Be lifted and see. Allow the field to be altered, and agree to the field that is in comparable pitch in what is around you. Let all things be made new, and allow yourself to see. Behold the Divine expressed as all things in manifestation, as what you see, as how you know, as what you claim, and as what can only be in truth. And now you may say this, if you wish:

"God Is. God Is. God Is."

And allow the wave of the Divine to move through you to all you see in its lifted state. Let yourself float in this wave, of this wave, and allow this wave to be what you know, realize, and be as and in.

"I am in the Source of all things. I am one with the Source of all things. I Have Come. I Have Come. I Have Come."

Now, as you are here in this high pitch, in this wave of vibration, allow yourself to be led to right action as it is required of you, allow yourself to know as it is imparted to you, and allow this claim to be made real:

"I know who I am. I know what I am. I know how I serve. I am free. I am free. I am free."

If you feel yourself expanding in this field of vibration, know that the expression of your being is being utilized in consort with Divine Will to translate not only what you see, but all that can be seen, to the high strata that is the Upper Room. The Divine has come as each of you. And as you sing, as you are this one note sung, you behold a world made new.

We will stop now for the day. Period. Period. Period. Yes, in the text.

Q: What seems tricky is having the experience without imbuing it with one's expectations of there being a big experience. This could be very subtle.

A: It's less subtle than you think. It's actually quite large as you align to it. It's the alignment to it, which is a forgiveness of the small self for not being the one to dictate it as he or she would have it, which is the result of fear that stands in the way. The largeness of this experience, we would like to say, is an expansion of the energetic field that is reclaiming what it encounters in a comparable pitch. So your experience of translation becomes one of manifestation and not ideology. You will do this again, as you wish, as you like, and begin to have this encounter as you can align to it. Thank you.

DAY TWENTY-TWO

What you see before you in history, in the obligations to history, are those things created in fear that must be re-known in a higher amplitude for the trajectory of humanity to assume a new stature. The detritus of history, those things you've created in fear, you are actually now obliged to, one and all. It is in the field you hold, the collective field, and is asking to be lifted to a higher frame. When we have spoken in the past about the transition humanity is undergoing, we have spoken of it as a wave that can carry forth great change. But in this wave is carried those things that humanity has claimed and must now know and be seen anew.

The times you sit in are times of celebration, if you understand that what is being witnessed are the ramifications of past action born in fear. Inclusive of this, it must be seen that the actions of fear that provoke other fears must now be attended to. And this is true for each human being as well as the collective. The refuse of history, that which you have accrued, has floated to the top—to be seen, to be cleansed, to be reclaimed in the Upper Room. Now, this feels like too great a job for Paul. He says, "I can barely manage my own refuse, let alone the refuse of humanity." You must all understand, first and foremost, that the individual's job is to align to its highest potential, and in this agreement the movement of the old, brought to the surface, is allowed to be re-seen and re-known. As an individual does this, the individual grants permission to those things that it encounters to be lifted as well.

The great act of re-creation that you are currently undergoing is as a typhoon, is as a great wave, lifting all things that have been entrenched in dirty soil to be lifted and known anew. The reclamation of humanity must take place on a higher ground than you have known thus far. To understand this— that a great wave has come, is encountering all things in the action of change, stirring up the old that has been somewhat buried or denied, and lifting it to the top so that it may be re-seen—you will understand that those carried upon this wave are actually being delivered to a new shore, a higher ground, a higher acclimation to a reality that is undergoing vast change.

Now, you're used to small changes, perhaps incremental changes. You move the couch from this wall to that one. You end this marriage, begin another. You take a new job or two as you find your way and a path to a livelihood. The change that is being undergone now by humanity is of a magnitude that you have not seen for thousands of years. And the resurfacing of the old, that which has been denied by you as of God, must be re-seen. How you undergo this process of re-seeing has been discussed. But the amplitude of the changes, while we have referenced them, is still abstract to you. If you understand that what humanity has believed itself to be is what is changing, in a high way, you will begin to accept that the new agreement on the higher shore must require humanity to announce itself anew.

Now, an articulation, whether it be a bunny rabbit or a tree or a human being, has identity. The identity humanity has held as a species, operating in a sense of separation, has been the cause of the pains you see—the wars fought, won or lost, the poverty on this plane, the idea of scarcity itself. If these things are to be re-known, they must be re-known at the level of consciousness where they cannot be held. While you are facing the old, the lack, the old ways of being, you fear them. But you must understand, friends. They are being shown to you to be resurrected, and reclaimed in higher thought, higher tone, for the benefit of all.

How this occurs from the Upper Room is a new equation of vibration. Understand this. You are in vibration. The manifestation of this vibration is the species you have known. In a re-articulated state, while what you resemble is what you have been, how you are announced in vibrational tone is quite different. When humanity is no longer claiming fear as part and parcel of its identity, when humanity says yes to its innate divine nature, the requirements for being human are actually altered, and even your understanding of how you operate in the idea of time is transformed. It is not that you are moving beyond time. You hold bodies. There are seasons you understand your lives through. But you are no longer bound or entrenched in the meaning that time has held, which must be inclusive of your idea of death, and the fear of it. In a re-articulated state, consciousness itself, while manifest in form, may also know itself beyond form. And even death is seen as leaving an idea of what the body is, leaving an agreement to form, to simply have another experience of consciousness. When the idea of death itself, so entrenched in fear, is lifted to the surface, claimed anew, much of what you have acted upon in denial of death, fear of your own mortality, locked in an idea of linear time, is moved, transformed, and claimed anew.

Now, you cannot imagine this. Paul can comprehend a friend or two who have said, "I am not really afraid of death. I know it is a transition." But if you understand death in a new way, getting into an elevator and off at another floor, as something to be understood, appreciated, and part of the experience of being, the choices made in fear, which are always in an agreement to death as censor, as end, as terminator, will also be made new.

Now, a transition undergone by a species has happened prior on this plane. You've believed yourselves to be one thing and later deemed yourself to be another. You didn't understand you could swim until you navigated the seas. You didn't know what fire was until the first flame was lit. This is what happens now. The requirements humanity is facing for its survival will be seen and known, and ultimately attended to, because you cannot destroy the earth and expect that it will support you indefinitely. You cannot pollute the air and expect to breathe easily. You cannot drink the water that is poisoned. So as you are beginning to understand the ramifications of past choice as they agree to your very livelihood and ability to maintain a body, you will awaken to the requirements that change will bring you.

Now, nothing will be reclaimed through the act of fear. The wave that we have spoken of, which has begun, will indeed place you in a higher landscape where you may attend to the business of re-creation with a higher template in place. The idea of self as singular is slowly being moved to an agreement to universal truth. Singular truth, "what I believe to be so at the cost of what others believe," will one day be a remnant of history. This is not to say that your individuated self and emotional experience will not be unique. It will be unique, but it will not be singular, or exclusive to an awareness of who you are as of a great body, a great being, that is in incarnation as a species. A cat knows it's a cat without knowing what a cat is. It identifies with the herd, as do most species. You have understood yourselves in a tribal sense, but the tribes have been warring. One tribe creates wine, one tribe grazes in the field, another tribe does something other. A universal agreement to being does not decide that a tribe exists in separation. It understands the tribe as of the whole.

Each of you here, who hear these words, is undergoing change through this transmission to support you in riding the wave that is now present. As long as this wave is agreed to as opportunity, you will be supported. As long as you try to fight the wave, swim against this tide, you will find yourself trying to cling to a history, an identified way of being, born in past thought, past creation, that is all being unmoored and transformed in this act of being—this act of being, being the resurrection of a species, the lifting of a species to its own innate divinity for the well-being of all.

We will stop today for Paul. Thank you for your presence. Period. Period. Period. Yes, this is in the text.

(PAUSE)

What you ask for, what you request, what you are seeking, is an assurance that the lives that you have lived thus far will continue as you wish them. This will not be the case. Humanity itself, undergoing a great change, is now accountable to its creations in a way it has not seen yet. You are actually compassionate to one another when you believe it serves you, if they agree with you. You are kind to your neighbor if your demeanor says, "I am kind," and it is safe to be kind. But much of what you see by way of division is the result of fear in a time of change. "When what I have known is no longer, cannot be seen as I would have it be seen, I must reach for something other to find my balance, to find my assurance." Some of you say to Spirit, "Keep me safe. Grant me my wishes." But, in fact, you too are being carried on this wave of great change that humanity has claimed in its ascension.

Now, when we use the word *ascension*, it simply means lifting in vibrational accord, and any idea of fear that you have amassed at this level of vibration is not expressed in the higher octave, cannot be held there. So in some ways what is happening is you are moving beyond fear as a collective, but you don't move beyond something without a transit through it or an encounter with it. And the challenge of the day for almost all of you is a demand, that will not be met, to an adherence of a status quo that you once thought was real, but is no longer present or true.

Now, reconciliation with your true nature, the Divine Self as who you are, has been the teaching thus far. And your ability to receive the gifts of the Kingdom, or the plenty that is available in the Upper Room, is simply meaning that who and what you are has the ability to hold a level of vibration in inclusivity to the manifest world that you have denied yourself thus far. You think this is about getting something, accruing more. In fact, it is about alignment and reception to what is already true. Because you have lived so long in a world born in lack, foundationally, in an agreement to separation, you claim most things with the idea that separation is implicit in them— "It is us against them, what I want and what she wants at the cost of what they want"—and decide again and again that your sense of well-being is born in a security that has its basis in the known. The known is releasing and will continue to for years to come. And the basis you will then stand upon, once the floodwaters have cleared, once you have landed on a higher perch on a solid foundation in what we will call the Upper Room, is a way of being in agreement to Source that you can barely comprehend because you have been so entrained by fear and the belief in separation that even the kindest God you can think of is the one that would throw a few pennies your way, save you from a disastrous outcome, or keep the job you never liked so that you can keep the food on the table.

The idea of God itself as supply is very different than the idea of God as supplier. Your idea of a supplier, perhaps an employer, perhaps an institution, perhaps a bank that sends you payments, are all born in a sense of individuation and limitation—the God that favors one over the other, the bank that doesn't shut or foreclose on your mortgage, the employer who can guarantee a job until you die. This sense of self as the recipient of another outside self, who may have a limited source of supply, includes for most of you a God that will love you if you behave or appease your idea of what God must want. Once upon a time, it was a sacrifice. Now it's a tithing or something other.

We must correct you now. To understand that supply is of one Source and only one Source, and once you are aligned to that one Source, while what it may offer may be through different avenues, be it an employer, a bank, a job, what have you, you must understand that the limitlessness of Source must be comprehended by you as a reality. Your sense of Source through religious upbringing is of one who parses out the good and the bad, favors this one over that one. That has never been this teaching, because that is a teaching born in separation, which contributes to your idea of lack. The realization of the Divine as of all things, inclusive of all things, quite simply means that you are in the Source of supply when you are in alignment.

Now, when you are in the Source of supply and the recipient of it, the idea of lack first is diminished and then released, because the Source of all things cannot be diminished. You may impede your comprehension of it. You may deny your alignment to it. And this is what you do when you are invited to fear and claim separation and agree to lack and then go grasping for the known to fill your needs. The times you stand in are rich in understanding, create a buoyancy for you, a wave that will lift you to the Upper Room if you ride the wave well. If you decide to surface, gasp for breath, cling to a log of old history, you will find yourself afloat, perhaps, but clinging to the old. If you allow the wave to claim you and lift you and plant you firmly on the new perch, the Upper Room, the new foundation, you may move to a receipt of what has been beyond the known and beyond the small self's comprehension.

Now, the small self holds a legacy of lack. This is not its fault. It's how you have been taught and trained. The idea of a merciful God or a loving God has even been abstracted by you to a God that must favor one and have mercy over another, and you replicate this through your own behavior and treatment of your fellows. "Those people there deserve what they get." "Those people there will never be right." You decide another's fate, but you don't understand that you seal your own in your own actions to deny the inherent Divine in another. The opportunity now for all of you is to acquiesce, agree, and align to the great Source who loves all equally. Now, you may say, "Well, perhaps God can do that, but I certainly can't, and certainly not with these people over there." That is your choice. That is your legacy. That is the act of separation replicating itself and using any advantage it can get to confirm an idea of separation that separates you from God itself.

Now, Paul interrupts: "You said we cannot be separate from God." But you can agree to deny the Divine, and because you have free will, you may claim your circumstances in lack, in separation, or in the disavowal of the Divine in another. That gets you darkness, and you try to claim in darkness. There is no fruit on the tree in darkness. The sun does not shine to allow its branches to bear fruit. You have lived in a world so separate from the Divine that you've denied yourselves entry to the very Source of all things, which has always been present, always will be, and is simply saying yes to itself as it has come as you.

The offering you make, "I am willing to know myself anew, be claimed anew," allows you to be participatory to a great action of transformation that is actually occurring now. When all are caught up in the same wave of change, when what you see before you that you once believed was transitional is now seen as ever changing, what you once thought would always be there is unmoored, you release your idea of what should be and you hold your brother's hand, you hold your sister's hand, because you are in the same tumult. The idea of being is highly transformed at this level. And for humanity itself, the need to be shaken from its sleep has been the choice of humanity itself. The process of awakening to one's divinity requires each of you, like it or not, to claim the denial you have held of the Source of all things, of the worth of the one beside you, or those people that you may never agree with. You need not agree to an idea, but you need to claim the truth, the inherent truth, that there is no one unworthy of God. The moment you decide someone is, you have put yourself in shadow.

Now, the teaching we are offering you is in the text. We are saying this for Paul, who is wondering. But it is also specifically geared to an introduction to the idea of change that you are all participating in and supporting each other through, whether or not you are aware of this, because, dear friends, you are not separate from your brother, you are not separate from your sister, and indeed you clasp hands as you ride this wave, because that is how humanity says yes to the new land it arrives upon, *new land* being new equation, in vibration, in consciousness, to a world made new.

DAY TWENTY-THREE

You ask for things in a presupposition that only certain prayers get answered. In fact, the life you are living, individually and collectively, is in manifestation through thought and agreement, or the expectations of what will be. Because you are aligned to reality that is known through the collective, an individual prayer, in many cases, must release the requirements of the collective, whatever they may be, to align to the high octave where they be known and freed.

Now, we will explain this for Paul, who is questioning. A prayer for peace, however well intended, is claimed in the lower octave where peace is merely an idea. To realize peace is to move to the Upper Room, where peace is in equivalency. A prayer for peace, the realization of peace, perhaps, as may benefit the totality of the world, can be claimed here without the resistance that the collective has conformed to. Now, we use that word intentionally—*conformed.* The collective has conformed to ideologies of war, born in tribalism, born in a belief in lack. The collective has decided, at one level, that they can no longer continue in the old ways, and the residual affect of this choice is the world that you are witnessing now in disarray. When you clean a house, the house will often look far worse than it did when you started, before the cleaning is complete.

The idea of who you are—"I am an individual being with authority, I make my own choices, I will not be told what to do, I have free will, I decide who is welcome in my house and who is not"—must be understood, in some ways, as a vestige of a belief in separation. Because you believed you were separate from your Source, and then your neighbor, the idea of self and self-will have become codified, in some ways, as exemplars of a kind of independence. Separation from Source is independence from Source, but the rules of a world known in separation, ruled by fear or belief in lack, can no longer sustain the collective. So you stand at a juncture now where you comprehend individual need, individual choice, and the ramifications of all choices. Yes, you may leave the marriage, but you are still responsible to your children's well-being. Yes, you may leave your job, but you have to still have some way to support the self in your daily needs. The ramifications of choice in accountable ways must be understood by you as a high use of will.

Now, some of you will say, "Well, in true freedom, I leave my family. God will take care of them. I will leave my job. God will provide." And then you are back to an idea of a God who will meet your prayers, even when your idea of independence from God is the underlying issue. "What does that mean?" he asks. There are many jobs, there are many ways to love a family, and perhaps to leave one. To know the Source of all things is not to demand of it. It's to agree to it. And in times of radical change, where the old is being released from you, taken from you, in some ways, because its amplitude cannot lift to the new by your old ways of being, you must trust that the Divine knows more than your small self, who you deem sovereign. When many people say, "I am sovereign," they are lying to themselves. Indeed, you are all sovereign, but not at the level you think. The True Self is sovereign, and in an embodied state, or realized state, that sovereignty serves the collective, because the one who is sovereign knows who she is, in participation of the whole, to the whole, and for the whole. The idea of a glory born in separation is to make oneself an idol, and that will never be the case in a true teaching. When you idealize the small self, and the will of the small self—"My will, not thine, be done"—you contribute to the catastrophe that you claim through war, through poverty, and through all the emblemizations of these things that are claimed in separation or fear.

Now, of course you have free will, but your idea of self as willful in participation to collective will is still confused. You think that being in the collective is ascribing to a tribal belief. "In my country we pray this way. In my town we vote this way. In my suspecting of my neighbors, my distrust of others, I claim separation, and then rest in my tribe, where we believe the same things." To understand collective will is to move to the Upper Room, where you may know it, where you may comprehend it. In some cultures, the culture itself believes itself to be separate from the rest of the world they live in. This is an illustration of arrogance born in separation and anointed by fear, because then the acts of the culture eschew the well-being of the collective because they think they have the right, or pre-suppose a kind of sovereignty where even the idea of collective will is used as a battering ram or an ideology that will claim separation at the cost of others' freedom.

To understand the country you may sit in today, wherever it may be, look at its borders. The borders of a country that is in alignment to a higher will is a welcoming border. The border itself is understood as a symbol. A county line, a picket fence, whatever the border may be, the symbol itself an idea of separation, may actually be porous. You invite the neighbor to talk over your fence, perhaps come inside for tea. When a country has decided that they are separate from the ones beside it, they will rationalize anything they like to conquer their neighbors, or refute the well-being or the ideologies of the ones who don't agree with them.

At this time, in this history, in this plane, you are going to see walls tumble, because the idea of a state, the idea of a country, even a township, may be replaced by a higher ideal of one people, one species, one holy expression. And while you may have the name of a town, or the name of a country, you understand them as designations on a map, and not structures that operate to keep others out. The well-being of a country in the years to come will be claimed by their independence from fear, and nothing more.

Now, when we say *independence from fear,* we are speaking of trials that you might claim in aggression to foist your will upon another in ways that may not be beneficial. When you are acting in fear, you may claim any excuse for any behavior.

But we will tell you this: As you align in the Upper Room, you are no longer pretending. You are knowing. And any act by the collective in aggression or fear can be met by an individual through their awareness of Source.

Now, the awareness of Source is not understood by most of you. You still believe God is on a cloud, or somewhere in the ethers, deciding what will be and what will not be. When we speak of realization, we speak of knowing. And to know the action and presence of the Divine from the Upper Room upon a situation, a border, an act of violence, an act of tyranny, will actually claim in the resonant field of the thing, or the idea that the action has taken form as, in a higher octave of expression.

Paul is seeing bubbles. Each bubble is an idea that is floating in this realm of shared agreement. When a violent act, which must be preceded by thought, is reclaimed in the Upper Room, the bubble itself explodes. There is nothing to it, anyway. When you restore structure to idea—and idea always precedes structure—you may re-know the structure through the alignment to a higher idea. This is, again, how a world is made new.

Now, you are not conquering the lower realms with your light wand. You are not the fairy floating down to the lower to make the flowers grow. You are in sovereignty at this level, which means you are knowing and you are not in deceit. You are not drawn by tribal logic to outcomes that the tribe would see. You are knowing yourself as of the whole, but an individuated aspect of the whole. You are not correcting others' behavior. You are re-knowing others. And the behavior you

might wish to correct, you must re-see from the high vantage
point in order for it to be transformed, not to what you say it
should be, but to the Source of all things.

Paul interrupts: "I did see the bubbles explode. What happens to the ideas that may later become violent acts?" In the
Upper Room, the action of fear is not present. Separation does
not express. You cannot be in the Upper Room and say, "Give
me what I want, what is best for my tribe, my politics, my religion, my idea of what should be." This is all the small self in a
masquerade pretending to be higher than it is. When one aligns
to the Upper Room, one has a new obligation, which is beyond
the small self's requirements, to a realization of the inherent
Source of all things that cannot be claimed in the lower realm
or lower vibrational field. The claim we have given you—"I am
free, I am free, I am free"—claims you in agreement beyond the
collective, or the collective will born in tribalism.

Now, to understand yourself as of a species is not tribalism. It
is a far more universal focus. And you do understand, friends,
that if there is one child starving, one woman grieving over
the murder of her husband, there is work to be done in consciousness for the collective. The idea that you may be privileged in your country, take up the battles of the neighborhood
or the moment and ignore the well-being of others, cannot
be claimed from the Upper Room, because you have access at
this level to what makes you human but what is always divine.
And *always divine* means the being that you think that you are
in the lower realm, or idealization of self through separation, is
re-known in agreement to Source in a resurrected state.

Now, the text we write, *Resurrection,* is about embodiment

at this level. But you claim this in agreement to Source, and you know yourself as of Source—sovereign, yes, but an expression of the great whole. And you move to a plurality, if you wish to use that word, of understanding your individuation through a new lens, which is of the whole. There is no human being on this planet, whatever they have done, been accused of, think they have done, may have done, who is not loved by Source. And until you understand this, you will be throwing rocks, you will be stoning the woman known in adultery, you will be burning the witch, and if you can't find one, you will create one.

The artifacts of old, the idea of *conqueror*, the idea of *warrior*, as exemplars, must be replaced with *peacemaker*. You don't know how to be a peacemaker in the lower vibrational field. The ones that have come in form who have tried to do the most good were murdered for their efforts. To move to the Upper Room, where you are no longer choosing in fear, and you may claim peace because fear is not present, will be the first step in a peaceful kingdom. And if we use the word *kingdom*, it is simply to mean location, area, whether it be small, large, local, or global. It really matters not.

Now you don't know, almost none of you, that there is an aspect of you now who knows peace, who is peace, who is the expression of peace, seek to come to claim itself in the world. Indeed, this is the Monad, True Self, the Christ, if you prefer that word. They are all one and the same. And it is this light, in its resurrected state, that is peace. And the decree of peace, in manifestation, can be known quite simply as "God Is, God Is, God Is," because in God, at the true level of vibration that is God, separation does not express, and you may know peace as you know God and yourself as of it.

The requirements of this teaching today are quite simple—to understand that the being that you are is in great participation to the changes that are occurring. But how you align to these changes, with a rock in your hand to stone the neighbor that you disagree with or the torch to light the way for others, will be in some ways not only your experience, but the experience of the collective.

We will take a pause for Paul. This is indeed in the text. Period. Period. Period.

(PAUSE)

We would like to say a few more things about what just occurred. We spoke words. We offered ideas. You heard the ideas as you chose to. The small self's will decides what is worthy, or perhaps what is not. You put some information in the dust pile, some others on the shelf to think about later. While this is all well and good, we must inform you that the aspect of you that thinks she is in discernment is seeking to align our information to what you already believe to be true. You seek confirmation for the old ideas to support a continuum, what you think should be because it has been—your idea of God, your idea of change, all of these things, bubbles if you wish, that can be re-seen and re-known in a new way in the Upper Room because the old is not present. The old idea is not present in the old form it had taken.

Now, for some of you we suggest that the teachings we offer

must be thumbed through or deliberated upon at the level of the heart. Your heart will not lie to you, because the Divine as you, at the level of the heart, can translate any experience to its implicit truth. Your realization of what we teach in your own lives must be the evidence for this teaching. When we work in language, we do our best through Paul to instruct, to teach, and to support. When we work in vibration beyond language, you have your own experience of us. And who we are at the level of vibration is as the Monad that can be expressed at a level of consciousness in spoken form. In some ways, we are risen from old identity of the Christ, or as the Christ. We use the name Melchizedek in comfort to Paul and in the truth of its expression, but even Melchizedek is of the Christ and an expression of Christ that may be known beyond form.

We are authorized as instructors to support a world in transition to aligning to its highest potential. We have been here, we remain here, not as idea, but as presence in support of those who seek realization, and, finally, embodiment, at the level that can be held while in form. Your individuation as the manifest Word, or the Monad, or the Christ, your realization of your true nature, is the journey we have been taking you on, and indeed will continue to, even if there is only one student who, with an open heart, commits to this journey in fullness.

"How does one commit to this journey?" Paul asks. By agreement, and by supplication. And by that we simply mean the offering of self to the journey as it seeks to manifest through you. You are no longer driving in the old way. You are in consort with the True Self seeking its expression through you. And it is this journey that is the alchemical marriage, if you wish.

Now, our agreement to you as to be made whole is simply to know you beyond the idea of self so moored in separation that you can't imagine yourself as other. Because we know who you are, what you are, and how you serve, we may love you when you cannot love yourselves. We may see you at peace when you desire to war. And we will still your hand when you wish to throw the rock at your neighbor. We come as peace. We come in love. We honor you, wherever you may sit, wherever you may be. And we demand nothing of you, except that you trust the aspect of self that truly knows.

Blessings to each of you. This is in the text as well.

DAY TWENTY-FOUR

Some of you decide what your life should look like based on an idea that you have inherited. Some of you decide that your lives will not live up to the expectations that you might mandate. You live in disappointment, or in a sense of failure, because you have not accrued the evidence of success that you believe you are worthy of or could not gain. When we ask you questions about your lives, we are asking to the self who seeks realization, who wishes for more, but is not deciding in advance what that *more* should look like or entail. Your own realization, you see, indeed comes at the cost of the known. But the aspects of self that you still seek to utilize to gain success or recognition on this plane must now be re-known in service to the higher.

Now, this means very simply that any experience you have in the manifest world is your teacher—your ideas of success and failure as well. When you realign to the Divine Self, or the Monad, things may seem to fall away—the self that you thought you should be, your idea of culture and what it should be, what religion should be, what an economic structure should be or resemble. These ideas that you've inherited, that you have seen out-pictured in your lives thus far, will in fact be disassembled by your own experience. In other words, friends, you are no longer captive to them, to an idea of success or failure or what it means to be in circumstances that others may not wish, or think are high choices.

Some of you believe that if you are truly living spiritually, everything will be handed to you. And while we teach that in the Upper Room you move towards reception and receipt of all that is, you comprehend the Source of all things, you still have lessons here in the material realm that you need to move with, in accord to, and perhaps surmount. Anything that is perceived as an obstacle in anyone's path may be seen as an opportunity to learn. In some cases, you find that the road that you are taking, now fraught with obstacle, was not the highest road for you. Others of you decide that what you thought was so important must not be important, and then you lose all hope of choice. "What is worthy now? I no longer aspire to success as I did. Now what do I do?" You still are learning that the act of being, which is impressive in the True Self, and embodied as you in your experience, is the reason you have come. A life well lived, you must know, is a life in high choice where things were learned. The expression of the Monad as

230 THE BIRTH OF THE NEW

the life lived, also a high choice, is claimed by those who seek realization. But the one who does not seek realization is still embodied at a level of tone or vibration and is seeking realization through his or her experience—what it means to be a father, what it means to be a colleague, what it means to be responsible to one's actions, all lessons learned and part of the being that you have chosen to experience life through.

Now, transcendence of a reality is not escape from a reality. And some of you who wish transcendence are seeking to escape, to discount the physical realm, to deny its opportunities to learn. In transcendence, you actually become more accountable to this realm because you understand that you are accountable to all of your choices, not for selfish reasons, but because you are one of the whole. The man in the Upper Room does not hoard his food. The woman in the Upper Room does not close her door to strangers who may require shelter.

Each of you says yes to the transition you are undergoing with us. However, some of you decide that it should resemble something that it's not. "I will float away on a cloud in the Upper Room. My choices will be made experientially. I will want for nothing." Well, we say that's fine. But dear friends, if it is raining outside, best to shut the window. If there is a fire burning out of control, best to do what you can to put it out. The actions that you take in consort with the physical realm are still present, but the alignment you hold to a higher level of vibration transforms your experience of them.

Now, Paul is asking, "Are we still afraid of death in the Upper Room? You are giving examples of self-protection, closing the windows from the storm, putting out the fire." You do these things because they are high choices, and maintaining the well-being of the body in certain circumstances that require action, such as shutting a window or dousing a fire, are also part of your lessons—that you are capable of maintaining a body and a home and a life in which to live through.

Some of you decide in advance that what we are teaching you is a way to rule the universe. "In the Upper Room, I will be the king. All things will come as I say they will. I will rejoice in my kingdom. I am in God. Everybody else better hurry up and get there, too." Again, this is the small self with its paper crown, seeking doctrine, seeking rules, seeking methods of control of others. It has not worked on this plane. The highest priest embodied in form is still here to learn, and the priest's lessons may be very challenging. The same is true for all of you as you align to the higher. You are continuing to learn and realize who you are and what you are not through this passage.

"Now, fear of death," Paul asks. "Do we have to encounter this on this journey?" Of course you do. And you all will. You will all lose the body at one point. Now, the fear of the loss of the body is really the only issue. In fact, for most, the release of form is perceived, once it happens, as something of a gift. A new expression emerges, a higher tone, and a level of ease that was never found fully when you were in dense form. But the fear of death is the fear of your actions prior, and what you assume will be there for you. The template of the old reality, with its delineations of good and evil, heaven and hell, are problematic now. You don't understand that whatever your experience has been on this plane, you have undergone learning through it. And the choice to embody, to come into a body to learn, is itself a high choice. And you must understand that each of you who says yes to embodiment is applauded for that simple act.

Now, once you understand you are not immortal in form, but you *are* in vibration, that consciousness is eternal, you are no longer frightened. When you leave one home and move into another, there is perhaps excitement. A new experience awaits you. And this is also true when the body is released. But many of you decide this is the only home you will be in, or perhaps whatever home waits for you next, in some other reality, will be a disappointment, claim you in punishment or fear, and that you will not know God.

The idea of heaven and hell must be understood now as metaphor of different levels of tone or vibration. The presence of the Divine, which we call the Kingdom, the honoring of this, the alignment to it, is a way of understanding heaven. But heaven in most cases is a creation, a way to describe a state of consciousness that exists beyond form. And there are levels of vibration beyond form that are not terribly pleasant, but also offer opportunity to learn. The Kingdom is not heaven, as we teach it. It is the realization of the omnipresence of the Divine in all things. It is a level of agreement or vibrational tone where you are in the presence in a unified state.

Now, hell can be understood very simply as the result of the denial of the Divine. Now, any choice made in fear, in the dishonoring of another, creates what you call karma. And when you incur karma, you incur a vibrational field that has much to learn through, and every life lived becomes opportunity to learn anew. The idea of hell that you've been given, the absence of God, a place of fire and brimstone, a place of torture, is also metaphor. You understand that fire burns away the old. And the burning of the dross, the release of the old, is part of the practice we claim in our teachings. We support you in releasing the ideas of self that are in the denial of the Divine that are the cause of much pain. When one dies, one cannot go to hell because there is not a geographical location for it. Hell becomes an idea of the absence of God.

Now, you must understand that the Divine Self as you already expresses in the Upper Room and seeks to be your counsel, seeks to be the aspect of you that reclaims reality in a higher accord. Paul interrupts. He is stuck on the idea of hell. He wants more explanation. When you claim in fear and act in fear, you are in denial of the Divine. The choices claimed in fear call more fear to itself, and you may align to a sea of fear and become somewhat lost or adrift in it. Now, violence itself, or what you understand as violence, is fear in action, another way of denying the Divine. And that which would deny the Divine would find a way to excuse itself, or claim itself as independent from God, or in its right motive. "It was right to kill. It was right to harm."

Now, self-protection, caring for the body, is understandable. At a level of vibration you have no need for arms. You know who you are, and realization itself may transform situations for you because you are no longer aligned to the level of fear through past agreement to the collective that you have known yourselves through. But as you lift to a higher way of being, as you begin to realize self, the idea of vindication, "I will get my way," the idea of revenge, "he or she will pay for what she has done," are released because you cannot align to them. But Paul interrupts: "But what about the one floating in a sea of vindication, desiring revenge, who cannot forgive?" He or she has placed herself in a hell because the act of unforgiveness actually precludes the action of the Divine, and until that heart is changed, that heart may suffer. But it is choice, and you must understand this. A loving God, if we can say those words, still loves the one stranded, but will not intercede unless asked, unless the aspect of self that is in the refusal of the Divine can be respoken, and the claim "I am free" can truly be announced.

Paul has questions. "There are some of us that suffer. We cannot imagine peace. There are people who are tortured in the mind who've been through terrible things who cannot imagine themselves as healed. What becomes of them?" You are all here to learn different things, and finally, we must say, there is no one left behind. Finally, all humans, or all souls, if you prefer, will reunite with Source. When someone comes in a life and incurs great suffering, they may be receiving what you may call the lessons of karma, or they may have other lessons to learn. They can be re-known. They can all be lifted, and ultimately will be.

You must understand grace, perfect grace, which is the presence of the Divine upon one who could not understand it, may not even know to ask for it. To be in the receipt of grace is to allow the soul itself to align to it, beyond the fragmented mind or emotional body that would refute it. You must always remember that there is an aspect of any human being

who knows who it is, what it is, and how it serves. This aspect
has been precluded through fear, through prior choice, and
through alignment to a collective field that has operated in the
renunciation of God. Anyone can be healed. And finally, we
suggest, all will be met in grace, because God is love. Those of
you who decide to deny the Divine, find a way to justify it, seek
revenge or recrimination, design outcomes that are exclusive of
some of your fellows and consequently exclusive of God, will
learn through these choices. Any karma, finally, is opportunity
to learn. But the high choice is present, and will continue to be.

The title of this chapter is "The Wave." We will continue
later. Period. Period. Period. Stop now, please.

(PAUSE)

We have several things to discuss based on the prior teaching and how it may be misconstrued. While you are accountable to your acts, the Divine Self as you may actually re-know
everything. This does not mean you may not be accountable
to things done. It means that your understanding of self as
bound to them has been released.

The idea of forgiveness from the higher has also been so
misunderstood that most of you seek forgiveness or believe
penance must be due. If you harm your neighbor, make it right
with your neighbor. To deny the Divine is to deny the action
of God within you, and when you are no longer doing that,
you move back into alignment through forgiveness. In other
words, you have always been forgiven, but in denying the
Divine you have blocked that expression. The Resurrected Self,

the aspect of self that comes into being once the boulder is removed from the cave door, is the one that forgives all things. Underline *all things*.

Now, this sounds horrible to some of you. "We cannot be victims. If we forgive, we will be victims." This is not about that level of consciousness at all. You may understand that the idea of forgiveness may conjure, for some, allowance. But it is not the case. To truly forgive another is to liberate the self. If the small self is not capable of this, and it may well not be, you ask for support from the Monad, from the True Self, in order to forgive.

When one is forgiving, one is releasing karma and attachment to the other that will play out in other ways in your idea of time. To forgive another is to release this and allow something to be new—again, the claim "Behold, I make all things new," which supports realization beyond prior subjectiveness, prior understanding, or prior creations.

When you ask questions of the Divine, why don't you discuss how you may heal, what it may require, what is required of you to support healing of the self that refuses to forgive? Most of you do this because the idea of forgiveness is frightening, and you think your only authority comes from anger. Have your anger, if you wish it. But do not stay there.

You will not be angry in the Upper Room. There is no place for it. But some of you must understand that you have been harmed, that it is not acceptable, in order to move to forgiveness. Blaming the self requires self-forgiveness, and many of you become locked here because you believe you are unworthy.

Again, God loves all its creations, regardless of what has been done. It is you who say no.

Yes, this is in the text. Thank you for your presence. Stop now, please.

DAY TWENTY-FIVE

You stand before us today in an awareness of what you seek, how you wish your life to be, what you presuppose could be, given the evidence you've accrued about what your life should look like. Some of you say yes to the unknown. "I am willing to discover. I am willing to know. I am willing to realize who I may be in a new way than I have thus far." Others of you may say, "I wish things were different. I want things as they were. I demand that the times of change be over so I can understand myself through the knowledge I had accrued prior."

When you're on a voyage in a new sea, the ideas of who you have been are altered through the transition you make from one shore to the new one that awaits you. To understand who you are, in times of great change, is to truly understand the essence of your being, that which is revealed to you through your own recognition of how you respond to what is around you. The one who is indignant, the one who is frightened, the one who is joyful, the one who is in trepidation but seeks to step forward anyway—all of you are present in this wave of change, and consequently your experience of the wave will vary greatly.

The times you sit in now are about a release of an idea, born in separation, that you are singular, only one, and not of a collective. The refusal to agree to being of a collective gives you a splinter to hold on to in this wave of change, whereas your agreement to the well-being of the whole, in times of transition, provides you a raft for many. Now, the game you play is always equality—who has a right to the seat, who gets the splinter, who wins the prize. But the game is over as it has been played, and the wave of change that is carrying all does not care what you do for a living, how good you are at this or that, or what you would like it to end as. When a wave completes itself, it rejoins the sea, and it will leave you, as we have said prior, on a higher ground than you have known thus far.

The agreement you are making now is to be realized through your experience of an altered reality that does not offer you the guarantees that you had come to expect. If you see this as a gift, you are carried high. You ride the wave with an awareness of what is before you, where you are carried to. Or if you are within the wave, in the tumult, you are claimed in the utterance of confusion: "Take me back to what I have known." It will not be so. The world will not return to it as you knew it or as you would agree to it. But the change that you are undertaking now, a requirement for the evolution of the species, can bring great joy if you allow joy to be present in this experience. Every morning you awaken to a new day, a new promise of an experience as you know yourself in form. In the high alignment that you may choose to claim, "I am in the Upper Room," the residual affect of change becomes as a wave lobbing against a lower cliff. You can see it from the high vantage point. You can see where the wave strikes. But your view is unobstructed because you are not dictating how changes should occur and what they should be seen as. You are bearing witness to change. Your life is informed by these changes, yes. But from the viewpoint of the Upper Room, your experience of self as of Source transforms what might be frightening to what might be held in a higher way—a new potential, still unseen, seeking to be born.

Some of you say, "Yes, I am willing to know who I am beyond the ideas I have held, beyond what has been taught me." Some of you say, "No, I will have it my way or no other way." We will say this once and for all: The times you sit in hold great promise. But the magnitude of change that we expect you will see in this lifetime is actually unparalleled in human experience. Now, this is not a frightening thought. Please do not make it so. If you look at the world that you live in now and compare it to the world of seventy years ago, it is vastly different and will continue to change at a speed that you are not prepared for through common history, but *are* prepared for through the Upper Room, where your ability to see is not informed by fear or a desire to claim what was and capture it in time. You know your seasons, you know your holidays, you know your ages, you know the country of birth. They are ways of knowing the self that are not altered here. But what is altered is a structure of agreement to what it means to be one of many, how it feels to know yourself as of the whole, what it means to put the needs of your brother first when you have been taught to refute that. Again, the lifeboat. You are in it together, know it or not, and you are being carried forward.

The new shore that you embark upon is humanity at its next level of incarnation, or next stage of expression, where what is irrefutable is the True Self as an aspect of being. What you may think now is theoretical becomes your expression, and as it becomes your expression it aligns the landscape you experience yourself through, through a shared tone or vibratory echo. "Behold, I make all things new."

The transition you are undertaking, one and all, must be understood as a requirement for the well-being of the whole. And if it comes at the cost of what once was, that can no longer be held in the vibration of truth, you will adapt, you will learn. You are not being punished. You have not been forgotten. You are simply being asked to let go of an idea of what it has meant to be, so that you may truly understand being. You are releasing the refusal of the Divine, the denial of God, and claiming instead an agreement to Source, by any name you choose, that you must be participatory to.

When you understand that the wave itself, great change itself, is of God, you can begin to articulate or manifest in a new way. When you fight this level of transformation—imagine a child seeking its way back into the womb—you will fail. You are being reborn, re-known. Re-articulation, the manifestation of the Monad come in form, is indeed resurrection. And the time has come for all humanity to say yes to what is new. Period. Period. Period.

Indeed, this is the end of the chapter. Period.

7

THE GIFT OF BEING

Each of you says yes to your potential when you say, "I Am." That potential is realized through aligning to the claim made. "I am in my highest good, highest awareness, highest agreement to be" supports you in acclimating to that level or tone. If you release the idealization of what that should resemble, you can allow the Monad, the Divine as who you are, to claim itself in its own recognition, which may have very little to do with what your personality structure assumes it should be or that something should appear as.

Your spiritual paths are dictated at a level of the soul. You are given the right to say yes, to say no, to what is before you as you wish. The Monad, you see, the divine principle operating in and as you, is seeking its own reclamation through your expression. And the I Am Self, which is the Monad, sings into being what it requires to express through. *Sings into being.*

Understand what this means. It means that an intention, set at the level of Monad, an invocation in tone, claims expression just as a song does. Now, a song has an intention behind it, be it a love song or a march to war. The intention of the song in the energetic field is resonant. In the claims you make with us by way of attunement, you are singing into being or transforming your expression, inclusive of the truth of the claim. And the manifestation of the claim occurs when you decide that how it appears need not be as you say it should. Some of you get tired of God. "Well, I prayed a lot. Not much happened." Or "I prayed a little. I didn't expect too much anyway." The idea that prayers need to be fervent is simply confused. Prayers need to be earnest, but everything is a prayer that is thought into being. And any claim made in I Am—"I am free, I am free, I am free"; "I am in the Upper Room"—sings into being its equivalency in your own energetic field.

Now, some of you wish this to be other than it is. "I want a path where I am told what to do and how I can expect it to be, and when and where I meet God, and what I need to wear for the meeting." You seek prescription through organization. What we have given you are symbols of vibration, through language, that support you in the escalation of tone or field, where your experience may be translated to confirm the claim you have made. If you do not have confirmation from the claims we have offered you in your own experience, you may choose another path. We do not bind you to ours. We have no authority to do that, nor would we. However, we will suggest that if you are operating with these claims, some of what stands in the way of manifestation is the small self's expectation of how it should look or feel.

In the alignment you claim to what we call the Upper Room, you are bypassing a level of vibration that you have been in collusion with. Now, by *bypass* we don't mean *avoid*. We mean *move beyond*, just as an airplane rises above the clouds. The turbulence that you experience on the way up is indicative of your moving to a higher jet stream. The idea of who you are, in a translated state, has a comparable value in its voyage, which simply means you know it's working when your sense of identity, your sense of certainty, your sense of what has been or should be, has been shaken. Now you are witnessing a world whose identity is being shaken—*a world* meaning a population, any segment of any culture, who has been aligned to fear, that is now being provoked to move beyond it.

Now, the alignment to fear is not an action another does. It is what is already present that is finally being seen and addressed. Paul sees the image of someone shaking the dust from a rug. The rug was dusty, but you didn't know how dusty until the room was filled with its remnants. The dust was there, you were walking upon it, but as it clears it creates a cloud that obscures what is before you. But unless the rug is cleaned, it will continue to amass detritus and you will continue to suffocate, wondering where all that dust might be coming from.

When you say yes to the passage that is before you now, you are agreeing not only to the unknown, but to a path that has been trod historically by the mystic, by the sage, by the one who was the holy one in her community. What is actually happening is that the alignment that is present now supports an awareness that was confirmed prior by a level of dedication and discipline that was available and met fully only by the prophet, by the sage, by the medicine woman, the one in his or her culture who was dedicated to a new level of being. In all instances, these individuals became doorways to the upper realms, and the benefit of their presence in any community was to claim the divinity that would otherwise be denied.

Now, imagine this. The act of re-articulation that we have introduced does not make you the medicine woman or the sage or the prophet. It simply claims you in an agreement to a level of tone where you might meet a level of articulation in manifestation that you did not know you could, or were told you would never. The possibility that exists now for full articulation is no longer there only for a few, but any who say yes, fully, at the level of agreement that they may agree to. And what that means is the yes from the heart strikes a chord in the energetic field, where the energetic field then becomes indoctrinated by the Monad or the aspect of the Divine that has always been present as you, but has prior been refuted or ignored. The choice to embody or manifest, as we instruct, is not a mandate for an individual. It is merely the mandate of the Monad, who works in tandem with the soul on this act of re-articulation. You will not spend your life in a cave or a nunnery. You will not be the high priestess as you see in the tarot cards. You will be Jane or Jonathan, Friedrich or Alice. You will be any name you may choose, embodied in a higher way.

Now, the Christ presence, or the Monad in articulation, is present in all human beings. So never for a moment believe yourself to be separate or special, but one of the whole. Paul sees the image of a popcorn machine. One kernel is popping, and then more, and finally all. This is what happens through co-resonance. Paul interrupts the teaching: "But what about wisdom, please? Not all are wise. Some want the idea of ascension to seclude themselves from others or to feel superior to others." We will say this, Paul: It actually matters not why one chooses God or the Source of all things. There are many doorways, many portals, many ways to enter, and while there are mazes that you may be confounded by, traps that you may meet of the egoic structure seeking specialness, God itself does not deny anyone who seeks its presence. It cannot. It will not. And once you have begun this journey, this journey will continue in its own perfect ways. The self that you have known, perhaps relied upon a bit too much, is altered in some ways by the realization that even the structure of personality is of God, and can and will be re-known in this field.

The joy of expressing at this level is expressing without fear, without shame, without a belief that you should be other than you are, appear differently than you do, be more well educated or wealthier or more beautiful than you believe yourself to be. You show up as you are, as this expression of God, and you join hands with the ones beside you in song of celebration of being. *A song of celebration of being.*

We will say this. You may say it after us:

"I have come to know. I have come to express. I am free in my knowing. I am expressed in fullness. And I say yes to the road before me."

Now we say this for you:

To all who hear these words, we announce your presence in liberation from any artifacts of history, any misconceptions, any idols you have worshipped, any fear that you have justified, so that you may know yourselves without the mask, without the fear that the mask implies, and know yourself as one with all around you, all that expresses, that is of God.

You may say this after us:

"I know who I am in truth. I know what I am in truth. I know how I serve in truth. I am free. I am free. I am free. I am in the Upper Room. I Have Come. I Have Come. I Have Come. Behold, I make all things new. It will be so. God Is. God Is. God Is."

And imagine beside you the students of this text. Those who hear these words extend their hands. Take the hands of the ones beside you, and please say this to all of them:

"I see you in the Upper Room. You are in the Upper Room. You Have Come. You Have Come. You Have Come. It will be so. God Is. God Is. God Is."

We see you each as you truly are, and we say these words to the collective:

Behold, I make all things new.

Allow yourselves to be, simply be, and say yes to what you have chosen.

Indeed, this is in the text. Stop now, please. Period. Period. Period.

DAY TWENTY-SIX

When something stands in your way, when you have a perceived obstacle in your path, you have an opportunity to grow. There is nothing stopping any of you, really, except what you believe to be. And the choice to align to the Monad in realization of who and what you really are calls to you those things that you must understand and move beyond. This happens in sequence for all of you, and the sequence that you understand yourself as experiencing is what is before you, what the teaching of the day is. And how you attend to what is before you each day will claim you in wisdom, in a new alignment, and in a true sense of the word, your own authority in a higher way. What frightens you becomes the wind that moves you. What challenges you becomes the muscle of your arms. What lifts you is your awareness that nothing before you is permanent. There is no such thing as a permanent obstacle, and everything that you encounter in your alignment to the Upper Room is brought to you so that you may know yourself through it— underline the word *through*—to know the self *through* the obstacle or the encounter or the experience that the life that you are living provides you. Some of you say, "Well, it should be easy. If I am doing this work correctly, I should be floating from cloud to cloud." Well, even a cloud has a thunderstorm or a great wind that breaks it apart. So your understanding of how things should be is based upon a false presumption. The weather continues in the Upper Room. There are challenges to be met because your growth is ongoing.

Now, when a community is in change, a group, a system is in change, you are all encountering perhaps a singular event through an individual identity. In other words, when the church is on fire, those singing the hymns upstairs are having a rather different experience than those downstairs, and the pastor is having a different experience than the one who lit the match. You are all experiencing singular things in different ways and contributing to what you see in your unique fashion. When you lift to the Upper Room, the identity that begins to perceive is so very different than what you were taught to be that it takes some time to grow comfortable with the new view. The self that has seen things in fear is still present and unlearning. The True Self that knows she is safe is having a different experience. And as you coalesce or move into a higher accord, the dissonant notes are released. But this happens in sequence, again through your encounters. Realization of the Divine is not about denying darkness. It's about claiming the Divine where the darkness has been held. It's about knowing the action of God, and *knowing* means realization, where it has been ignored. It is about re-knowing what was put in darkness as worthy of the light, to transform your own individual experience and contribute to the collective availability to perceive a world anew.

Now, when we teach a world made new, we are speaking of structures, we are speaking of landscape. We are actually speaking to the weather, in some ways, because what you know of as weather has been so deeply subjected to the ruination of this planet by some, that your contribution to the healing of this plane is part of the alignment to the Upper Room. But when we speak of landscape, we also speak to consciousness—how anything is held, how anything can be lifted and perceived anew. When a community undergoes change, the individuals first seek to decide how to attend to the change on an individual basis. Imagine you have three families down the street. Some may pray, some may act, some may build a bunker. When great change comes, the community itself must rally in a new awareness of the collective. Anything that comes to the collective, not just a bill in the mail for you, but an expression of manifestation that informs many, must be attended to by the many. And as the collective shifts, the old ways of coping, building the bunker, laying the foundation for change through fear, are disassembled so that the new may be made.

"Well, what is the new?" he asks. In times of change, we invite you to look to the ones beside you as allies, in support of a regrouping for the benefit of all. To the extent that you believe your neighbor to be your enemy, you bifurcate, you polarize, and you claim separation, which is the fear that you have all known yourselves through. "Well, I don't like my neighbor," you may say. "I don't want to be friends with the one next door." Well, when a great wave comes, you are all impacted by it, and if you don't put your differences aside, you will be fighting your neighbor for resources when in fact there is more to be shared when you move to a collective action.

What you experience on this plane now, in agreement to

fear, is a polarization of people, of identities, of politics, of religions, of finances. You understand each other through the name tags you've chosen and the identities that those things claim. "She is the Muslim, he is the Jew." "She is the wise woman, he must be the fool." You play these games of identity at the cost of a collective agreement. All humanity is one species, and in fact the species itself, in re-articulation, is about to receive an enormous gift. "What is that?" he asks. It's the gift of awareness.

Now, for some of you, awareness is terribly painful. "That pain that I ignored in my knee was far more serious than I wanted to know." "The marriage that I hoped would last will not last." Awareness can be challenging because you are being invited to a new experience. But the awareness of past action, what you have collectively chosen through fear or misalignment, has been reckoned with. You are facing the refuse of your past choices. You seek to deny them still, but they will not be denied. And as you say, "Yes, I understand, I understand how I have been complicit to separation, how I have denied my brother food, how I have said no to the opportunity to be of service," you will understand the great significance of this moment of awareness. It means you are about to make a higher choice.

Now, a higher choice need not be a more moral choice, a more productive choice. We will never use the word *better* to describe a choice. But by *high* we mean in alignment to a higher truth. Now, a higher truth can be very simple: "God is the source of all manifestation." It can perhaps be more complicated: "I am willing to leave a life or livelihood I had chosen, in participation to collective fear, to grow beyond the old choices." Any choice may be made, you see, from the Upper Room. And a choice made in truth, from the perspective of the Upper Room, will always lift you higher.

Some of you say, "Well, that sounds possible, but here I sit today, confused about what to do about much of anything." We would offer you this: The life you live is your teacher, and the obstacles you are facing are the opportunities for continued growth. And unknowing what you expected to be there gives you the opportunity to truly know, to truly perceive, from a new vantage point beyond the self that denies its role as a creative aspect of the whole. We will underline that phrase— *creative aspect of the whole.* Now, what this means is that the idea of self that permeates your life is actually contributing to collective structures. How you perceive everything and anything informs the structure of the thing seen. Well, you didn't make the tax system or the medical system. You didn't create religious doctrine. But each of you are informed by their experience, by their existence, and by your experience of them. How you think of anything claims a thing in agreement or vibrational accord to you. Again, what you damn, damns you back. What is blessed by you is blessed for you.

Now, to agree to the world that seems to be in chaos is not confirming chaos, if what you are agreeing to is radical change, productive change, productive potential being realized through the movement of energy and the realignment of structures to a higher velocity. At a certain level or pitch, the manifestation of fear cannot remain. You've heard the stories of walls tumbling in response to a horn played. If the horn is truth, if the vibration is truth, the wall will indeed tumble.

Now, sadly, most of you mistake truth to be somebody else's opinion, the data of a culture, an idea of what you would like to be. So every time we have used the words *in truth*—"We know who you are *in truth*"—we are claiming you beyond the mask, beyond the political self, beyond the religion of your birth, and beyond your status in the culture you may be living in. To align to truth relegates every aspect of you in this vibrational field. And what releases, or what is lifted in a reclamation, is in alignment to truth that may now be seen. When a world is made new, it is made new in truth. And we promise you this: What will not occur is a disassembling of structure to leave you in ruination. We are not blowing up the building so you can see what the building once was. The building may be lost so that the new may be born, but the act of re-creation, done through this level of consciousness, will not hold the seeds of fear. What crumbled was born in fear, or infested with fear. What is claimed anew will be present well beyond your lifetimes, because what is built in truth will be everlasting.

Each of you says yes to the idea of being in the Upper Room. But we wish you to know what it means to be here. Paul is interrupting: "Is this in the text?" Indeed, it is in the text. Now, let us continue. The idea of being in the Upper Room, of expressing there in a glorified state, is appealing to you. But please imagine for a moment that where we are taking you is to a level of tone where what you have held in falsity, what you have denied, what you thought might be true but was not known, is all re-known so that you may understand yourself as you truly are. To be in the Upper Room, to be expressed at this tone, is to be as that horn that breaks the wall

down, that claims the obstacle that you find in your path gone
and dissolved. It's what offers you the peace that this road that
you are journeying is claiming you, beyond the old and in a life
that you may rejoice in.

We will stop now for Paul. Period. Period. Period.

(PAUSE)

We would like to begin. We would like to continue as we
are allowed to teach.

The idea you have of who you are is so transformed when
you are no longer operating in fear that the sense of liberation
you hold is not only contagious in a sense of being, but in an
actualization. In other words, the one who becomes free of
fear is liberating the one she encounters, and not through any
action, but through an alignment.

Now, because what is true is always true, and in the Upper
Room you don't hold fear or choose from fear, you are witnessing others as they truly are, beyond the fear that they have
known themselves in, beyond their politics, beyond their religions, beyond what they think they are through the cultural
edicts they have been born into. Now, when you do this for
another, you are reclaiming them, you are re-knowing them.
You are not forcing them to be other than they think they are.
You are knowing them in love.

Now, to know someone in love is not to judge them, but
to agree to their essence, the True Self, or the Monad that
expresses as them. Paul sees the image of a woman weeping
when she is gazed upon with love. Each of you know what it

feels like to wish to be loved. Some of you know what it is to be loved, but most of you do not. You have ideas. The experience of being loved, in the truest sense, releases you from all that would be an obstacle to love. And as you embody at the level of love, where you may hold another in this field, you are a liberator, a game changer, an idealization made manifest.

The idea of the Word—that one note played that manifests as all things—made flesh is confused for so many of you. But indeed that is the teaching of resurrection. And the realization of this, from the Upper Room, invites all to join you. You cannot enjoin with those you judge from the Upper Room. You cannot align to those you fear from the Upper Room. What you do instead is love them as they are, beyond any other claim, and let them be lifted, re-known, and re-seen through this love.

The gift of this teaching for some of you will be the realization of who you truly are, and you will begin to realize the truth in others as a result. The gift for others will be actualization, a manifestation of the Monad as the energetic field that will allow you to serve as a doorway between the octaves. And we say this to each of you: You all have the right to be re-known, spoken into being anew, as you align to the True Self, who speaks the truth into being.

We will stop now, please. Yes, in the text.

DAY TWENTY-SEVEN

Each of you says yes to the degree that you are willing to claim an idea that you cannot know the outcome to until it transpires. The agreement we are making to you, that you will be re-known, re-

claimed in the high order of the Upper Room, is made in agreement, not only to your individual potential, but to humanity's
potential as well. Now, the claim is made from the Upper Room.
We know who you are, and in your own re-articulation you may
know as well. The self-deceit you have used to camouflage identity, the fear you've held about reckoning with your own creations,
is actually discarded at a level of vibration, because what is present
is true, and fear, a lie, will not be held in truth.

Now, the requirement for this class today is reconciliation
with the idea of self that could ever believe itself to be in separation. If you are understanding what we are saying, the idea
of separation itself, in its own dense creative form, is what
you have been contending with. But it is an idea, finally, and
nothing more than idea. The idea of union itself, you may say,
is calibrated through the release of the fear, the release of denial, as you are re-known beyond the template that the idea of
separation has encased you in.

Now, the original idea of separation that you contend with
was as if you drank water from a sour well. The taste of the
well let you understand yourself in a new experience, and
you did not trust the water that you drank after that, so you
looked elsewhere. Paul interrupts: "What was the sour well?"
Your own demands in fear, your own requirements for gain,
and your belief that what you would be given would never be
enough, the idea of self as unworthy, "Look at what I am given
to drink," are far too potent and powerful. "I will not drink
what I am given." The idea of the well, the eternal well, Source
as well, has been discussed in prior texts. And you do drink
from the well daily, because you are participating in a reality

that is of the well, the well as all things. But the dismantling or release of the one idea of separation, the first idea of separation, must be understood as a reclamation of identity that you have not encountered yet.

Now, while we have taught you what union is, while we have taken you on a journey through great change towards union, you are precluded from union by your adherence to this one idea: "I am not. I am not." Now, the *not* that is attached to the claim "I Am" is as creative as anything else you could summon. "I am holy," a statement of truth that will align you to your true sacred nature. "I am not holy" will discard that and perpetuate separation, which is how you've been denied, at the individual and collective level, the realization of the omnipresent Divine. "Can it be that simple," Paul asks, "that we re-know an idea?" Yes, indeed. Everything is an idea that you have attachments to, that you emblazon with meaning. The idea of God itself as idea, confused for most of you, is the thing you seek a relationship with. The idea of God is what you are seeking to relate to, not God itself, which is the source of all idea, which is the expression of all things. The moment you release the need or the requirement for separation, which is in fact present in the energetic field, you are reclaimed, not only in the Upper Room, but in an agreement to embody at a level you have not done thus far.

Now, you understand that there have been some who have been realized, and they have undergone this passage as well. It is not a comfortable passage, because to release the need for separation, to release the need to deny the Divine, is to propel yourself into a level of tone or vibration that you don't believe that you can hold. Imagine a rocket ship that burns when it trespasses the border to the next reality it is moving towards. Imagine a balloon that is burned by the sun as it lifts too high. You have many warnings of not trespassing to the top of the mountain or to the pinnacle of a potential towards realization, and you have heard these things and agreed to them and kept the self low. Now, to become high is indeed to become visible, but not with human eyes. You are not seen as a savior, as a prophet or a sage. You are seen as whoever you may be through the tone you emit. And in the Upper Room, beyond the idea of separation, the energetic field you hold is actually unhindered from what it may claim. So much you cannot claim, or would not think you could, is addressed through the idea of separation and your idea of a potential that is born in scarcity, limitation, and fear of self. The True Self is unafraid of itself. Do you hear these words? The Christed Self, the Monad, is unafraid of itself. It is the aspect of you that has claimed separation that is operating as fear, and still, at this level, seeking to refute the Divine that has come as all things.

"How does this release?" you ask. "What is done? What is asked of us? What do you do for us?" In song, in tone, we have claimed you in a higher pitch of resonance, and we sing together now, in this collective, towards a high broadcast that actually releases you from a binding agreement made by the small self to replicate separation, the first idea of separation. The agreement to replicate was not made at a soul level. It is something the species chose, through its own act, through its own denial of the Divine, and decided it would do its best and learn through what it has. And now we say this is not only transformed, but you are reclaimed beyond it through the release of an idea that you actually could be separate. You cannot be separate, but you can amass the dense vibration, through the denial of the truth, to align to a world that would seek to support you in the claim of separation, "I am not."

Now, the claim "I am not," as we teach it this way, is used to refute the Divine. The simple claim "I am of, I am of the whole, I am of God" is already the step to release you from the need for separation. As this one note is sung—"I am free, I am free, I am free"—as you re-articulate from the Upper Room, the idea of self that could believe itself to be separate is unmoored and begins to detach from the energetic field. Imagine, if you wish, that there is a thumbprint in the field that you hold, and the thumbprint announces an agreement to separation. The self that agrees to this, that came into a body, that chose to learn through whatever experience she claimed, has been unaware, but under the intention that the thumbprint has claimed it in, which is indeed separation. To release the one idea, which we have been coming to throughout this text, is to release a mandate: "It could be so. It could be so that I could be separate. It could be so that there is no God. It could be so that I have no right to it even if it is there." This crack in the armor allows fear to claim itself in every crevice. When that idea is no longer present, only the light may shine through you.

We will say these words through Paul. You may repeat them, if you wish:

"I am choosing to release any idea, from any time, born in any world, that I could be separate from Source. I am claiming

the release and the reconciliation of that first idea of separa-
tion that has perpetuated my name, 'I am not,' and reclaims
me in the fullness, in the beauty, and in the alignment of the
True I Am Self."

Now, the I Am Self, which is the Monad, or the Christ, whatever you wish to call it, can only and always be present. But in the dense field you have known yourselves through, you have aligned first and foremost to the separate self, or small self, that has accrued much information and data to support the idea of separation. "How could there be a God if . . . ?" "There could never be a God if . . ." "I could never be of God because . . ." And all of these agreements, which sit as thumb-prints in the energetic field, claim a collusion with fear, with separation, and all the ideas that separation might perpetuate.

The reclamation to the one idea of union—"I am of, I am of the whole, I am of Source, I cannot be other than what I truly am"—will actually gift you with a level of alignment that you may learn to sing in. "What does that mean," he asks, *"learn to sing?"* Well, when you are aligning at this level of structure and tone, even the self that you have thought you were is actually re-known beyond an idea of separation, and the evidence that it has accrued to support separation must be dismantled. Now, the claims we have given you prior— "Behold, I make all things new; God Is, God Is, God Is"—will indeed support you here. But the realization of this is held by the individual who has released his footing, or her mooring, in a belief in separation, so that she is fully lifted to the spirit of the whole, or the manifestation of the Divine come as her, as him, that is no longer bound to that single idea that is the cause of your challenge, your fear, and your sorrow.

The gift of the day is the choice of the day, and the choice of the day, as you wish it, is reclamation of identity at the cost of the idea of separation, and any investment you may hold in it. "I will not be who I want to be. I will not have what I have had. I will not know who I am or what I am." If you look back at our teachings through you thus far, to each of you we say the claim "I know who I am, what I am, how I serve" has all been in preparation for you to acknowledge, claim, and accept this level of embodiment. It has always been true. It is true now. And the song that is sung in reconciliation lifts you to agreement to be as you truly are, without the key to the old lock that has claimed you as separate informing any aspect of you.

"What does that mean," he asks, "*any aspect of you?*" You understand that the body has a structure, and that the body that you hold is separate from the woman next to you, or the man over there. You understand that identity operates at a singular level, and also at a collective level. While you know your body, and while you know your identity, you are no longer aligning to the need to dictate who and what you are through an old system that denies God through separation. As you do this, you are actually lifting not only the body in tone, and the energetic field in tone, but everything that you encounter. You become as a sphere, in oscillation, in radiance, and in love. And it is this love, the sphere that you are in agreement to the larger sphere and the spheres beyond that, all of which are God at different levels of manifestation and tone, to claim you anew, and the world you are in agreement to.

We sing in love. We sing in tone. We sing in truth. And we sing in an agreement to who and what you truly are.

We will continue with this teaching tomorrow. Stop now, please.

DAY TWENTY-EIGHT

What stands before us, in totality, is one true light asking expression, claiming expression, designing through itself perfect outcome for its expression. Each of you here, in this agreement to embody, to align, and to express, becomes sovereign, as of the whole, and the completeness of your expression can indeed be announced. "I know who I am, what I am, and how I serve."

Now, the agreement to embody comes at the cost of the old, but it also reclaims that which has been disinherited, disavowed, and chosen to stay in separation. The reclamation of history has been begun, and much of what you see before you is the uprooting of the old so it can be re-seen. Our day before us, in tandem with this teaching, is reclamation of what was disinherited.

Now, when we spoke last, we spoke of the singular idea—the claim of separation, the denial of the Divine, and the impetus for all separation that has followed. When this is claimed and seen anew, recognized, responded to, and known anew, there is actually no tether to the old field that would deny the Divine. In fact, this single thought, "I am not of, it will not be so," has claimed you all in a relationship of separation to that which is already present and only asks expression through the being that you truly are.

When we say these words through Paul in instruction, we are offering context to the teaching so that you may comprehend the shift and the ramifications of it, so you may feel steady when entering a new environment, a new way of expressing. But finally, we say, it is the realization of this teaching in its completeness that transforms all you see. Now, *all you see* must be understood to include all history, and all ideas of history, all ideas of time, and all ideas of separation. The realization of the Monad at this level doesn't discount what has been. You know where you stand and where you have been. But the ideas you've attached to historical data are actually reclaimed in the Upper Room, and hence the claim "Behold, I make all things new" is perfectly and accurately a descriptor of your experience. When what was once fraught with fear is seen anew without fear, it simply is. When it simply is, you may work with yourself at a level of relationship where you are no longer attached to the historical data that you leaned upon to support you. It simply is. You simply be. And the claim of your expression, "I Have Come, I Have Come, I Have Come," announces you fully in a landscape that is untainted by fear.

Now, because you no longer oscillate at that level of tone or vibration, because you have agreed to release the initial idea of separation, there is no attractor. You do not tell others they are wrong for their beliefs. You know who they are beyond what they have claimed. But because you are whole, at a level of alignment or agreement to this manifest truth, "I Have Come, I Have Come, I Have Come," you are claiming them in the resonant field where the fear is not present by nature of expression. When any of you says, "I am free, I am free, I am free," you are actually anointing those you encounter because the claim in the field holds the opportunity to agree to all that it encounters as free. Each of you says yes at the level of tone that you have aligned to thus far.

Paul interrupts the teaching: "Did you complete the teaching on the release of the one idea, or the first idea, of separation?" In fact, we are continuing it, and we are going to continue it until there is nothing there to claim you, or the resonant field you hold, in alignment to what was never true. The significance of this release, which is reconciliation with Source, claims you completely without a binding to a collective belief in separation. You may feel untethered because your experience of your expression is transformed, and you may choose for a period of time to stay in the old until you understand the safety of where you now stand.

The claim of separation has been chosen and agreed upon through the collective, and its disassembling is what is occurring before you. And the manifestation that separation has accrued is visible now, and will continue to be, because nothing is released until it is first seen. And your refusal to see, the collective's refusal to see, how it engages in fear and how it claims separation has come to a term that cannot continue. In other words, you have chosen to see what you've denied. This is the reckoning, this is the re-seeing, and it is a requirement for the transformation that is before you.

Now, those of you who say yes to releasing first cause are actually challenging a much larger field that you might say is somewhat determined to maintain the old. The idea of logic as you have utilized it is not your friend in this moment, and only in this moment, because when you are transposing a reality, logic itself, accrued in the old frame, is not necessarily applicable to the new. You understand that birds fly. It is an accepted reality. "That thing has wings. It should fly." But you don't understand that there is, in some ways, a parallel reality in the Upper Room where the statistics and the rationales that have been cemented through collective agreement are not present. This does not mean that your kitten will fly. But it simply means that what you believed must be so, and the logic that you would use to confirm the old, actually is not present here. Time itself, a construct that is utilized well in the old field, is not present in quite the same way. And your experience of time and how you move in and through time is also transformed because the weight or density of the old frame or the old template is not present in the Upper. If you can imagine consciousness, unimpeded, allowed to go anywhere, as creative and love, you will have an idea of the freedom that is expressed in the Upper Room.

Now, Paul interrupts: "But we're still bound by form. We're still bound by time." In fact, in some ways yes, and in some ways not at all, and this is what must be understood. This is a transition of identity, and this identity that you are reclaiming holds a very different alignment to manifestation, because it is not separate in its experience from the Source of all manifestation. So what was delineated in hard lines—we show Paul a coloring book with clear parameters, you fill this in this way or that—is actually not the experience of the Upper Room at this level or degree of tone. There are no hard lines, because frequency itself is actually aligned to the material realm at a level of pitch where what was once solid is actually experienced somewhat differently.

Paul interrupts: "I don't understand this. I pick up a teacup, I expect to have a teacup in my hand." And indeed you will, Paul. But your comprehension of self and what you engage with is now at a level of alignment where the old solidity, or the experience of the solidity, which was in fact an illusion, a claim of the lower vibrational field, is not present in the higher. So indeed there is tea in the teacup, but your reality, which no longer dictates what should be in the old way, is having a relatively new and then fathomable experience of a new delineation. If everything is God in form, operating in tone, the higher you lift in tone, the higher the agreement is to what you experience. And the barriers of manifestation, how a thing is claimed, how a thing is known or received, is very different when there is not the dense field to preclude it.

Understand, friends, that prior to the belief in separation, your experience of being was in a less solid atmosphere, a reality that was somewhat different than you can imagine. The idea of Eden, where all ideas are met, is a metaphor for this plane of vibration. The reality that you have accrued and confirmed through separation has mass and an experience for you that continues to confirm itself until you lift beyond it. Now, those of you who have had experiences that you might call spiritual, or a piercing of a veil, have been given an invitation to realize that there is more. And part of the reason, as we teach through Paul, that we confirm energetic structures in

ways that you may feel, is to support you each in a comprehension that there is far more present than you can see with
the naked eye. When you feel vibration, you are feeling tone.
There is no color to it, necessarily, or mass, as you understand
it. But you may feel it moving through the body, or elevating
you. This is the first step in beginning to experience the self
in another level of tone. The tones you have been singing, by
way of attunement or invocation, are all of the Upper Room.
And the manifestation of these claims in the Upper Room is
the gift of the Kingdom. Now, the experience of the Kingdom,
as it unfolds before you, is of a system of tone and vibration
that does not hold the density that you have accrued in the
lower. So you may find yourself quite simply taking off your
backpacks, releasing the luggage, the weighty ideals that you
thought that you would be required to hold. You will be navigating a world in a different strata.

Now, the belief in separation, which you are moving
beyond, one and all, has a choice attached to it. "I am truly
free," "I am in liberation," "I am untethered to the first denial" are statements of truth, because at the level of the
Monad this is always true. But free will, as you understand
it, is offering the self to this higher and new experience while
you have consequence in the lives lived for the untethering
that you are embarking upon. "What does that mean?" he
asks. It means nothing is as it was. "Behold, I make all things
new." Your experience of form, your experience of memory,
your experience of logic, your experience of God or what you
thought God was, is all in re-articulation. "Behold, I make

all things new" is a statement of being. It is not a statement of improvement.

Imagine you've lived in a country where one language is spoken. There is one currency and one way of driving down a street. Imagine you move someplace other, where the language is different, there is no currency, and there is no need to drive because you are where you think you are. Now, while this is a stretch of a metaphor, it is actually apt. The structure of reality that has been informed through separation is in translation in the Upper Room, and your experience of being is in fact transposed, which means your reality, how you comprehend yourself within a structure or template, has been made new. Are you operable at this level? Of course. But the structure cannot hold density. And the relief that you will find as you release your baggage, as you are untethered, is that the manifest world lightens with you.

"How is that so?" he says. Through co-resonance, yes, but through the chink in the armor, the break in the field, the lifting that has occurred is making this reality highly available to those who are willing to receive it. And the level of escalation may happen at a level of rapidity that has not been known on this plane. In other words, your alignment, and the alignment of others, through whatever teaching they may have pursued, whatever process they may have engaged in, must create the space to release the density that has precluded the light, so that the light now shines upon all. As this happens, all are moving to alignment, but in their own way, at their soul's jurisdiction, choice, and agreement.

We will stop this lecture for today. We will continue to-morrow as we are allowed. Period. Period. Period. Stop now, please.

DAY TWENTY-NINE

We ask you this now: Who have you become? What have you aligned to? What has been the claim of being that you are now resounding as? We will tell you what we perceive. Through this instruction, you have claimed an alignment in the Upper Room that has surpassed the level of tone that you have adhered to thus far. You have claimed victory over fear and you've announced yourself in a high way through the claim "I Have Come."

Now, ongoing realization is what must occur, and how you attend to this on a daily basis becomes the way you live your life, less a thing done than a being of self from this level of amplitude, without the tethers to bind you to historical data that would limit your perceptions, denounce the Divine, and claim you in separation. Each day now is the opportunity to be sung anew, and as you sing, which is your expression in vibration and tone, the freedom you hold in the energetic field supports you in a new adventure of experience. What was once seen in one way is seen anew. Any idea of self that you had held in limitation is about to break through to a new potential. The idols you've used, the things you've prayed to that you thought would take care of you—be it business, be it relationship—are all being moved to their rightful place so that you may know yourself in union and in support of a realization of what union really is.

To come to union is to come to a place, or expression of being, where the design of self that has known itself in singularity becomes participatory to the whole organism or the whole realm of experience that you have never been apart from. Imagine a snowflake that believes itself to be singular, now of the storm. Imagine the raindrop that thinks itself as separate from the ones beside it, now of one storm, one expression, one way of being. The design you have held in the energetic body in support of separation has held an amplitude which denies the Divine simply because it is. If you understand this, that there is something in the energetic field whose sole purpose is to claim separation, that has been moved and will continue to be moved through your alignment to the higher. Paul sees the image of a screw becoming unscrewed from a piece of wood. There is nothing pushing the screw to the right new support. It is simply being moved, because in the amplitude of the Upper Room what has been in denial of the Divine cannot remain. Underline *cannot*.

Now, because this has been so foundational to the entirety of your experience, the belief in separation and the agreement to separation, and a world has been created in support of this, you are in some ways operating in a new way, because while you express in the world you have known, your alignment is to the higher, where separation is not present.

Paul interrupts the teaching: "Is this *as in the world but not of it*?" Yes, in some ways, but it's actually a larger statement. While you are pretending in some ways to an accrual of evidence that surrounds you—"That is where the bank is located," "This is the time I have my meeting"—you are actually operating at a strata that understands that these structures, as they have been known, are present for convenience, but your reality and your experience of the meeting or of the bank are rather different than you would have ever thought. While you are in time, you are also in an awareness of the eternal now in a way that actually transcends the idealization of time and, unfortunately, the agreement to time that you have used so dearly. "What does that mean?" he asks. Well, when you understand that time as an idea is losing its grip on your perception, you may find yourself forgetful, or ill at ease, or suddenly feeling bound by structure that has never bothered you prior. This is simply growth. Paul again sees the screw becoming undone, unscrewed from the piece of wood. What will happen eventually is that when you are unbound to what you have known, you are able to operate effectively in the two strata—your reality of the Upper Room, and your ability to advance, to live and choose, and experience a manifest world. But, again, your perception of this world has been altered, and there will be a period for most of you where there is some confusion.

Paul is seeing the image of someone trying on new glasses. It is very blurry until the prescription is set. Once the prescription is set, things are crystal clear. That is exactly what is happening at this level of adjustment to the degree of vibration that you are now becoming accustomed to. So when you understand that the lines are blurry, you actually understand that you are being altered in perception. When you understand that the momentary lapse of memory is part of a process of re-establishing knowing beyond the data of history, when you understand that time itself as useful structure is present, but you are not moored to it at the level of density it would seek to use to claim authority, you are enjoying life and the new sense of liberation that you have indeed come to.

Now, when you know yourself in truth—"I know who I am, what I am, how I serve"—the vibrational field has moved to a chord, c-h-o-r-d, of tone and vibration that has actually shifted the entire field to the Upper Room, where the simple knowing and being and expression of who and what you are is established and qualified by your experience of it. This does not make you delusional. That was for Paul, who interrupted and said, "Oh, no, people are going to say they have ascended again and they may not have been." In fact, Paul, the process of integration in the Upper Room, while a process, is done at the level that the soul can manage so that the integration is not violent. Again, we have said so many times, we will not bring you to a bright room until your eyes can become accustomed to it. There is no need for that level of drama in an awakening. Those that seek that level of drama may indeed find it, but it will not be the Upper Room they have discovered. It will be someplace other.

We move our students in love, and we claim them as they truly are. When one is ascended, one is not announcing it. When one is aligned at this level, one is not screaming it from a rooftop. One is simply having an experience of a reality that was always present that was hitherto denied and is now present and is becoming the new that has been claimed. Again, yes, "Behold, I make all things new" is the claim, and your experience of this *new* is the reality you have aligned to. When a student says to you, Paul, "I have ascended, I have all the answers," you are hearing an aspirant, and he or she will be taught in love at the level that they can agree to love. Again, the one who has aligned at this level is operating as love and a humility that is known by one who completely understands that he or she is of the whole, not the only star sparkling in the sky, but one of billions.

We sing your songs for you so that you may learn the words. But the word of being, "I Am, I Have Come, I Am, I Have Come, I Am, I Have Come," as realized, is a step towards realization that is available now. And its complete expression can be known by those of you who say yes, and have said yes, to the process of release, reclamation, and of course integration, which is necessary. To have a large experience of the Divine, in any way you may come to it, is highly useful to the progress of the soul. But the experience itself, unless there are fruits and benefits that can be seen and known, is simply an experience. To understand yourself as continually unfolding to greater levels of realization is to understand fully that everything in this universe is in movement, and you are no exception. Every one of you who says yes to these teachings actually is being tutored in your own experiences of it, of the teaching itself. "What does that mean?" he asks. Well, because your life is actually your lesson, because the lesson of the day is ever present for you, and because the instructions you are receiving are happening both in a context of language and of vibration, you are being met by us in language and in tone. And the level of mentorship that is available is happening through a collective agreement to support each of you to learn what you need to learn so that you never feel abandoned, lost in the dinghy, as the great boat that you are riding continues to cross a difficult sea.

We know who you are, and as we know who you are we will of course support you as you need it. What we will not do is tell you what to do or answer the questions about your lives that are left to the heart, so that you may become the student of the heart, or the one in her true knowing, his availability to know. As mentors or teachers, we support a large collective of beings who have said yes to a level of support so that they may be aligned for the good of the whole. So we teach the whole, and the individual as part of the whole. But we are not fairy godmothers. We are not coming to fix things. We are teachers, and we support the teaching, the comprehension of the teaching, and the availability of the student to learn.

The choice you make every morning is to be, and how you be, the level of alignment you have come to, has been altered through this instruction. When you feel yourself in low vibration, you may come to think of this as an anomaly and something that you may understand that you can learn through. Restoration to the Upper Room is established by you through the agreements you make, and have made thus far, to say yes to the Monad or the Christed Self as the basis of your expression. Understand that line—*the basis of expression.* It is ground zero, the fundamental truth, the one truth that you may know in all things. And the claim we have supported you in—"God Is, God Is, God Is"—is an invocation of the Monad, expressed as you, to align everything that it encounters to the Upper Room, where at a certain level of amplitude it is already expressing.

The denial of the Divine will no longer empower itself when it is not fed. Do you understand that? Fear no longer operates as fear when it is known as something other. The denial of the Divine, when it is not perpetuated, languishes and falls away. It may be re-known, it will be re-known, but the claim you have made—"God Is, God Is, God Is"—announces itself in the face of every lie, so that every lie may be re-known. And the world you live in, in its own way, is made available to this through your perception of it, through your agreement to be in it, to ride the wave of change and be in the Upper Room while maintaining a habituation in the lower realm, where you have your diary, and your datebook, and your bank, and the children as well. All things will be made new.

And we will say this to Paul: Indeed, this is in the text. Indeed, the text is not completing. This is of the chapter we are writing. It is not the end of it. We thank you all for your presence. We will stop now for the day. Period.

DAY THIRTY

When we speak to you about what is before you, you anticipate outcome, when in fact all we are doing is preparing you for the vessel that you have become. The regarding of a reality that is in transition, that is moving from one level of tone to another, is deeply challenging to those who are frightened of change. But those who are willing to perceive these times in their true light—a reckoning of past choice to claim a new life, a new way of being—will understand themselves as participatory to the new world that is unfolding.

Each of you who says yes to a level of manifestation where you are inclusive of the totality of wonder, that you are present for all that *is* present, you may understand that the beings that you are, are creating opportunity for others to sing. Now, when we teach through Paul and he listens too closely, he can interfere, so we're going to invite him to go back to bed so that we may continue this transmission. The reliance you have on what you knew is being moved from you, sometimes quickly, sometimes slowly. All of you are being asked, out of necessity now, to transition from one agreement, one way of being, to another. And the choices that you are making to align to the higher are made, not just for the self, who seeks security within the new, but the supporting of others, who are coming to you, regarding you as on the other side of the shore and perhaps a beacon in the stormy seas they travel to a new kind of safety. A new kind of safety—a new way of comprehending being, in the immediacy of time and not in the foretelling of it, in the moment you sit in, not what will happen in two weeks or two years or two hundred.

As you all decide that where you sit is the only place you can be, in agreement to what is, you all begin to align to the present moment, where what is before you is apparent, can and will be seen anew, and the challenges that you have faced through past creation are allowed to be re-known. "What does that mean," he asks, "*allowed to be re-known?*" Well, in most cases, because you are complicit and in agreement and in accord to all these past structures, because you've believed them to be intractable and solid, you anoint them in their solidity. You agree that they cannot change. But because of the times you sit in, they will be changed, and your agreement to these changes is what allows them to become new. You cannot say, "Behold, I make all things new," and demand a thing be as it was.

The totality of your experience on this plane is about to be surrendered to one new moment, one perfect moment, where the light that shines through you reclaims every act, every thought, every choice made, in the light of the Upper Room. When this occurs, re-articulation, or the Manifest Divine, is completely sung through the frame that has held darkness, and as the darkness is reclaimed in light, the being that you are is indeed re-known. The idea of being born again, so misunderstood, can now be understood as a re-articulation of the Christ vibration at the cost of the old. And while there is no death, but resurrection, the Resurrected Self no longer holds the detritus of past history, and a new thought, one new thought, replaces all prior thought. "Well, what is the one thought?" he asks. *God Is.* The spectacular simplicity of the one note sung. Being itself as manifestation.

Now, the consequence of becoming what we teach, aligning to what we teach, and receiving what we teach will not be comfortable to those aspects of self that would seek to cling to an old history. We have done what we can up until now to support you in high choice, to relinquish those aspects of self that are so tethered to darkness that you cannot imagine them moving. But the great wind that we see that is now moving through will actually untether the creations of humanity at a level of rapidity that they are not accustomed to. And your willingness now to be in receipt of this teaching indeed must support those who will be grasping for anything to keep themselves afloat in the wave of change. Re-articulation, as we teach it, is becoming new. And the True Self that holds no fear, as manifest, is the gift that is given to the world. Now, you are not becoming Christ. As we have often said, indeed the Christ becomes you. But you seek to deify this idea, create a totem from it, when in fact all it is, is the being of self in an aligned state without the fear that has claimed other fear and moored you to a lower field.

As we sing through Paul today, we sing in memory of his life and his own ideas of who he has been that are now being translated, re-spoken, in a new tongue. A new tongue, we would suggest, is a language not spoken through reference or attachment to the old meaning. To be spoken anew, to become this new tongue, is to embody as Word, and this is the process that we have spoken through you and that you may now sing. When even memory, or the idea of history, can be re-seen beyond the structures that have claimed it in fear, you will find that your legacy as a species has great love, great fire, great joy present within it, and this will be what claims you when it is fully allowed to bloom, to light, to sing, and be expressed.

We will complete this chapter in a few moments, but we have some direction for the channel that may be useful to all of you. To receive this level of vibration requires integration in the body, and to the extent that you allow the body to be in receipt of this vibration, to become accustomed to living here, it will not tax you as you have experienced it. The fatigue you have been receiving is simply the result of an adjustment in the energetic field because you are lifting beyond what you have known, and the form that you have taken is actually asking to become lighter, to be lifted with you. So as you say yes to the body's needs for what this entails, as you agree that in the Upper Room the requirements are met before you ask them, you may become in receipt of what is required to support you, both in spiritual and physical ways, through this process you are undergoing.

For all the students who hear these words, each time you take a step forward in this work you release a little more, or re-see a little more, or reclaim a little more in the life that you are truly being. This is the passage you are all undertaking. And "The Gift of Being," which is the title of this chapter, will be known to you in fullness. Period. Period. Period.

Stop now, please.

8

UNITY

When we teach you about life, we use your frames of reference, the language of everyday usage, the ideas that are commonplace, so that you may have a mooring in what expresses beyond the old, so that you may have an understanding that the language that you have used to describe experience still has a place, but will be re-known in a new way.

The idea of *self,* what it means to be an individual, how you participate in a world through identity, now must be understood as altered. The requirement for being, at this level of vibration, is an understanding and agreement to the whole. You can no longer stand separate from another, decide who he is based on prior expression, the names another might give him. Instead, you are asked to see the one before you as of yourself, as participatory to this agreement to be alive in this shared experience that you call life. If indeed all men are your brothers, all women your sisters, if indeed there is one Source that is responsible for your presence on this plane, you must begin to claim them as of you. "I am not alone" is a statement of truth, whatever you think or whatever you may feel. "I am not alone"—a simple claim that announces you in an agreement to a collective reality.

Now, you don't want a collective reality. You want separation, in some ways, because it agrees with what you've been taught. And every myth you have ever been taught, anything about superhumans, has decided for you that what it means to be divine is somewhat separate, somewhat loftier, somewhat different than the ones beside you. In fact, the opposite is true. As one gains in awareness of her divinity, as one steps into his own authority as the True Self, he realizes others with the deepest compassion and love. And understand this, friends: This is not done by you as personality, but it is how God witnesses its own creations.

Now, some of you think that if you arrive at that level, you are anointing others, separate from them, blessing them with your presence. In fact, you bless them with your presence because they are one with you, and you one with them. The agreement to the collective is not to your friends or your neighbors or your countrymen. It is to life itself, and the acceptance of union that is already expressing in the Upper Room. Paul is seeing an image of a man who thinks himself alone in a misty landscape. As the mist is leaving, it reveals the others who stand and walk. And as the mist continues to shift, he understands himself as of them as well. And the idea of identity, so cemented in the lower levels, has changed, has lifted, has moved into an agreement to love at a level of totality.

Now, compassion, if you wish to understand it, is the deep awareness of what it means to be, the deep awareness of what it means to be at any level of vibration. You do not eschew the one who is operating in low vibration. You see him or her, you realize him or her, you know him or her in love, and your agreement to them is to a *we*. "We are not alone. We have never been alone. We could not be alone. We can only imagine it." Now, the imagination that has first conjured separation, or agreed to the idea of it, is still elastic and can agree to anything. In the Upper Room and what expresses beyond it, the level of vibration is far less dense, and a wall that was erected in fear can be dismantled instantaneously by one who knows the other in love. To know another in love is to accept them, say yes to them, at the deepest core of their being. You are not telling them what they should be or do, how they should change, how they should correct their behavior. You are perceiving them as of you, and as of all. And it is this knowing that reclaims a world in agreement to truth.

Some of you will say, "Well, I don't have to like people," and we will say you're correct. But *like* is a personality structure. It is a simple preference. "I prefer my coffee black." "I prefer mine with cream." You understand preference through the idea of separation, that one thing is this and one thing is that. But at this level of vibrational accord, the idea of *like* is actually shifted to an agreement to be. *Like* is a very low-level way of deciding what something is. And while you may enjoy preference, you cannot at the Upper Room change or value another in any lesser state, because the True Self, who is the one perceiving and knowing, has moved beyond that.

Our teaching today is of union, and agreement to the collective as in love. Now, to understand what it means to know the collective in love is to agree to an idea of participation that you have heretofore not known, or believed could not be. If you imagine yourself lifting now to a new place of being, where the idea of separation simply does not exist, what does it mean to have a body? What does it mean to have a neighbor? What does it mean to have others who create in their own ways, through their own being? Each of you says yes to this potential the moment you align in the Upper Room. And the release of the old, in its completion, leaves you present in agreement to love, and this love cannot be contained by a self, because it is not of self. It is the broadcast of God, love as God, that claims a new world in its choice to receive itself in union. God sees God, yes, in all of its creations, and God loves as God, the agreement to be love through and to its creations.

The borders that you have created, that you have chosen to decide who is where and what is what, will be changing. The idea of a landscape, a shared terrain, will be changing. The idea of a country is changing before your very eyes. What has been may still be, but will be in an altered transformation, an altered agreement to be new. Now, when we say *altered*, we do mean changed. But the level of change that you are participatory to now on this plane is still the beginning—a world made new, a world reclaimed, a world in agreement to the mandate that all are of the same Source. You say, "Well, I have free will. I don't want to be one of the whole." Friends, you must understand. That is not choice. That is truth. Your idea of individuation at the level you have known it has been exclusive. You may be inclusive in your unique expressions, knowing that what makes you, you also makes the one beside you who or what they are. A transformed world is a world where one is seen as worthy of being, worthy of love, and worthy of an agreement to know itself as it truly is.

We will ask you this now: What might it feel like to know the self beyond borders? What might the experience be of knowing the self beyond any edict of separation claimed by another? What might it feel like to celebrate your unique qualities while claiming the same for others, knowing you are of one tapestry, that the thread that makes the tapestry is one thread, and the tinctures that color this tapestry, while altered, are of the same Source. Your reality, you see, is indeed as a tapestry, and when you are no longer operating in a claim of separation, you see all things as of the same, while comprehending self without the old—the borders, the walls, the moats, the idea of separation that has claimed you in fear.

In the Upper Room, fear is not present. Anything created from the Upper Room, from this octave of being, will not hold the seed of fear in it. When humanity aligns at this level of vibration—and we will say it will, it is, and it must be—the idea of self as in fear is dismantled. And the creations of humanity, that which will come in place of the old, will be fearless, will be in love. You don't understand yet because you understand all things through the filter of fear, and fear permeates even your idea of being alive. The most basic expression of your being

is still tinted with fear. You anticipate death. You fear desti-
tution. You don't know if you will live until tomorrow, some
days. The small self, you see, is doing its best to navigate an old
sea, polluted by fear, and even the boat that you ride the sea
in is fraught with fear because you do not know if it will carry
you safely to a new shore.

The truth of your being, in a higher octave, claims a world
through nature of presence and being. But what you don't see
yet is what happens to the systems of your world, how gov-
ernment, how religion, how medicine, how all things are seen
from a new vantage point. Now, because you have operated in
factions, because you have used tribalism as a source of pride,
but also as a source of fear—"Our tribe needs this, our tribe
needs that, that tribe cannot have what we have, there will not
be enough"—because you understand yourselves still through
the structures you've held, you assume that any structure that
will be created must resemble the old. And this is what you
must understand. When we speak of a world made new, we
are teaching you that what has been, in a state of vibration
claimed in fear, cannot exist as it has, so the altered reality may
not resemble what you've known. While we use the language
of the ordinary to describe circumstance, to illustrate states
of consciousness, where we are taking you is actually beyond
what you have known. And any way of describing it that we
might claim for you must still be impressed with the old, the
language of old. Your imaginations, you see, are unbounded, but
only limited by what you allow it to be. Imagination itself,
aligned to Source, claims a world in a much different way,
because imagination need not be bound to what has been.

We are moving you beyond the old to a new expression. And the value of this expression, in vibration, will surpass any idea you have of what it means to be. Now, Paul asks, "How? What is this you are talking about? What is this new thing?" We are simply saying, Paul, that where we take our students is to a level of tone and expression that may be held in body, but allows perception to be experienced beyond what has been limited by prior language, by prior structure, and by the idea of separation that is no longer present as a value in the Upper Room.

You are learning to sing with a sound that has not been heard here. And this is a sound of union, of love, and of being. We sing your songs for you so that you may learn the words, but the one note sung, ever true, is always present, and now will be known.

We thank you for your presence today. Stop now, please.

Paul: When it feels too impossible, I just want to pull the shade down at a certain level. I think that's where I get challenged with this. Okay, I get it conceptually, but is this doable?

A: Yes. If you want it to be. If you don't want it to be, you will have what you've had, and that's what you'll get, and what you're getting now is far less than you're capable of receiving. It's really that simple. What you've been living with, and used to, is minimal compared to the real experience of being, in an awareness of union. You don't lose individuation. You experience it completely dif-ferently. So while Brent knows Brent as Brent, he also knows Jerilyn beyond an idea of Jerilyn, which right now is the best he can do. You have your ideas of one another, and that is how you negotiate a reality. An idea is not knowing. Brent does not know Jerilyn, and cannot know at the level of personality structure. All you can do is have your preferences. "I find him interesting. I would like to learn more of what he has to say." "She is quite lovely. I would like to get to know her." Your idea of *interesting,* your idea of *lovely,* is what you are engaging with. When you truly know another, who and what they are, you are dealing with the aspect of Source, come as them, that is a reframing of your expectations and demands and *shoulds* and *would-like-to's.* In fact, what happens is you've changed an idea, a separate idea, to an inclusive being. To know another is to love another. You do not love the one who is other than you, or separate from you, because the best you can have is an idea of them. Most everything else is a projection—"my job, my child, my house," these ideas of things and ways of being with others. When you move beyond that, you are experiencing the Kingdom. The Kingdom does not align to separation because the separation that you have known yourselves through is born in an agreement to the denial of the Divine. It really can be reduced to that. You are no longer denying the Divine, and that is the gift in your relations. Period. Period. Period.

DAY THIRTY-TWO

You speak of the day that you stand in as an idea. "Today I will do this or that." "Today was such and such a day." You have ideas about who you are, and you know less than you think about your makeup or the quality of being that you are actually engaging in. While, indeed, every day, an opportunity to learn is before you, even the idea of the day and what a day is comprised of is somewhat lost to you. The eternal now, where we invoke this teaching from, is present for you always. And the realization of the eternal now, the Kingdom in presence, will claim you each in a realization of what matter is, what being is, what love is, what truth is. And if you ask for it, the requirements of this will be made known for you.

Not one individual is denied the Kingdom, because the Kingdom is comprised of love. And the responsibility of the individual to ask admittance, to allow herself to enter, is always the key. Some of you say to us, "I want it now, and I want it my way. My heaven will be such and such. My spiritual life will be such and such. I will have what I want as I want it, as I deem it, as I say I shall have it." And you fool yourselves that you sit in the Kingdom. You are in your room conjuring what might be if you stepped out of your way and allowed yourself to know truth. When you know truth, you know the causation of manifestation. When you know the causation of manifestation, you are realized. When you are realized, you know yourself as of the whole. When you know yourself as of the whole, you are one with your brother, one with your sister, and you are known as of Source by the aspect of you that is now realized as such.

The claim "I am known," a realization of Source in presence as and through you, will be taught in further books. But for now we suggest that the opportunity that is present to know and to be known as of God is paramount to where you will be taken. Realization of self as of Source is a first step. But to maintain this, you must grant it, and know it, and be it for others. To be it for others is to be inclusive as it, not withholding, not denying. Some of you want what you want. "I want to sit on my throne in my kingdom. And those over there, well, I will tolerate them. Those over there, I will seek to know. And those behind me, I will happily ignore." You are in a fool's kingdom if this is what you believe. The claim of truth, "I Am," must extend to all you meet.

Now, how do you stand in your knowing in the face of cruelty by others, or bigotry, or fear? How do you know another as of God, as of truth, when every act they may take seems to deny it? The harder one denies the Divine, the more they must be loved. And you are not the one who loves, because the personality structure cannot love as God loves. The personality structure has its likes and dislikes, its proclivities. But it denies the Divine when the Divine does not suit its purpose. Hence, we describe it as small self. We do not make it wrong, but we honor its limitation.

When we speak to you of true love, we speak of the act of God, and the beingness as of God that is love that you are now experiencing and cannot deny another. When we say this, we mean the frequency you hold in love must be available to the one you don't like, or you deny it for yourself. Some of you say, "Well, they don't want it." That is their right. They may choose as they choose. But you love them anyway. They may deny God. You love them anyway. And the aspect of you that loves is the one that cannot deny the Divine. So you are one with what you love, as God is one with its creations.

The template of the old ways, born in personality, agreed to by the denial of the Divine, which you have all chosen to know yourselves through, is so constricting that if it could, it would deny the Divine in all things because it believes its survival is paramount. The personality structure is indeed of God. It will be aligned in the Upper Room, reclaimed anew, and utilized in high ways. The template of the whole that has served to deny the Divine, the constrictive aspect of the self that is in accord to that, is what is relinquished in the claim "I Have Come," because it is God, the seed of God, the flame of God, that has come, and overtakes, and realigns, and supports you each in a realization of true union.

Now, true union cannot be explained here because it can only be experienced. You can imagine it. We can give you indicators for it. But true union is to be known and to know, and its realization is what you come to when you have undressed, unmasked, released, and overcome the one belief that you could ever be separate.

Now, for some of you this remains conjecture. You wish to close the text. "Well, this will not happen for me." And if you wish to confirm that, you may. But we will say these words, and say them in truth: You have come to be known, you have come to sing, and the song that you sing now is in preparation for a new world born. The claim of the Kingdom, "I Have Come, I Have Come, I Have Come," the realization of the Kingdom, "Behold, I make all things new," and the knowing of the Kingdom, "God Is, God Is, God Is," are present in the energetic field of all who have invoked them. And in true invocation, realization must occur. Underline *must*. The denial of the Divine may say, "Close the book, close the window, draw the blind. Let me know myself in my shadowed room." But the light that is present now will be known by you, and we say by all. The consequence of fear and separation are before you now. The denial of the Divine is seen clearly so it may be remedied. And each of you who says yes to this potential aligns to it in agreement of truth. In truth a lie will not be held. And the belief in separation, the great lie, will be remedied by the amplitude of light that will not claim all things in separation, because it cannot. The light that is you, in claiming manifestation, "Behold, I make all things new," claims the new template of the Upper Room in all that is seen and known. And the alignment you will come to—underline *will*—is the agreement to this.

The realization of the True Self in you, in all, in all that can be, is the agreement you make to be who you truly are. And who you truly are, what you truly are, is not separate from its Source. Union, you see, is your natural state. To be in union, while knowing a body, while walking on earth, knowing the one beside you as of Source, is the gift of the Kingdom. Your proclivities and preferences may be engaged in at this level, but the moment you deny the Divine in another, you have denied it in yourself. You agree to the Divine in them regard-

less of what they say, how they act. And you love them, because
when one is loved, one is claimed in light, one is known, and
when one is known, one will not deny God. "Well, what if
what I see and know *is* the denial of God," you may ask. Then
you love them more. The Christ loves all. It does not have a
list of yeses and nos. The Christ knows all, because all must
be of God.

Now, when you see shadow, those engaged in shadow,
those denying light, and you are the light, you illumine what
you encounter. You don't take a hammer to it. You lift it to the
light so it may be re-seen, re-known, and encountered anew.
Again, the claim "Behold, I make all things new." Realization
is the least convenient path for the egoic structure that you
could ever claim, but it is the only structure that must be
transposed to the Upper Room. The egoic structure or personality self is an idea of who you are, who another is, and all
you see from that perspective is an idea of someone, born in
your own history and the morals of the day, the proclivities
of the self that agree to what they are told, what it is told to
do and believe. Because the Divine Self knows all things in
truth, it is unashamed to love the one that has been in darkness. You have all come to learn, and the path that is most
difficult will often claim the most learning. Your need to be
vindictive, to put another in shadow, to be right at the cost
of others being wrong, is separation. It's play, it's game, to
deny even the seed of God that must be present in the ones
before you.

We speak these words now for Paul. This text is not done.
We will have one more chapter after this one. This is the

chapter on unity. You may call it thus. We are grateful for your presence. We will reconvene and teach you more tomorrow.

Stop now, please. Period. Period. Period.

DAY THIRTY-THREE

When you ask questions about what will be, you predicate outcome on a basis of history. "This could happen. It has happened before. This may happen. It's a potential." Everything is a potential. Anything claimed in truth may be a true potential. And when we say this, we mean when you divine, when you know, from the truth of your being, you claim a manifestation of outcome that will echo in the higher realms. To claim a world anew is to know who you are in truth. And in this truth, the claim of being, "I am free, I am free, I am free," releases you from the old, and a new potential, a new idea, if you wish, about what will be can be understood and made so.

When we teach through Paul, we are obligated to use language so that you may understand what we mean. The discourse that is occurring today is actually happening well beyond language. We are actually claiming each of you in new potential, in a new understanding of what union is. And because we use language to codify, to explain, to prepare, to support, and instruct, we will use it as we may. But please understand that the day's lesson is in the energetic field as we move you to an amplitude of vibration where what was will not be thought of as outcome, and what is, what truly is in truth, may be claimed.

Now, in the Upper Room, you have opportunity to grow. It is not a static place of expression. In alignment in the Upper

Room, you become an expression of the Divine in action. The manifestation of the Divine in action is what is being spoken to now, and your agreement to stand still in the midst of a great storm, your willingness to rise above the fray when the fray is tumbling, your agreement to sing when others may whisper, will be what supports you. The expected acts, in times of change, will get you the expected outcome. To understand that the ramifications of change now are indeed to lift all to a new level of tone, a new plateau, supports you all in a recognition of the potential of these times. But when the potential is outlined—"It will be as I think it should" or "as I suspect it may be"—in fact what you do is limit what will be through your old ideas or designs of potential. "Behold, I make all things new." We have instructed you in this claim, but to truly understand the presence of it is to understand that what is new has not been known yet. You are not upgrading a new model of a car. You are not building a nicer home. In fact, what you are doing is claiming a world in truth, in recognition to truth, and in truth a lie will not be held, and the great lie of separation is what is being disbanded and made new.

Now, how do you agree to a potential that you cannot imagine? We are doing this with you now in frequency. All who hear these words, all who say yes to this promise, will be re-known at a level of amplitude where their contribution to the release of the old will be known to them by their own experience of the new. Now, when we say *the new,* we are saying a new potential, that which has always expressed, but that you have not been party to through the level of alignment in the template that you have known. In the Upper Room, you are lifting and agreeing to a new way of being, and the being in the Upper Room is in agreement to union.

Now, understand what *union* really means. It is the knowing of your oneness with the Source of all things. The Source of all things must include what you think of as other—other than self, other than what you've thought, other than what you would decree through the language of history. To move to union does not disband individuation as much as re-know it in a higher agreement. Susan is still Susan. Brett is still Brett. But the one that you think of as *self* has moved to an agreement to the truth of *them* that reclaims them and the experience of them. Because Paul has only had glimpses of this state of being, we cannot draw on his history for him to illustrate. But we will say this much: The agreement to be, in inclusivity, in the awareness of the whole, is the first step towards a level of alignment where you are not dictating what should be, based on past presumption.

When we sing through Paul now, and we intend to today, we support you each in rising to a level of vibration where the known may be re-seen with new eyes, where what was once thought to be present in a certain way is now re-seen in a new state of consciousness. And this means that the one who perceives is re-seen and re-known in order for this act of re-articulation to be made manifest. In re-articulation, there is re-knowing. And the manifest Word, the Divine that has come as each of you, in its own amplitude, in its own expression, is what does the work. When we sing to you now, we are going to speak one word. And the word is *yes,* the *yes* that embodies, the agreement to embody, the song of embodiment, to restructure, re-see, and decide for itself that it is re-known in the Upper Room as it can only be in truth.

We say these words now through Paul on the behalf of all who will hear them:

> *On this day we claim that each one present, that all who hear these words, will be summoned and re-seen at a level of amplitude where they may know union, claim an agreement to participation in the act of resurrection wherein all things are made new, all things are seen anew, and supported in re-creation through the presence of being. We say this in love, we say this in agreement to who you truly are, and as we say yes to you, we invite you to say yes to all that will be seen and known anew in union.*

Paul, on the count of three.
One. Now two. Now three.

[The Guides tone through Paul.]

Allow every aspect of self, every cell of your being, to go into agreement, a great *yes* of re-articulation in an awareness of one's union with the Source of all things. The *yes* that you sing—of the heart, of the soul, of the expression of being— will be sung through you with your permission.

"*I Have Come. I Have Come. I Have Come.*"

Allow this to be. Allow yourself to be known at this level of vibration. Allow the great *yes* of your being, the consent to embody at this level of tone, be announced in every cell.

We say this for each of you now: The work of this day was a transmission of union. It will continue. We will teach you more tomorrow. Stop now, please.

DAY THIRTY-FOUR

When we discuss the opportunities that are present for you now in the Upper Room, we speak to a potential that you may know as absolute. What we mean by this is very simple. The desire you have to hold this level of vibration indeed will be met in the increments that you can manifest. The realization of the Upper Room, the True Self in embodiment, is claimed for you—underline the word *for*—more than by you, by the Monad that holds itself in truth and cannot be denied. Realization in the Upper Room at the cost of the old has indeed claimed most of you to a level of alignment that you did not perceive, could not have perceived, prior to this encounter. And the realization that ensues, the potential in manifestation, must be understood as consequence or affect of the work to date.

Now, the work to date, in prior texts and in this one as well, has been about alignment to a level of tone and vibration that was heretofore unavailable, easily ignored, on this plane of dense frequency. The alignment that is present on this plane now actually affords the opportunities for this level of integration, and you must understand that the releasing of the dense planes, the creations of havoc, the fears you've held, are releasing now for the benefit of all. But the movement from density to a more refined state are in fact cataclysmic to the self that wishes things to be as they were, or thinks they must be, to perceive a world in an old way.

The consequence of this teaching, the ramifications of the teachings thus far, are supporting you each in and at a level of tone that you may begin to hold, acclimate to, and surrender to as you grow comfortable in the new atmosphere. When you move to a new room, all you perceive is the newness. When you become accustomed to the room, it becomes home. Once you know you are home, and confident that you can return there, you can venture outward, explore the worlds around you. And we said *worlds* intentionally, because from the Upper Room you may move without the density that you have accrued in the lower field, and this liberation actually allows you to explore potentials that you may never have considered.

Realization of the Upper Room, the Monad in manifestation, the acclimation to a higher level of tone, supports each individual who comes here at the level that he or she can hold it. But you must understand, friends, that the Upper Room in entry, the place we have taken you to and supported you in holding, is merely the first stage of adaptation to Christ consciousness. The availability to hold this, to integrate, to participate in its great love, is what awaits you now.

The temptation for some of you will be to rest here. "I like my new room. Let me enjoy it for a time." But in the Upper Room, you are indeed empowered to act, and the transformation that you are beginning to undergo—and notice we said *beginning*—will continue as you advocate, by nature of your own presence, for this level of tone and embodiment and its availability to all that you encounter. As you are an emissary of this tone because you hold it, because it is sung through you, because you have acclimated to it, said yes to it, and support this yes through the maintenance of the tone "I am free, I am free, I am free," because you say yes to the absolute as all things, "God Is, God Is, God Is," you have said yes to becoming what you have always been, the mastery of this expression as may be known in form. "I Am Word."

The first text we dictated through Paul holds the template for what has followed, and the students who have agreed to this level of agreement, manifestation, and choice are being met in the great *yes* that you spoke yesterday, the great *yes,* the great choice, the manifestation of the Monad and what it claims in this world. What it claims, Paul, in this world—he is asking—is truth, and the truth of all things, and the return to the holiness that has been denied, and the refuting of shadow by the light that you become. The lantern that you are grows in strength, grows in amplitude, as you continue to say yes to the Christ principle, which is the Monad in its amplification. The residue of the old, that which tarnishes the lantern, inhibits the light, continues to be attended to as you align, again and again and again, to the truth of your being. You are no longer deciding what should be. You know what is. You are no longer saying, "Someday." You are in now, you are saying yes to now, which is the only time that God is known. You will not be more holy tomorrow than you are today, although your recognition of your True Self may amplify as you continue to agree to your essence. The field that you hold, which has been altered through this encounter, will continue to say yes for you, because the small self or personality structure that you have thought you were is becoming re-known and agreed to as the light, as of all aspects of you—which simply means, Paul, that even the personality in its restoration, the Resurrected Self, can deny no aspect, and you are lifted to the song of being, as you are.

On this day we claim that all who hear these words will sing a new song, will sing in a new voice, will sing the song of truth and love as their expression. And as this is done, the Divine as all things is now the encounter of consciousness, of being, that you now know.

We sing your songs for you, yes, but you sing with us now, and you sing in joy, and you sing in agreement to what you can only be. You Have Come. You Have Come. You Have Come. And as the world is made new, we sing with you the one note of being: I Am.

Thank you each for your presence today. We will continue this dictation tomorrow. Period. Stop now, please.

DAY THIRTY-FIVE

What stands before you now is all that may be known from a new vantage point, new comprehension of the inherent divinity that is all things. Your reliance on history to be your director is actually waning as you begin to re-articulate or manifest from the Upper Room. The Divine as who and what you are sees all things with new eyes, and the reclamation of all things—"Behold, I make all things new; God Is, God Is, God Is"—will be surrounding you as you align to it.

The choice to sing at this level has consequences for the individual and the life lived by the individual. What was once important, so important, may now seem like very little. What you thought was unimportant, gave little attention to, may well rise for focus because it needs to be re-seen. The octave you are now singing in has its own properties, and the dense vibration that has been your training thus far, now anew, will be seen anew through your experience. Underline those words, friends: *Through your experience* means how you experience, what you experience, from this altered vantage point. Reality, you see, is not what you thought it was, and the first glimpses to a higher truth must already be available to you through this instruction. But this is the beginning, as we have said, of a great adventure of being. The choice to embody to serve at this level, and with its consequences, supports you all in the life lived. The challenges you will now face will be rather different than you might expect. Because you are no longer in the octave of fear, but the memory of fear is still present, you will still see fear, but you will begin to find that your prescription for what fear should be or how you should be responding to it will be very different. In fact, it will become a whisper when it was a din, and then it will become silent, because you understand that it has just been an idea that you have acclimated to. And the energy that has been presented through this idea, which has permeated your old life, need not be known, need not be conjured, need not be decided upon from the new place you stand.

The song that you are singing now, "I Have Come, I Have Come, I Have Come," the embodied Divine, makes you no better than the next man, the next being beside you. It makes you one of the whole, and the one of the whole always knows who she is in consort with her fellows. She is not seeking deification, nor is she hiding from the light that she is. She simply is, and all simply are. Because you are no longer relying on the old, no longer labeling people through their occupations, their physical attributes, how much money they may have or how very little, you are moving to a space of inclusion of all through the recognition of what is always true. If you are asked to help, you help. If you are called to help, you help. But true service, you see, at the level we are teaching, lifts you beyond even what you think service is, because the song sung as you, in tone and in field, the re-articulated state of being, calls all things to it in co-resonance. And the claim, again, "I Have Come, I Have Come, I Have Come," the Monad in presence and in action, is the service that is provided through you.

Now, a re-articulated being serves in some ways as a tuning fork for its environment, and you must understand that consciousness is not limited by physical presence. Wherever your consciousness is, this level of tone or vibration is. And your claim of being, wherever you are, "God Is, God Is, God Is," actually reclaims all things seen, all things known, in the collective field or new template that is the Upper Room. You are no longer fixing. You are knowing. You are no longer deciding through the old template, but in the experience of the new, and in a foundational way where choices made are all present in an awareness of requirements of the moment you stand in. Self-deceit will fall away because it serves no purpose here. You have no need to lie to the self, pretend this or that, because you simply be. And because you be, you know, and as you agree to this knowing, the consequences of this are a life lived in a new way.

Some choices may be made by some of you to confirm an old identity. Paul is seeing the image of someone with a nameplate, as would sit on a desk, trying to carry it to the Upper Room. The weight of the old identity will not stand here. So your investment in how you should be seen or called will also release, and to the good. When we say *to the good,* we simply mean that what is left behind is what is not required. And we will say this for Paul: The things that you seek to bring to the Upper Room are the things that make you unhappy. When you make a list of what makes you unhappy, you will see how moored these all are to old ideas of self, claimed in fear or past experience. When you see these things for what they are, you can say thank you to them, understand that they were required at a time, but you don't need to bring your dirty laundry to the Upper Room. "Behold, I make all things new" is a re-seeing and reclamation of what was. You do not have to carry pain and seek to sort through it there. If it must be seen, it will be seen, because it will make itself present in your momentary life.

The skill set that you have utilized, Paul, to support this dictation is being well used today. We are speaking without any effort, and we are reaching many people with these words.

The trajectory of this text, unlike the others, will be quite large, and the proponents of this text will speak to the truth of it. The ones who dislike it will do their best to say what they say, but their words will not last. This is a teaching of truth, and the vibration of truth informs it. In truth a lie will not be held. So there need be no concern of misuse or even misunderstanding of the essence of this teaching. The vibration that this teaching holds will be present for a long time as you each integrate it and, in some ways, become it. As you become it, the pages of this text may wither and fall away. The text is alive in its students. The song is sung through the reader, and we are graced to hear this song from where we sit, from where we know ourselves, the high light of being that we know as love and God itself.

These teachings are coming to a close shortly. We are actually completing this last chapter today, and we will speak again with an epilogue when we reconvene soon. The teaching itself on resurrection will of course continue as we have more to teach, but the distillation of this teaching, as you all understand it, must be held first. In other words, friends, we prepare you for what comes through what we teach today, and you are prepared for what comes after by your alignment to the energy, and indeed the ideas and the presence that we offer. For some of you, this means that you want it done now. You don't want more. Have what you wish. We do not tell you what to do. We only offer a way forward, and in this case *forward* means upward, or in escalation, beyond an old agreement to a much higher one.

All of you who hear these words have indeed been called. All of you who indeed say yes to these words are in alignment to that *yes,* and your permission has always been required for this work to proceed. This is the book of re-articulation, resurrection, and the Upper Room. The idea of resurrection, which is re-articulation, the Monad in risen state and expressed through all, will be comprehended by you in your own experiences of it.

We say these words in joy: The Christ is risen. It Has Come. It Has Come. It Has Come. The universal truth of being, the inherent Divine, is now known, will be known, will be expressed, and you will sing for a very long time.

Blessings to you each. We will return tomorrow. Thank you for your presence, and stop now, please. Period. Period. Period.

EPILOGUE

DAY THIRTY-SIX

When we sing to you about purpose, we sing about the reason you be—the realization of the identity that you can only hold in truth. We see you each now, not only prepared, but in agreement to manifestation, and the alignment that you hold that indeed supports this will accrue its own evidence. Understand that, friends. *Accrue its own evidence* means your world will teach you, your identity will claim you in a higher way, and the world will make sense at this level of accord.

Now, the choices that are before you every day are to hold the alignment and claim the agreement, the True Self in manifestation, and align to what comes. Understand those words, friends: *Align to what comes,* to what you call to you at this level of tone, because this will be the choice to be in service, to be in realization, from the Upper Room. Each of you who comes before us has made a claim, "I am willing," and the reason for this teaching is to meet the claim of the willing, the ones who wish to know themselves in high accord.

When we teach through Paul, we honor the body, we honor the idea of the self that he has accrued, in order to claim him in this experience of re-articulation. The same is true for you. Now, some of you say before us, "Teach me to be the channel. I want to be the vessel who speaks." The opportunity for all of you is to move to a level of identity where what is known, what is spoken into being, is that which is always true. You need not be a radio for us, to embody at this level. And, in fact, when you are operating in your knowing, any other word spoken from any other will be secondary. The choice to be, the idea of being, the realization of being, in the Upper Room, claims you as you require it. And what is known by you here, in a balanced way, will indeed support you in choice, in reason, and in agreement to truth.

Now, we will say this to all of you: Indeed, this is an epilogue for a text. But this is the first of three texts that teach embodiment and manifestation. And the work of this text has been done through this transmission, and what follows will be what claims each of you in the new awareness that can only be sung from the vantage point of True Self. This is a new agreement we make with our student. We will teach you as you come to us. We will not take you higher than you can hold. We will claim you each in agreement to the level of choice that can be claimed by you with the soul's permission to ascend. Each of you says yes at the level or octave that you can align to.

This is a purposeful work. And the work of this first text in

Resurrection is the manifestation of the Monad from the Upper Room in a state of being that will accrue its own evidence to your participation in a world made new. What we will dictate next through Paul will be the text on knowing, true knowing, and the realization of true knowing that can only occur from the Upper Room. When we are ready to begin dictation, we will convene a group again to be participatory to the transmission. But each time we speak through Paul, the transmission moves far beyond those assembled in the room. In fact, each of you who hear these words, who read these words, become a transmission of them as well.

We will say this now: This will be the final day of teaching, and only for one reason. If we keep discussing this, we will prepare you too much for what comes next. If we say thank you now for your presence, and give you the opportunity to say yes to your own experience, this work will have been done well. We are your teachers, yes, as you wish to be taught, and the song we sing is and always will be sung in love, sung in agreement, and sung in an awareness of your true nature.

We will say goodnight. We will say, again, thank you.

You Have Come. You Have Come. You Have Come.

Stop now, please.

Acknowledgments

Dustin Bamberg, Noam Ben-Arie, Tim Chambers, Joel Fotinos, Jerilyn Hesse, Kenn Holsten, Amy Hughes, Joan Katherine Cramer, Jeannette Meek, Noah Perabo, Brent Starck, Olivia Thirlby, Christine Warren, Eric White, and Hanuman Maui: Ram Dass Loving Awareness Sanctuary.

About the Author

Born in New York City, Paul Selig attended New York University and received his master's degree from Yale. A spiritual experience in 1987 left him clairvoyant. Selig is considered one of the foremost contributors to the field of channeled literature working today. He served on the faculty of New York University for over twenty-five years and is the former director of the MFA in Creative Writing Program at Goddard College. Information on channeled workshops, online seminars, and private readings can be found at www.paulselig.com.